And those who were seen to dance were
thought insane by those who could not
hear the music.

Friedrich Wilhelm Nietzsche
1844 - 1900

The Incomplete Pyramids

by

Stephen Brabin

Published by Stephen Brabin

Published by Stephen Brabin

www.giza-pyramids.com
Manchester, England

First Edition , December 2010

ISBN 978-0-9566588-0-7

ISBN 978-0-9566588-0-7

9 780956 658807

Printed in Great Britain by the MPG Books Groups Group, Bodmin and King's Lynn

Contents

Appendix

List of illustrations

Unas and the Egyptologists

A room full of clues

Unas the ruler

An unusual inclination

Another brick in the wall

A long line of pharaohs

The forgotten chamber

A very primitive triangle

A view from the heavens

The model pyramid

A twist in the tail

The world is not round

The invisible pyramid

In through the out door

Finding your roots

One small step

The time scale

Which way out ?

The satellite pyramid
and the sphinx

Second great pyramid

Unfinished business

Another twist in the tail

Welcome to Luxor

The Giza Pyramids
Astronomical epoch

Making sense of it all

Appendix

INTRODUCTION

Four and a half thousand years ago, at the very dawn of civilisation, the pyramids of Egypt came into existence. Their utterly immense proportions are so out of keeping with the known construction abilities of mankind at that point in our history that they have provided a source of fascination for all those who have come across them. They have been studied professionally by Egyptologists and also written about by those with little more than a instinctive feeling that something about the origins of these monuments cannot be correct.

The work of the Egyptologists is exemplary and their archaeological reconstructions, detailed surveying measurements and highly structured reporting methods leave little room for doubt about the origins of the pyramids. That they were built when the Egyptologists say they were is without question because the science of radiocarbon dating which has been applied to them is an accepted scientific dating method. That they were built by the Pharaohs of the Old Kingdom of Ancient Egypt should also be beyond question because the linguistic experts who have studied the hieroglyphic writings for more than a century are in agreement with each other about the translation of the ancient scripts which adorn the walls of many of these ancient monuments. And since it is from these ancient writings that the time line of the ancient Egyptian civilisation has been reconstructed, we should be certain about the succession of Pharaohs who ruled the country at the time the buildings were constructed. There is no room for debate about the dimensions of the monuments or their exact locations because the exhaustive survey work of the archaeologists has the stonework of the monuments and their surroundings mapped out down to the very smallest of details. In summary, the Egyptologists have investigated these monuments in the most astonishing detail and have documented that work and cross referenced it to provide anyone who is interested with the most wonderful collection of source material that one could imagine.

During the vast majority of the time that these scientists and linguists have been diligently putting all of this work together they have been dogged by a problem. They have been relentlessly pursued by the second group of people mentioned before who have rigidly stuck to their belief that the pyramids were not built by the Ancient Egyptians and that there is something mysterious about these buildings. There have been fashions in the general public where the Egyptian pyramids have caught the imagination of the masses, and at these times numerous books have been published on the subject. Without exception, the scientific and disciplined approach that is the trade mark of the Egyptologists is lacking in these works and the conclusions that are drawn from them have no solid foundations.

Yet human beings are emotionally much more complex than the scientist that we can find within ourselves. We have instinctive feelings and, as most people experience at some point in their lives, we have the ability to just 'know' when something is not quite correct. It is difficult to argue against these feelings when one is standing next to a building as massive as the Great Pyramid of Giza. No matter how much the scientists tell you, and no matter how much factual information is presented to you, there is still the tingling feeling in your nervous system that tells you that something is not quite right. And it is not just the tourist or the 'new age' follower that has these feelings, it is the scientist and academic as well. One of the world's leading Egyptologists who currently presides over much of the excavation work on the Giza plateau apparently first went to the country from his native United States with the notion of uncovering or investigating the esoteric secrets of the Ancients. And the director of the Egyptian government's antiquities department is also on record as having experienced strong emotional experiences during his career in and around these monuments. So the question arises as to why, four and a half thousand years after these monuments were built, do we still have any instinctive doubts about their origins.

One reason is that the Egyptologists have yet to provide a single piece of corroborating evidence for their story. There are absolutely no records whatsoever from the ancient times that document the design and construction of the pyramids of the Giza plateau. The intricate details of the constructions clearly indicate that these buildings were designed with the utmost forethought and planning. There is quite obviously some sort of logic in the layout of the dark chambers and atmospheric corridors which can be found within their walls. Yet the Egyptologists have to resort to the minor details of the archaeological sites to try to bind the historical deductions that they have extracted from the hieroglyphs to the archaeological evidence in front of them. They use the existence of ancient bakeries and sleeping quarters surrounding the Great Pyramid to help to prove the methods of its construction. And when you contemplate why this would be necessary you return to the same overwhelming fact each time, that there is no independent substantiated evidence of the history of the construction period of the pyramids. There is no written documentation from a contemporary civilisation that can conclusively confirm the Egyptologists deductions regarding the building of the monuments.

It is into this academic void that the other group of people, known rather amusingly to the Egyptologists as 'pyramidiots', rush head long. Realising that until such time as the archeologists uncover something more substantial than an ancient bakery at the back of the Great Pyramid to prove beyond question that their theories are correct, then the subject is open to speculation. This speculation makes for fascinating reading and appeals to the intrinsic emotional nature of human beings. That the Gods of the ancient world were involved somehow in the design of these pyramids is a subject title that will always attract attention from the general population. If the more unusual features of the pyramids are explained within a this context then the 50 tonne roof stones inside the Great Pyramid's main chamber and the 2 million or so massive slabs of rock that were used to construct the building start to take on the air of a fascinating mystery. The academic void that the Egyptologists have left wide open has been filled with pseudo scientific fiction and that is how we ended up in the situation that we currently find ourselves.

This dilemma provides a fascinating challenge for anyone with the inclination to study the subject. The overriding question that presents itself is whether it is possible to close off this gap in our knowledge and thereby provide the solid foundations to the academic discipline of Egyptology that will allow the subject to progress in the future without the hindrance of the sceptics. It is,

I suspect, this very thing that provides the motivation for the Egyptologist to spend another day in the searing heat of the Egyptian desert uncovering another few ancient stones beneath the sands of the Sahara desert. They are searching for that one piece of evidence that will lead to the closing of the academic void and provide the world with the definitive answer to the origins of the Pyramids of Egypt

This book, the result of ten years of research into the architectural design of the pyramids, was written with the intention of closing off that void. By meticulously analysing the results of the archaeological surveys on each of the pyramids and looking for the logical design of the architects within that data, it has been possible to reach conclusions which will go a long way to finally bringing to rest the battle between the Egyptologists and the sceptics. It was during those ten years of research spent retrieving numerous books from Egyptology libraries and reconstructing the details of these buildings on computer systems that I built up an enormous respect for the community which dedicates its professional life to the restoration and preservation of these ancient buildings. Their survey work and attention to detail is exemplary, the archaeological maps and drawings that have been put together are highly informative and the presentation of the findings organised to perfection. There is however one minor point which detracts from their work : the conclusion that can be reached after a diligent scientific analysis of the pyramid's architectural design has been carried out is that it is the sceptics who are correct about the origins of the Giza pyramids, and not the Egyptologists.

This book is essentially divided into two parts. The first part covers the fascinating internal architectural design of the pyramid of Unas, and shows with clarity how the Egyptologists have been completely deceived by the architects of this building. The rooms within this pyramid have been cleverly designed to confuse anyone who looks at them, and the chambers are full of optical illusions and visual riddles throughout. By looking very carefully indeed at the small details in the building it is possible to identify the opening tricks that the architects have placed into it, and once that those have been identified the whole of the structure's architectural design starts to fall into place. By the end of the first section of the book it is abundantly obvious that this building is not just a simple bronze age burial chamber, that whoever designed the building's architecture was very clever indeed, and that the currently accepted story that is told to us by the historians must by fundamentally incorrect. This then allows the second part of the book to be placed in a realistic framework. If the Egyptologists have been deceived to such an extent in the relatively small confines of the chambers of the Unas pyramid, then the immense proportions of the Giza plateau's construction can be looked at in a fresh light.

The second part of the book deals with the pyramids at Giza and systematically shows how the architectural design of each of the pyramids has been put together. The mathematical framework onto which the building's architecture has been attached is carefully extracted from the pinpoint surveying data that the Egyptologists have provided, and chapter by chapter the Giza plateau starts to come to life. The culmination of the second part of the book is the discovery of the astronomical details which have been carefully concealed within these buildings' architectural design. The final picture that is presented at the end of the book is beyond anyone's wildest dreams.

Because of the nature of the work, and the immaculate detail which is concealed within the pyramid's architectural design, there are pages of this book which are particularly time consuming to read. The subject is not simple, and each of the pages of this book has taken 11 days on average to write and research. When reading the book it is worth keeping in mind that fact, and when the sentences and paragraphs appear to be becoming difficult to read, realise that it is most likely a result of the architectural complexity of the buildings that is causing this to happen. I have attempted to edit and re-write the book so that it is as easy to understand and read as is possible, but ultimately the flow of the book is dictated by the architects of the pyramids, and not by me.

The subject matter covered in this book is immense, and was not designed for one person to try to decipher alone. I hope that what is written and presented in this book does some sort of justice to the subject matter. There should be sufficient detail within my work for the true design and origins of the pyramids to be understood, and hopefully enough evidence and scientific proof that the work can act as a starting place for future diligent scientific studies.

SHBrabin

August 2010

Section one

The Pyramid of Unas

How the Egyptologists got it wrong

Unas and the Egyptologists

UNAS AND THE EGYPTOLOGISTS

The pyramids of Giza are by far the best known of all of the ancient monuments in Egypt, but if you stand beside the Great Pyramid and look to the south through the heat haze you can just make out another collection of pyramids 14km in the distance. They are located in an area known as Saqqarrah and it is the five largest pyramids of this region that can be seen shimmering on the skyline from the Giza plateau.

Nestled amongst these towering structures lies an utterly unimpressive mound of old rocks and sand which is known to Egyptologists as the 'Pyramid of Unas'. As can be seen in the illustration below there is very little left of the external structure of the monument, and the supposition that this pile of rubble was once an elegant pyramid is based on the existence of the few remaining face stones which can be found around its perimeter. The association of the building with the Pharaonic name Unas was a relatively simple task for Egyptologists because below the ruined external structure lies a series of chambers upon whose walls can be found the most stunning collection of hieroglyphs. Repeated over 800 times within these hieroglyphic inscriptions, artfully carved into the limestone walls of the chambers, can be found the name of the Pharaoh for whom the building was apparently constructed. And so this mound of ancient rocks has acquired the name of the 'Pyramid of Unas' and it hides itself away between the other pyramids of Saqqarah which have been its neighbours for the last 4000 years.

It would be reasonable to classify the underground chambers of the pyramid of Unas as one of the jewels in the crown of Egyptology, such is the state of preservation of the hieroglyphs and architecture found within the chambers. The building's rooms were first uncovered in 1881 by Gaston Maspero, one of the early band of Egyptologists, and a man who later went on to become director of the Antiquities Service in Egypt (the official government department which administered all archaeological excavation work in the country) from where he would oversee the management and excavation of all of Egypt's ancient sites. Being the first person in modern times to enter the building, an accomplishment which was much more difficult than one would imagine due to the massive build up of sand and rubble which blocked the entrance passage, he was the first to map out and draw the rooms' structure and layout. His plan, reproduced on the next page, shows that a long straight entrance passage leading into a series of three underground rooms : one long rectangular room ; one reasonably square room ; and one rather unusually shaped room which contains alcoves down its longest side. The side profile of the chambers on this diagram show vertical room walls meeting an apexed and inclined roof, and the only feature of

The pyramid of Unas

A view across the monuments of Saqqarah towards the north east corner of the pyramid of Unas.

*The original plans of the
pyramid of Unas from Gaston
Maspero's 1881 publication
showing*
  A- main chamber
  B -antechamber
  C- serdab

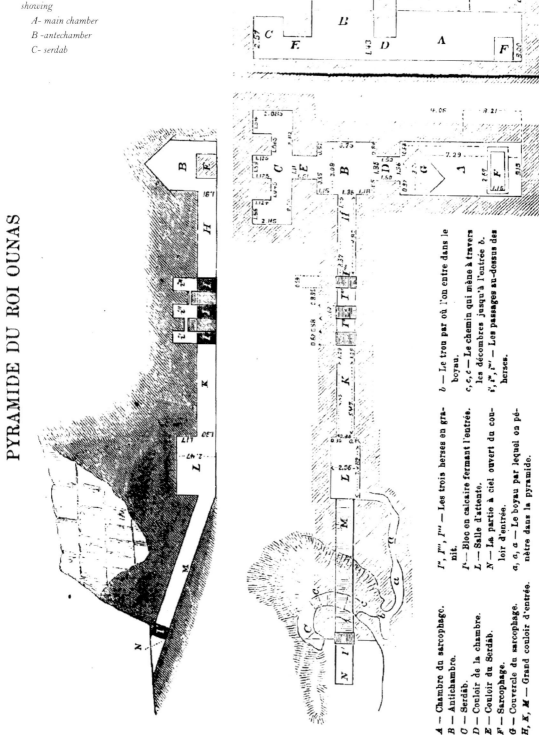

PYRAMIDE DU ROI OUNAS

A — Chambre du sarcophage.
B — Antichambre.
C — Serdab.
D — Couloir de la chambre.
E — Couloir du Serdab.
F — Sarcophage.
G — Couvercle du sarcophage.
H, K, M — Grand couloir d'entrée.

I', I'', I''' — Les trois herses en granit.
I⁴ — Bloc en calcaire fermant l'entrée.
L — Salle d'attente.
N — La partie à ciel ouvert du couloir d'entrée.
a, a, a — Le boyau par lequel on pénètre dans la pyramide.

b — Le trou par où l'on entre dans le boyau.
c, c, c — Le chemin qui mène à travers les décombres jusqu'à l'entrée b.
i', i'', i''' — Les passages au-dessus des herses.

note, other than the architecture, is a coffin and coffin lid which are shown on his drawings in the positions in which he found them. The measurements on his drawing are in the metric system and displayed in meters, and relate quite accurately to more modern surveys which have been performed on the building, with differences of only a centimeter at most between Maspero's measurements and the modern ones.

There are three features which are incorrect on his drawing. The first is that the vertical walls of the chambers do not meet the sloping roof as shown by Maspero, but stop 30-40cm short of the roof as can be seen on the illustration below. This incredibly unusual roof construction is one of the more noticeable features when first looking at the pyramid's architecture and it is surprising that Maspero neglected to include this point on the drawing which he published. The second incorrect feature is the west wall of the main chamber which Maspero shows as a single vertical face, but which is in fact composed of two sections as shown in the illustration overleaf, with the top gabled section set back from the vertical plane of the wall by more than half a meter. The third error is that at the very start of the entrance passage there is a small step which is significantly large enough to warrant putting

onto such a drawing, but which Maspero's drawing omits. A cut through diagram of the entrance passage and the step are shown on the following pages. These three errors were no doubt of little consequence to Maspero at the time of writing since the 26,000 hieroglyphs which he had just uncovered were of much more importance than the details of the building's exact construction. What one can reasonably deduce from these errors is that Maspero did not produce the drawing whilst inside the burial chambers but must have created it back at his place of study, relying on his visual memory as to the layout of the building and using the measurement notes that he had written down to complete the drawing's details.

Maspero's publication served as the standard reference document for the burial chambers from their date of publication onwards and many of the details that he first described in his work can be found again in later books concerning this pyramid. In particular Maspero created a numbering system for the columns of hieroglyphs (known to Egyptologists as 'racks') within the pyramid so that scholars would have a numerical reference system with which they could easily locate and describe the columns of hieroglyphs. Unfortunately, whilst numbering the

Cross section of the main chamber

The unusual manner in which the roof extends beyond the limits of the chamber's walls is shown in the diagram. The fractured wall section above the doorway illustrates the state in which Maspero discovered the pyramid in 1881.

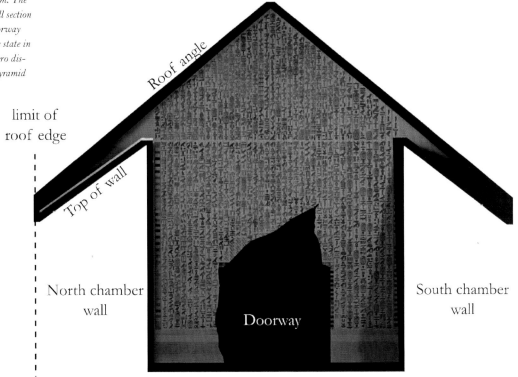

limit of
roof edge

Roof angle

Top of wall

North chamber wall

South chamber wall

Doorway

racks Maspero made several errors, missing out some sequential numbers and duplicating others. For example there is no rack numbered 129 and there are two racks numbered 61, and these eccentricities managed to find their way through to even the most modern of books. Maspero's numbering system, and a suitable alternative to it, are dealt with in the appendix to this book as it will become evident that a rationalised numbering system is vital to the comprehension of the riddle which is contained within the monument's architecture.

In 1908 a German Egyptologist named Kurt Sethe published the first comprehensive listing of the hieroglyphs that are found on the walls of the chambers inside the pyramid of Unas. Using Maspero's numbering system he diligently drew by hand all of the twenty six thousand hieroglyphs in a massive two volume work, along with all of the corresponding hieroglyphs from the other pyramids in the Saqqarah region. And so by the early years of the 20th century the pyramid of Unas had been well documented, and it was not until 1950 that the next significant publication on the subject was to appear, this being a book by the Russian Egyptologist Alexandre Piankoff. In this work appear the first detailed photographs of the walls of the chambers comprising of full views and beau-

tifully detailed close up photographs of the hieroglyphs on each section of every wall. By using Piankoff's close ups it is possible to create a mosaic of all of the walls on which the hieroglyphs are inscribed in sufficient detail so that every symbol can be clearly identified.

The final reference work for the pyramid was published in 1996 by the French Egyptologist Audran Labrousse and is a thorough scientific report on the survey that he and his team undertook in the underground chambers. The work includes accurate magnetic north measurements and the detailed dimensions of every stone within the pyramid's chambers, including spot heights of all the floor sections in relation to sea level. The diagrams included in the book contain comprehensive information regarding the stonework, hieroglyph racks, entrance passage angles and the coffin and contain none of the errors that are apparent in the earlier work by Maspero. The small step at the start of the entrance passage is clearly defined; the sloping sections of the roof are correctly shown along with the relevant distances between the wall tops and the roof sections; the west wall of the main chamber is correctly drawn with the recessed gable set back from the wall face by the cor-

The entrance passage of the Unas pyramid.

The step at the start of the entrance passage of the pyramid of Unas, a feature which have hindered the construction project and which was presumably added at the very end of the building process.

The west wall of the main chamber.

A photograph of the main chamber of the pyramid with the south wall removed, showing the gable of the west wall which is set back from the face of the wall by 50cm

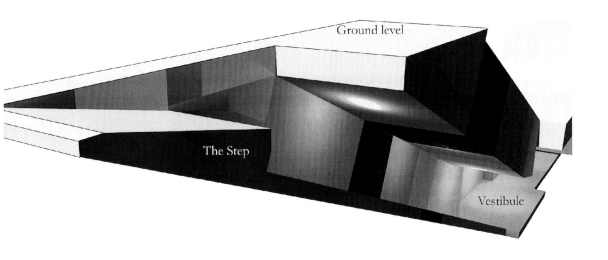

Ground level

The Step

Vestibule

rect distance.

    The only detail that is not shown in its original format is the lid of the coffin, since by the time that Labrousse came to carry out his survey work, the Egyptian Antiquities Organization (the renamed government department) had carried out extensive reparation work inside the chambers and had replaced the coffin lid into the position in which they assumed it was designed to be, resting on a wooden plinth to the west side of the coffin. There is one extra detail in Labrousse's work which cannot be found in that of the earlier books, that being the location and size of the square hole in the main chamber's floor which was created at the time of the room's construction to hold the canopic chest of the Pharaoh. (The canopic chest was a box which was divided vertically into four quarters and used, according to Egyptologists, to store the internal organs of the dead Pharaoh after the process of mummification had been carried out on the body.)

    By referring to these four authors, Maspero, Sethe, Piankoff and Labrousse an apparently accurate picture of the pyramid of Unas's underground chambers can be reconstructed. Egyptologists have diligently documented everything that can be documented, the Supreme Council for Antiquities (the governmental department renamed for the 3rd

time) have repaired all of the damaged areas of the walls and floors, the rooms have had an electric lighting system wired into them and the whole subject of the archaeological analysis of the chambers can be perceived as being closed. Indeed, in order to keep this stunning and highly important historic location in its best possible state of preservation, a metal door has been added to the start of the entrance passage which is kept permanently locked to prevent anyone from the general public from entering the chambers.

    So whereas the treasures of the underground chambers had previously laid in the dark for 4000 years, buried beneath a mountain of sand and rubble, thanks to the dedicated work of Egyptologists over the last century or so the rooms are now documented, preserved and available for scholars to study, bathed in bright white artificial light and almost as clear as the day that they were created. And what those scholars and Egyptologists tell us regarding the chambers of the pyramid can be summarised as follows :

    " *The three underground rooms in the pyramid are lined up along and east-west axis, all three are rectilinear and are accessible from the outside via a perfectly aligned north-south entrance passage which connects to the middle of the three rooms. The underground complex served as a burial chamber for the Pharaoh Unas who lived and ruled Egypt around 2350 BCE, and who was buried in the coffin which can be found in the main chamber of the pyramid. The hieroglyphs on the walls are sacred texts which were carved around the chambers in order to assist and protect the soul of the Pharaoh in the afterlife. The damage that is evident to some of the walls within the chambers was done by tomb robbers at some unknown time in the past, and these same tomb robbers account for the fact that when the rooms were first entered by Maspero in 1881, that there were no treasures of any type found within the building"*

There should be no reason to question any of what the Egyptologists tell us about the underground chambers of this pyramid for a number of reasons. First, unlike the sprawling archaeological site of the Giza plateau which covers millions of square meters, the total floor area of the Unas chambers is a mere 50 square meters - about the size of a small bedsit apartment. Second, the rooms were first documented in 1881 and they have been studied in detail for 128 years : when you spend 128 years studying the details of anything the size of a small bedsit apartment it is highly improbable that you will have missed any significant detail. Thirdly, the study work has not been carried out by members of the general public, but by highly educated academics from the world of Egyptology which is a disciplined and established university departmental subject, with a rigorous set of principles and research methodologies.

So it should be possible to come to a conclusion regarding the pyramid of Unas by looking at the published works, considering the source of these works, appreciating the depth of detail within them and comparing all of this information to the pyramid itself, whether in situ or by way of photographic records. By doing so the correspondence between the academic study work and the chambers can been determined and a conclusion should be able to be drawn that the subject matter does appear to constitute what could be called a 'closed book'.

Principle Problem

To find in these reference works that perhaps one of the twenty six thousand hieroglyphs had been documented incorrectly would not be that surprising, since the task of recording them must have been particularly la-

bour intensive during which human errors are always bound to occur. Similarly, to uncover a small numerical error in the surveying work where a distance varied by one centimeter between authors would also be on the limit of what one would expect to find when looking at the documentation of the pyramid.

However, upon examining all of the work by the academics and diligently comparing it to the pyramid itself, what we find is something quite extraordinary. The Egyptologists have completely missed all of the architectural details of this building, their beautifully detailed drawings of the walls are utterly wrong, their ground plans bear no resemblance whatsoever to the actual rooms which they purport to represent, and they have missed the most significant detail of the hieroglyphs. That the documentation of one of the jewels in the crown of Egyptology is scientifically bereft of all validity is a statement which requires exemplary explanation to back it up, and the first section of this book provides exactly that, and to a degree of detail which will satisfy even the most critical of minds.

How could it be that after 128 years of study that the principle details of this building have still not been discovered and how could the architects of this stunning construction have managed to deceive such a distinguished group of modern academics and scholars for so long ? The answer to all these questions has its origins in the series of subtle clues that have been deliberately left throughout the architecture of these rooms by whoever it was who designed and built them, and it is to those clues that we will first turn our attention.

A room full of clues

A ROOM FULL OF CLUES

Duplicate of
Piankoff's plate
number IV

The photograph
shows the northwest
corner of the
antechamber. The
doorway on the
right leads back
along the entrance
passage, and the
doorway on the left
leads through to
the main chamber.
The coffin lid with
its broken corner is
visible through the
doorway.

If you were to travel to Egypt today, make your way to the pyramid of Unas and stand inside the chambers which lie beneath the massive mound of earth, you would see exactly what the Egyptologists have seen. Having entered the pyramid via the entrance passage, stooping low as you walked the 27m of its length beneath the shoulder high ceiling, you would be able to stretch back to your full height amongst the four walls of the pyramid's antechamber. All the walls of this room would look rectangular, as would the floor, and looking back down the entrance passage which runs north-south you would instinctively realise that the passage met the room square-on, since the racks of hieroglyphs on the chambers north wall, the lines of the roof stars above you and the entrance passage are all perfectly visually aligned.

Indeed you could also take a photograph of the room on which you would see the very same features, such as the photograph shown in the illustration opposite. This photograph, as with all the others in this section of the book, is taken inside a millimeter accurate computer model of the pyramid of Unas in which both the hieroglyphs and the building's architectural construction are perfectly recreated. The reason for using photography of a model rather than of the real pyramid chambers will become evident as the work progresses, and for now all that is required is to understand why this particular photograph is important. It is a duplicate of one of the seven original photographs from the 1950's publication by Piankoff and by comparing the photograph taken inside the model with the Piankoff's original, one can see that what he photographed and what is available from the model are identical views from inside the antechamber.

Carrying on our journey and moving into the main chamber via the connecting passage, which once again forces you to stoop down to traverse its short length, you would be confronted by a room which perfectly matches the description given by the Egyptologists. You would see rectangular walls and floor, an ornately carved ceiling of stars above you, the front half of the room being filled with racks of hieroglyphs and the back half of the room decorated with intricate patterns of paint work, the pattern also having been carved meticulously into the alabaster walls onto which it was painted. Taking another two photographs, once again duplicates of Piankoff's photography and shown in the subsequent two diagrams, you can see that the main chamber of the building accurately resembles that which the Egyptologists have described to us.

Before continuing in this chapter, have a very good look at the three photographs that have just been presented. Study them carefully, look to see if you can see anything unusual in the architecture displayed within them and then when you are finished put this book to one side and attempt to describe the rooms to yourself without the aid of the photographs. If you are able to do that then we should be in a good position to continue, since you will have just come to a personally satisfactory conclusion regarding the building that you have just visited, in a very similar manner to the Egyptologists who visited the rooms in person.

If we now start to analyse the building rather than just look at it, the subject starts to take on a completely different feel. The anomalies in the architecture, or clues, that we come across can be divided into three sections. First we have visual clues which can be seen within the rooms during a sufficiently diligent visual inspection; second are the clues derived from the survey and measuring data which are only evident after a suitably detailed analysis has been performed; and third are the unusual features within the rooms which are all visually apparent from the outset but logically ambiguous.

Visual Clues

The first visual clue that indicates that something is not correct in the Egyptologists understanding of this monument can be seen on the north wall of the main chamber. To line up the compass points with a sense of spatial awareness, this wall can be found on your right hand side after walking through the connecting passage from the antechamber. If you look up at the top of the wall you will see that the wall appears to rise from left to right and that the architects and builders were fully aware of

Two views of the main chamber are shown, the first looking back towards the antechamber with the coffin lid in view, and the second looking down the main chamber towards the coffin and the west wall.

this fact since the first few rows of stars on the ceiling have been adjusted to compensate for this rise in the wall's height. The design of the stars is unambiguous and is shown on the accompanying diagram, and one can be quite certain of the fact that the stars have been carved to visually match the top of the wall section. You will also notice on the roof that there are a series of red lines which the builders used to help align the stars on the ceiling and which are now once again visible since the paint work that once covered them has now largely faded.

Now have a look once more at the second of the Piankoff duplicate photographs which you have recently studied and focus you attention at the corresponding section of the north wall. Remarkably you will notice that there is no evidence whatsoever of a rise towards the end of this wall. Although somewhat confusing initially this can be rationalised by deducing that rather than the wall rising at the east end of the chamber, it must actually be built so that it comes into the chamber towards the south wall, as this would give an identical effect when viewed from a standing position at the chamber's entrance. And what is so noteworthy about this, apart from the fact that it means that the main chamber floor cannot possibly be rectangular, is that the carving of the first row of roof stars on the ceiling is lined up with a *visual* perception of the top of the north wall and not an *architectural* one. Someone has gone to great lengths to carefully align the stars with an imaginary line emanating from the viewer's eye level (when standing besides the doorway) and being projected onto the

sloping roof section. Since Egyptologists tell us that the Ancient Egyptians who constructed this building did not understand what we consider to be simple mathematical concepts such as trigonometry, then the alignment of this row of stars must have been done by either guesswork or, more likely, done visually once the roof had been put in place. This is a particularly fascinating concept, since carving the roof stars inside the dark chamber would have required significantly more effort than if they were pre-carved whilst lying flat in the sunny outdoors prior to the roof slabs being fitted to the room.

The second visual clue is similar in nature to the first in that it involves visual perception in both its creation and functionality. On the west wall of the main chamber, on the portion of wall that cannot be seen from the room's entrance (due to the coffin blocking the view) there is no paint work, and a clear but somewhat faded line of terminating paint indicates that there never has been any paint work on this section of the west wall, as shown in the diagram. To understand why this feature is so unusual one has to return to the story that the Egyptologists tell us regarding the purpose of the building : that it is a burial chamber of the Pharaoh Unas. It's construction must have been a considerable logistical undertaking and its unique purpose was to serve as the sanctuary for the body of the dead Pharaoh which would have been surrounded by treasures and religious 'spells' to help his soul progress in the afterlife. Once the ceremonial burial had taken place, three enormous granite locking stones would have been lowered into place and the underground

The distortion in the north wall

The apparent rise in the north wall is shown, with dashed lines indicating the continuation lines from the wall's regular top and from the red builder's marks which were used to align the grid square of stars.

chambers would have fulfilled their purpose and become the *exclusive* domain of the soul of the departed king. Following this story to its conclusion, one would assume that the Pharaoh's soul, having left its body resting at peace in the coffin, and being surrounded by golden treasures and magical hieroglyphs, would be fully aware of the rather tatty lack of paint work situated just one meter to the west side of the coffin from which it had just emerged. It is a fact that the *only* beneficiary of the missing paint work behind the coffin would be a fully functioning and breathing human-being entering the chamber and visually inspecting it that makes the absence of paint on this wall section so remarkable. The visual craftsmanship in this section of the west wall does not comply at all with the purported function of the building and is more evidence that something is not quite correct.

The third visual clue which is apparent upon casual inspection of the chambers is the missing racks of hieroglyphs on the gables of the east and west walls of both the main chamber and the antechamber. In the diagrams shown across the following four pages all of these four sections of wall are shown. It can be seen on the east wall of the antechamber below the level of the gable that there are 36 racks of hieroglyphs bordered on either side by one rack of artwork, and that on the gable above there are 36 racks of hieroglyphs but only one rack of artwork which can be found on the south end of the gable. The end rack at the north side of the gable has been left blank or, to put it another way, is missing. It is a fact that could easily be overlooked and indeed was overlooked in grand

fashion by Maspero who did not allocate rack numbers to either the artwork racks throughout the pyramid or the blank racks, since he was primarily interested in numbering the hieroglyphs and not the architecture. The west wall of the antechamber shows a similar design where the wall has 37 racks of hieroglyphs bordered to the north and south by two racks of artwork, one at either end, and the gable has the same rack design but with the northern rack of artwork missing.

Moving through to the main chamber, the east wall is made up of 38 racks of hieroglyphs with a single rack of artwork at either end, but the gable contains 40 racks of hieroglyphs which sit vertically above the 38 racks of hieroglyphs on the wall and the two artwork racks. The west wall of the main chamber contains only the artwork that surrounds the coffin and so there is no way of comparing the wall and the gable. Much more importantly, as we noted earlier when looking at the errors in Maspero's drawing, the gable of the west wall of the main chamber is set back by half a meter in relation to the wall itself, so although it can be seen from inspection of photographs that there are 40 racks of hieroglyphs on the gable, there is no way of determining whether those 40 racks fill the same width as the chamber's west wall, or whether there are blank racks at one or both ends. In fact it is not even possible to determine if the hieroglyph racks could possibly extend past the northern and southern extremities of the chamber's width and since any visual inspection of this gable taken from a single fixed reference point will include parallax error, we have no easy

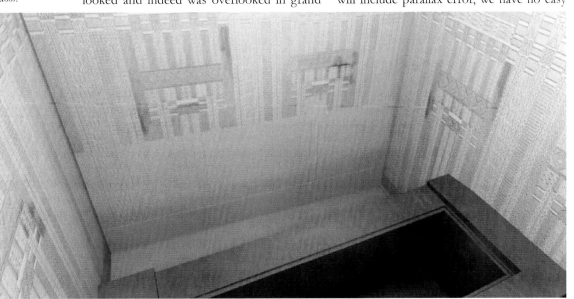

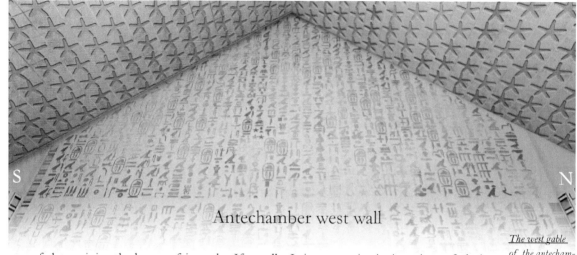

way of determining the layout of its racks. If we turn to the Egyptologists for an answer on this subject we can see in the work of Labrousse that in his illustration of the west wall and gable of the main chamber (figure 22 in his work) he shows the ends of the 40 racks of hieroglyphs aligned with the north and south walls of the chamber.

Alternatively we can look to see if there is a pattern to the architectural design of the 4 gable ends of the two rooms. If you study the diagrams of the gables and take into consideration the number of racks on each gable *regardless of whether they contain hieroglyphs, artwork or are blank*, then you will find that, looking at them in order from the east end of the series of chambers to west, they contain 38,39 and 40 racks respectively, suggesting that the west gable of the main chamber should contain 41 racks if the architectural pattern has been followed logi-

cally. It is a most intriguing piece of design, and one which the buildings creators would have known could only be solved by detailed analysis of the chamber. But therein lies the enigma, since this building was supposed to be sealed for eternity and as the architects went to considerable lengths to incorporate massive slabs of granite to block the entrance passage from possible intruders, for whom exactly did the architects design the west gable's riddle ?

The fourth visual clue within the chambers is so obvious that it has been missed by every person who has ever studied this building (as opposed to the three previous clues which are subtly hidden). On the north wall of the main chamber is a massive, crude scar which traces out a curved path through the limestone into which the hieroglyphs are carved, the slightly raised edge of which casts significant shadows in many

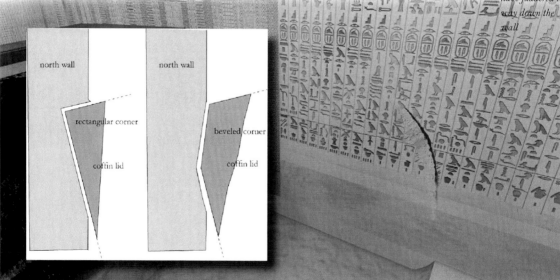

north wall   north wall

rectangular corner   beveled corner

coffin lid   coffin lid

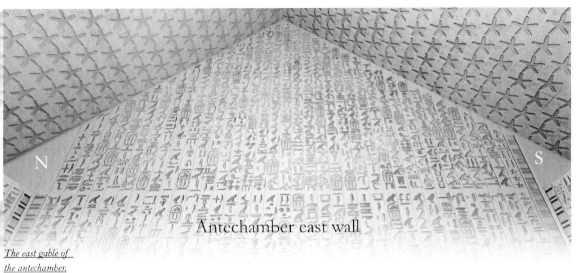

N
S

Antechamber east wall

The east gable of the antechamber.

On this wall it is the left most rack on the gable which has been left blank, and the correspondence with the west gable can be seen.

photographs of the chamber. The Egyptologists have presumably concluded that it was created by tomb robbers when they slid the granite lid from the coffin and allowed it to crash haphazardly to the floor, scratching the soft limestone walls as it fell and gouging out the enormous scar that can be seen in the diagram. In the second Piankoff photograph from earlier in this chapter the coffin lid can be seen in the position in which it was found by Maspero and the damaged corner of the coffin lid, which again presumably was the result of it crashing to the floor from the height of the top of the coffin, is visible at the back left corner of the lid. The explanation that the scar was created by the tomb robbers and the

lid is so obvious that one has no real reason to question it : the curved shape of the scar and its position on the wall clearly indicates that the coffin lid must have been its inadvertent architect. However, once you start to analyse this proposition rather than just ignore the scar as a piece of unintentional damage, things start to become significantly less clear.

The accompanying diagram shows two views of the coffin from which it is evident that the north west corner of the body of the coffin is chamfered. The measurements that were used in the 3D reconstruction of the coffin were taken from the survey work of Labrousse and compared to private photographs of the coffin, and I have no reason to doubt the validity of this diagram in relation to the coffin's general profile - there is indeed a chamfer at this corner. If the lid of the coffin had been slid off in the direction of the chamber's entrance door and then had scraped down the north wall, it is the angle where the chamfered section meets the north side of the lid that would have gauged out the scar on the wall and not the north-west corner of the lid. The cross section of the gauge in the wall, which is shown in the previous diagram, could only

The coffin of the Unas pyramid

The first view shows the coffin as viewed from the back corner of the chamber, and the second is a plan view. Both illustrations show the shamferring on the coffin's corner.

NORTH

27cm

27cm

NORTH

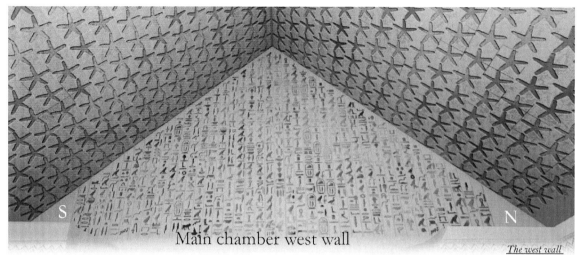

Main chamber west wall

have been made by the corner of the coffin lid since, had it been made by the angle of the chamfer, two things would have been apparent. First is that the cross section of the scar would have been significantly different as shown in the illustration and second, the height of the scar on the north wall would be situated 27cm lower than it is, that being the distance between the north-west corner of the lid and the angle where the chamfer meets the lid's side.

The only simple answer to this discovery is that the lid of the coffin was rectangular and therefore a completely different shape to the coffin itself, and that in the north-west corner the lid must have overlapped the coffin by nearly 4cm. To verify that this is the case one should simply be able to inspect the shape of the coffin lid, but upon doing so one is confronted by the fact that the corner of the lid that is damaged is exactly the same corner that we need to inspect and not even the fragmented section remains in the chamber for us to look at, which is a most unfortunate situation in which to find ourselves.

The fifth visual clue can be seen on the gable ends of the walls in both the antechamber and the main chamber and can be seen in all of the four diagrams. Have a look at the gap between the top of the chamber's side walls and the sloping roof sections and you will notice something quite peculiar. On the antechamber east gable the gap appears to be significantly larger on the north (left) side than on the right, yet on the corresponding gable of the west wall of the same room the gaps appear pretty much identical on both the north (right) and left sides. It is difficult to see this straight away due to the blank racks that appear at the ends of the gables, but with

a small amount of casual measuring you can very quickly see that the discrepancies do occur. The same is true on the east gable of the main chamber where the gap on the north side appears to be larger than that on the south, and this anomaly is much easier to spot on this gable since the racks of hieroglyphs fill up the whole width of the wall. There are a few possible answers which would explain why the gaps are different at either end of the gables : the apex of the roof may not be in the center of the room ; the angles of the roof stones may be completely different ; or the walls may not be the same height on either side of the room. Whichever of these solutions one chooses to adopt one is left with the same conclusion, which is that the rooms cannot be at all symmetrical in design - yet the Egyptologists tell us that they are. On the drawings of Maspero, Piankoff and Labrousse the gaps between the wall tops and the roof slabs are shown as being identical on both the north and south sides of the room, the apex is shown as being in the center of the two rooms, and we are once again left with a very strange feel about this building.

The sixth visual clue comes from a

The west wall of the main chamber.

It is not possible to work out the layout of this wall from casual viewing since the gable is set back from the wall by half a meter.

The west wall of the main chamber.

A group of Egyptology students standing infront of the west wall of the chamber, which shows a non horizontal incline along its upper section

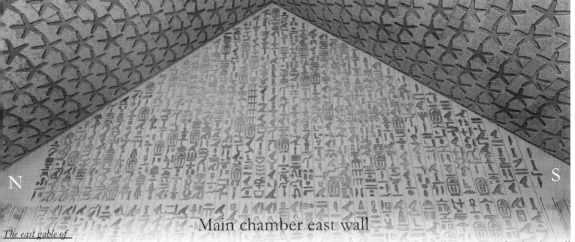

The east gable of the main chamber.

This gable displays a completely different design from those in the antechamber, with the hieroglyph racks extending to the far extremities of the side walls.

The drill holes behind the coffin

The asymetric nature of the drill holes behind the coffin suggests that the two holes may well have been positioned for a specific purpose.

photograph of a group of students who visited the Unas burial chambers in 2001 accompanied by the current director of the S.C.A., Dr. Hawass. The photograph can be found on the internet by searching for "fieldtrip6 Unas" in a search engine. It is located on the official website of Dr.. Hawass, and the photograph is reproduced in on the page opposite. The group of students in the photograph cover the majority of the foreground of the image and behind them can be seen the black shape of the coffin in the chamber. It is a simple task to determine that the high contrast line which defines the top of the lid of the coffin is roughly horizontal and that the camera which took the photograph was being held horizontally and the time the photograph was taken. If you now look at the back (west) wall of the chamber you can see that the right side of this wall is considerably lower than the left side, despite the repaired section of the wall in the center having no paint work which would have assisted the eye in seeing this fact. If you

draw a horizontal line across the back wall of the chamber, lined up with the back left corner of the west wall, you will find that the wall slopes down from left to right to quite a large degree. It is also evident from the positioning of the camera in the room, which is only slightly offset to the left of the room's center line, that this apparent slope on the wall cannot be accounted for by parallax error or perspective distortion. Compare what you have just seen in this photograph to third of the Piankoff photographs and you will see that the back wall of the chamber appears to be perfectly horizontal along its top surface in Piankoff's. The west wall of the chamber appears differently in two photographs.

The final visual clue within the chambers is located behind the coffin, where two drill holes can be found in the floor stone. The egyptologists have suggested that the purpose of these drill holes was to act as fixing locations for a wooden table

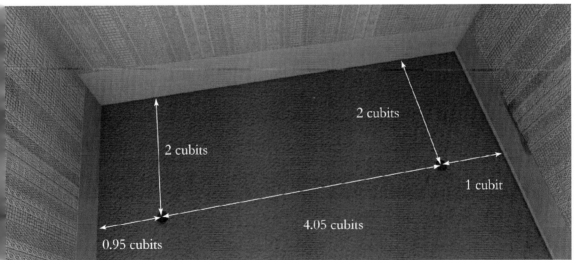

2 cubits

2 cubits

1 cubit

4.05 cubits

0.95 cubits

which stood behind the coffin and supported the coffin's lid prior to the ceremonial burial of the Pharaoh. The drill hole to the north side of the chamber is located exactly 52,5cm or 1 Egyptian cubit from the north wall, and 105cm or 2 Egyptian cubits from the west wall suggesting that its placement was a routine affair. However the southern drill hole is situated only 48cm from the south wall, and the lack of symetry in the system suggests that the two holes may well have served different purposes. If they were intended to simply fix a wooden bench in place then one would expect the holes to both have been placed 1 cubit from the two respective side walls with a 4 cubit gap between them.

Surveying Clues

With such an array on conflicting visual information it is only a matter of time before you need to consult the measurements taken by the group of Egyptologists to attempt to determine the solution to these riddles. Available to us is the drawing made by Maspero in 1881, a technical drawing included in the work of Piankoff from the 1950's and the detailed work of Labrousse from 1987 which has to serve as the primary reference material due to the detailed nature of the measurements within it. But upon a preliminary inspection of this work you find that rather than solving the riddles that we have just seen, that the surveying work simply adds to the problems, which in itself is a most unusual state of affairs.

The first of the surveying clues comes from the short passageway which connects the antechamber and the main chamber. In his work Labrousse states that the north wall of this passage is 156cm in length, yet the south side is 154cm with his measurements rounded off to the nearest centimeter. Two centimeters of difference between the work of Maspero in 1881 and Labrousse in 1987 would not be significant, but this is two centimeters of difference in the same survey work down the sides of a very short corridor. Consequently it is absolutely impossible that the west wall of the antechamber and the east wall of the main chamber can be parallel to each other and since the Egyptologists tell us that the two rooms are rectangular, they cannot share a common central axis line. What is even more remarkable about this fact is that the wall which divides the two chambers from each other is made from single blocks of limestone weighing nearly 40 tonnes, and since the passageway walls are different lengths, the opposing faces of the huge wall blocks must have been carved at different angles. The two centimeter difference in the passage wall lengths corresponds to an angular difference between the two faces of these blocks of nearly one degree and would necessitate a difference in south wall length in either the antechamber or main chamber of 4.5cm in order for the architecture to all join together. Unfortunately, since Labrousse made no reference to the consequences of this disparity in passage wall lengths and showed on the plan view of the chambers' walls that the passage and rooms were all perpendicular to each other and sharing the same central axis line, then we have no way of knowing what is going on here.

The second clue from the surveying is absolutely identical in nature to the first, suggesting that there may well be a common pattern between the two. The east and west walls of the entrance passage are composed of granite blocks from the start of the lock section onwards in the direction of the chambers, with no hieroglyphic carvings to be found on their inner facing surface. However, the last block on either side of the passage, prior to it meeting the antechamber, is made from limestone and contains the first hieroglyph inscriptions that one comes across when entering the chambers. The end limestone block on the east wall is stated as being 146cm in length, and the corresponding block on the west wall 143cm in length, again with measurements rounded off to the nearest centimeter. It would appear that we have the very same problem with the entrance passage as we did with the joining passage between the two chambers, but since the blocks of stone in question are, in this case, part of the longer entrance passage walls it is necessary to check that all of the survey measurements of each block of stone from the pyramid's entrance to the antechamber doorway correctly correspond on either side, so that the start of these final blocks can be confirmed as being on exactly opposite positions on the walls. The analysis of these stones is shown later in the book, and one can find that a one centimeter error is apparent in the cumulative lengths of the individual stones when compared to the stated passage lengths, and that the 3cm difference in the final blocks does indeed represent the exact same problem that we saw in the first surveying clue, that the entrance passage and the antechamber cannot be perpendicular to each other.

(Opposite) is the view back down the entrance passage showing that the lines of roof stars and the passage appear to be perfectly aligned with each other.

On this page is a photograph taken inside the antechamber showing a view back down the main passage and shows how utterly perplexing this second clue is. It is clear from the photograph that the lines of roof stars, the passageway's longitudinal axis and hieroglyph racks are all lined up. The visual experience inside the pyramid shows us that the entrance passage meets the antechamber north wall perpendicularly, yet the surveying information shows us quite clearly that this is not the case and we are left with an utterly confusing situation.

The third of the surveying clues concerns the construction of the north wall of the antechamber and, due to the unusual layout within the work of Labrousse, involves looking at his detailed measurements of the end of the entrance passage stonework as well as those of the north wall. The end lintel of the passageway is described in section F4 of his work and since the lintel also forms part of the upper level of the north wall, it is necessary to combine its details with those described in section G1 of the work, which lists the details of the other stones in the north antechamber wall. When you do this exercise you find that there is large triangular section of stonework which is missing from the north wall, and which is not visible on the photography from within the chamber - the stone simply does not exist.

The illustration on the next page shows exactly where the problem occurs. Labrousse states in the introduction to the antechamber section of his work that the length of the north wall is 371cm. He states in section F4 that the lintel of the passage is *trapezoidal* in cross section with a top length of 294cm and a base length of 309cm, and that at either side of this trapezoid are two blocks of stone. That on the east side (right) is angled with the top measuring 31cm and the base measuring 26cm, and that on the left side is the same height as the lintel and 37cm in width. Since he also states that the antechamber north wall is rectangular (as shown in all his illustrations), the combination of all these facts leaves us with a missing triangular section of stone work which is 9cm in width along its top.

The fourth of the surveying clues concerns the smallest of the rooms in the pyramid, known as the serdab, and to which we have so far paid no attention. In the 1881 work of Maspero, he states that the south wall of the serdab is 3cm shorter than the

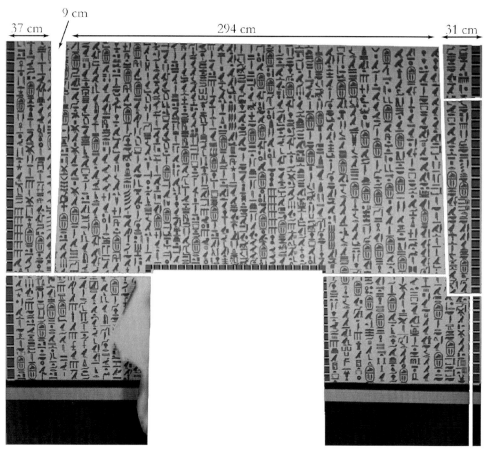

37 cm — 9 cm — 294 cm — 31 cm

371 cm

north wall, a difference that one could easily overlook if it were not for the fact that it is very similar to the discrepancies shown in the surveying clues 1 and 2. When we come to checking the values for these wall measurements in the survey work of Labrousse from 1987 we find that rather than individually specifying all of the sizes of the stone blocks, as he had throughout the two other rooms in the building, he resorts to generalised measurements stating that the alcoves in the room are all the same depth at 123,5cm. What is missing from his work in the serdab is the measurements of the individual pieces of stonework, and one gets the general impression that he paid only cursory attention to the details in this section of the pyramid. Also Maspero, in his work of 1881, states that the passage that connects the antechamber to the serdab is 1.51m in length, and yet Labrousse states that the passage is 153cm in length, giving us once again a disparity of two centimeters and raising the question as to whether the passageway could also contain the same difference in wall lengths that was seen in the

other two passages. Luckily in this section of the building we can easily check the surveying information against the known construction of the building because the east walls of the antechamber also form the serdab roof and the alignment of the join between subsequent blocks of roof stones can be checked against the alignment of the back wall of the serdab. When this is done we find that there is a massive 5cm disparity between the survey work and the visual location of this join line, which quite clearly is aligned with the left side of the central alcove of the serdab, suggesting once again that there is an angular error somewhere in the surveying information.

Unusual Features

So far we have looked at the visual clues that can be seen within the pyramid's chambers and the more complex clues that can be derived from the surveying work,

*The top layer of the ante-
chamber east walls are the end
faces of the roof stones which
make up the serdab ceiling
- note the alignment of the
roof and walls*

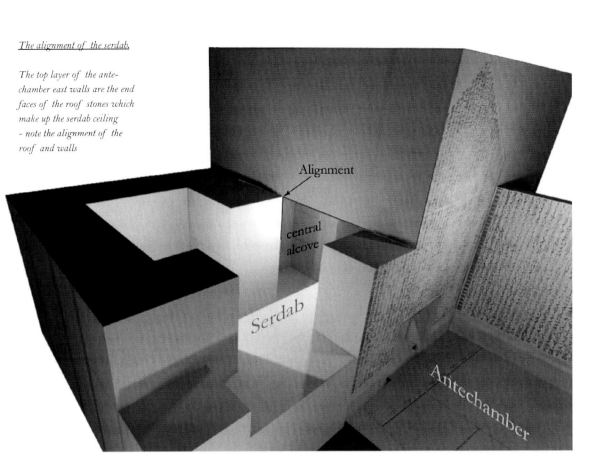

Alignment

central
alcove

Serdab

Antechamber

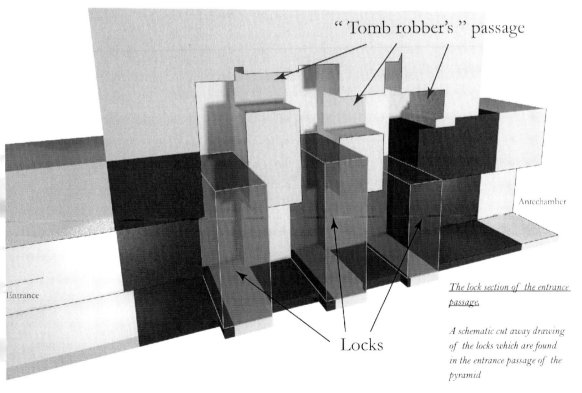

"Tomb robber's" passage

Antechamber

Entrance

Locks

*The lock section of the entrance
passage.*

*A schematic cut away drawing
of the locks which are found
in the entrance passage of the
pyramid*

and both of these sets of information give us hard factual evidence to work with. The last set of clues, which I am calling 'unusual features' do not contain hard facts, they contain suppositions and logical deductions and I am fully aware that they would not stand up to rigorous scientific analysis since they are nothing more than opinion. I have included them despite these misgivings since I consider them essential to the overall feel of the preliminary analysis of this building and they help greatly in getting the mind more involved in the subject matter.

The first unusual feature concerns the locking stones in the entrance corridor and tomb robbers passageway that has been cut above them. In the simplified diagram on the previous page the general layout of the locking stone section of the entrance passage is shown, with the three granite locks shown in the place they would have been at the time that the building was sealed. The drawing is an entirely fictional piece of work, since none of the locking stones was in place when the chambers were opened by Maspero 128 years ago. Indeed, despite the fact the stones must have weighed at least 8 metric tonnes each, no remains of them have ever been found and the explanation of this fact from the Egyptologists is that they were destroyed by the tomb robbers when they broke in to the pyramid. Leaving aside the curious decision that these tomb robbers came to, which was to remove all 24 tonnes of granite by labouriously dragging it back up the entrance slope of the pyramid, there is a much more puzzling aspect to these missing stones.

Directly above where the locking stones should have been, and shown in the diagram with red sided stones, is the tomb robbers tunnel which was carved through the limestone ceiling stones to allow the tomb robbers to get past the granite blocking stones and enter the pyramid. As is abundantly clear from the diagram, the tomb robbers would have to had removed the first of the granite blocks before creating this passage, begging the question as to why they would have created the tunnel in the first place if removing the lock stones was already within their abilities. Also, the combination of the tunnel and the missing stones makes no sense whatsoever. If the tomb robbers had to cut a tunnel above the granite locks than they would have had no reason to remove those very same locks at a later point in time, since they already would have had access to the internal areas of the building. Conversely if they had removed the locks first, then the tunnel would have been a ridiculous undertaking. Either of the two features, the tunnel or the locking stones, on its own would possibly make the tomb robbers theory a plausible argument, but the presence of both is quite bizarre.

The second unusual feature in the pyramid is the extensive but selective damage that was perpetrated by these tomb robbers, if the Egyptologists are to be believed. In many of the diagrams so far this damage is evident around the door frames, along the wall tops in the main chamber and also to the floor of this room. The damage to the north and west wall top sections in the main chamber can plausibly be explained by the robber's theory, as can the missing floor sections, but the damage around the door frames in both the main chamber and antechamber needs some more detailed consideration. If you have ever been to a museum that houses relics from ancient Egypt, and particularly if you recall the iconic golden death mask of the Pharaoh Tutankamun, you will realise that the treasures that one would expect to find inside the burial chamber of a Pharaoh are both precious and delicate works of art. Ever since starting work in the pyramid of Unas, I have had a comical vision in my mind of a band of robbers, working by naked flame light and in a rush to get out of the building before being discovered, smashing the golden death mask of the Pharaoh haphazardly into the door frames of the pyramid of Unas with such force as to remove substantial amounts of limestone masonry. If the door frames ended up in such a damaged state, then one can only wonder in what state the treasures were in once they arrived back into the scorching sunshine that bathed the outside of the pyramid. In short, the attribution of the damage caused to the door frames to the tomb robbers adds yet another layer of confusion to this building.

The third unusual feature within the pyramid concerns the position in which the coffin lid was discovered by Maspero when he opened the building in 1881. As was shown earlier, the coffin lid was found at the east side of the chamber, situated some 4 meters from the coffin and was put there, according to the Egyptologists, by the tomb robbers as they plundered the treasures of the burial chamber. Now if you look at the dimensions of this lid, and consider the density of the material from which it is constructed, you will find that it weighs about 2 metric tonnes, equivalent to the weight of about 30 modern day human beings of average size. One can only imagine the number of people and amount of effort that would have been required to move this object. Whilst we are quite accustomed to the remarkable achievements of the ancient Egyptians and their building accomplishments with very heavy objects due to the stories that are told to us by the Egyptologists, transferring these gifts to a bunch of tomb robbers is out of the question. Furthermore there is no evident purpose in the moving of the lid down to the far end of the chamber - the only thing that it accomplished was to make access to the main chamber from the passageway a more difficult affair. In addition to the logistic problems involved in the positioning

of the coffin lid, it is also quite fascinating to note that the lid was discovered lying at an angle in relation to the sides of the pyramid, and by careful analytical reconstruction of the lid's position from photography this angle can be determined with some accuracy. The angle is very similar indeed to that in which the coffin itself was found in, as this also appears to have been moved during the complicated process of the tomb's robbery. The coffin and the coffin lid were found in identical mirror image positions to each other.

The fourth unusual features is also associated with the coffin, which quite bizarrely can be found resting upon two pieces of wood. The coffin is carved from a massive piece of stone and weighs in the region of 8 metric tonnes. When coffins such as this are placed into modern museums, such as an example in the Egyptology museum in Vienna which corresponds quite closely to the coffin found in the pyramid of Unas, the museum floor had to be

The serdab door.

The start of the passage from the antechamber to the serdab has been left unfinished by the builders

reinforced prior to the coffin's arrival, such is its weight. It is most unusual therefore to find a coffin of such mass resting upon two pieces of timber upon which, one can safely assume, the builders of this pyramid placed it. Had they placed in on the floor stones it would have been in a much more stable position, since the floor stones are in direct contact with the bedrock into which the chambers have been carved.

The fifth unusual feature is the un-finished door frame which announces the start of the passage that connects the ante-chamber to the serdab, and which is shown on the previous page. It is worth looking at the photography of this section of the pyramid in the publication by Labrousse in which it is even more clear that the miss-ing wall sections around the door are cov-ered with plaster work which has been very roughly applied by hand at the time of the building's construction. The contrast be-tween this sloppy piece of workmanship and the most exquisite details that can be seen on the hieroglyph covered walls is most striking, and it is odd that this one unique section of the underground cham-bers was left architecturaly unfinished. As Labrousse deduced in his work, it is quite clear that something was intended to be fit-ted into this section but that the work was never finished, and he makes the reasonable assumption that the missing feature was probably a decorative door frame. However, when compared to the stunning finishing of the chamber walls and also considering the ultimate purpose that the rooms served which was to house the body and soul of the departed Pharaoh, workmanship of this standard would surely not have ben ac-ceptable.

The last of our unusual features in the pyramid has already been mentioned earlier in this book, and is the small step that can be found at the entrance to the pyramid. Although this step is now covered up by a wooden entrance staircase which has been constructed by the S.C.A., its existence is in no doubt. This feature will be looked at in great er detail later in the book, but for now it begs one simple question - what on earth is it doing there ? It appears to serve no practical purpose whatsoever and must have been a significant annoyance and hin-drance to those who constructed this build-ing.

So, with all of the major clues and anomalies listed, let us recap what we know to this point. In the first chapter we looked at the classical story of the pyramid of Unas as told by the Egyptologists in which this jewel in the crown had been ex-plored ,measured and documented and then sealed in a perfect state of preservation. In the second chapter we have uncovered that rather than being the perfectly studied and documented monument that we would ex-pected, the pyramid of Unas is still, after 128 years of research work, as much of an utter mess on the inside as it is on the outside. The only significant difference be-ing that there is now a large locked metal door blocking our way in. The question is whether it is possible to reconcile all of the features and clues that we have come across so far, and then produce documentation that is sufficiently well detailed as to serve as an explanation as to how and why this building was constructed and as to where the Egyptologists have gone wrong. The answer to that question is that we can, but when we do so we will find that the sum of all the small parts of the puzzle that we have come across up to this stage combine to make a master puzzle which is consider-ably more significant than its component parts.

To start the analysis of the archi-tecture we are not going to go in to the pyr-amid armed with laser scanners or ground penetrating radar equipment or any of the trappings of modern archaeological study. We are going to tackle the problem in the way that the architects intend us to do, armed with nothing more than a small wooden ruler and a head full of curiosity.

UNAS THE RULER

Before starting our analysis of the pyramid of Unas there are three things that will greatly help us on our quest : an understanding of the measurement units that were in use at the time of its construction; a comprehension of the depth of mathematical knowledge that the ancient Egyptian's possessed; and a simple yet effective analysis technique, known as 'vanishing point analysis', which will allow us to make sense of the features that we have so far come across. The first allows us to reconstruct the architecture of the building in the proportions originally intended by the architects; the second allows us to recognise structural design elements and compare them to the limits of mathematical knowledge of the civilisation who were supposed to have carried out the construction; and the third permits us to examine the architectural detail without the hindrance of visual distortions. In this chapter my intention is not to present a detailed analysis of these three subjects, since they have been written about extensively in the past, - books such as "Ancient Egyptian Science , A source book" by Marshall Clagett already explains the first two subjects to a depth sufficient for any interested reader. My intention is to give a broad overview of the subjects which will set the rest of this work into context and allow a comprehension of the structural elements of the monuments to be understood *from the perspective of the builders, rather than the perspective of the reader.*

Let us start with the 'Royal Egyptian Cubit', the standard of measure which was used by the pyramid builders.

Royal Egyptian Cubit

The unit of measurement used in the design of an object or building is of paramount importance when attempting to analyse the item when one does not have access to the original design principles or drawings from which the item was created. This is particularly true when analysis of ancient artifacts is being performed since their state of degradation will often preclude the possibility to determine their exact original physical properties. Depending upon the state of preservation of the object, it may well be possible to extract certain measurements, such as an angle of inclination or distance, but these measurements will always be open to surveying error, and at best will provide no more than an indication of the objects approximate original dimensions. Unless and until the fundamental measurement units of design have been determined, the comprehension of the objects design principles will remain illusive.

Indeed one can go a stage further into this postulation and state that within the design of an object it is possible to hide certain fundamental design principles within the units of measurement. A simple Pythagorean primitive triangle with sides measuring 3m, 4m and 5m will appear less regularly designed if it is analysed in inches, where the side lengths of 118", 157" and 197" do not reveal any information whatsoever to the casual observer. In order to realise the inherent design of the triangle, the observer would first have to recognise the implicit proportions of the sides, which remain constant regardless of the measuring units, and then correctly interpret the result to determine the designer's original unit of measurement. When the design principles are considerably more complex than the simple example stated here, even a comprehensive analysis of the object's dimensions *in the units of the observer* will seldom reveal any of the underlying fundamental design structure, and it is in this way that an architect or engineer could, if they so wished, disguise the whole of a design system within the system's measuring units.

It is of great interest and practical use to us that the ancient Egyptians paid close attention to the perfect duplication and preservation of the measuring rods which were used in the design of the breathtaking monuments and temples which today litter the Egyptian landscape as ruins. The measuring rods were handed down through the generations, and show us without any ambiguity whatsoever, the exact system of measurements that was used in the very earliest of these structures. Since so little detailed information regarding the Old Kingdom (approx.. 2200 BCE - 2700 BCE) monu-

The Cubit measuring rod

The royal cubit has an accepted conversion value of 52.35 cm giving the following metric lengths for the various subdivisions :

Cubit   52.35 cm
Palm   7.48 cm
Digit   1.87 cm
Hexidigit*   0.12 cm

*The hexidigit was the smallest division of the cubit marked on the ruler: it is 1/16th of a digit , and therefore 1/448th of a cubit.

Unit naming conventions

ⓐ digit
ⓑ palm
ⓒ handbreadth
ⓓ fist
ⓔ 2 palms
ⓕ small span
ⓖ great span
ⓗ 4 palms
ⓘ 5 palms
ⓙ short cubit
ⓚ royal cubit

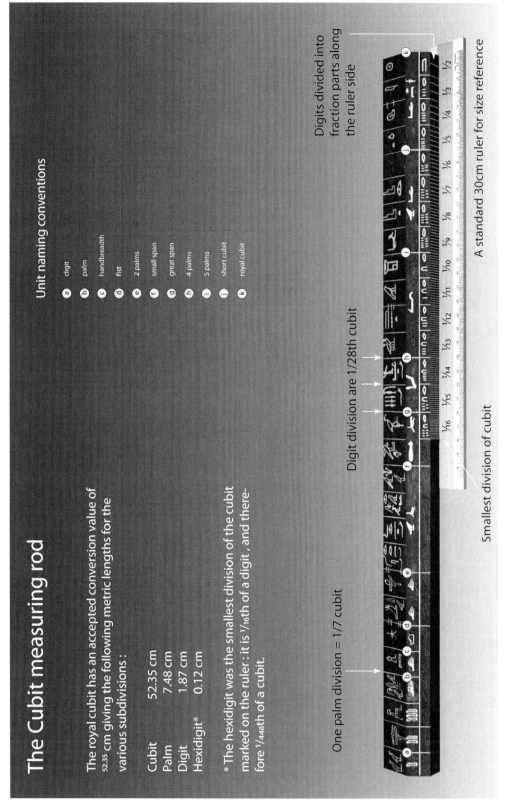

One palm division = 1/7 cubit

Digit division are 1/28th cubit

Smallest division of cubit

Digits divided into fraction parts along the ruler side

A standard 30cm ruler for size reference

The cubit rod

The illustration shows a computer modelled ancient Egyptian measuring rod with the original style of design painted onto the wooden rod.

ments has survived, by which I am referring to written documentation of the building methods and design principles, the knowledge of the measurement units incorporated in these monuments ranks highly in the available information and is a pre-requisite in the analysis of these buildings' architectural design.

There is a second method by which one can determine the original measuring units of these monuments, and that is by archaeological analysis of the remains of the building's structure. By using diligent surveying techniques accompanied by professional statistical reduction methods it is possible to extract a value of the builder's principle unit of measure in modern units to a degree of accuracy which is sufficiently exact as to be used as a measuring conversion standard. By far the best example of this technique that I have come across is in the work of William Petrie who not only surveyed the Great Pyramid of Giza with a dedication befitting the monument's grandeur, but was equally exact when it came to statistically reducing his results and publishing both the methods and results together, thus allowing independent verification of the conclusions. He is of course not alone in having published accurate surveying work from the Egyptian monuments, and as each of these works has become available to the public over the course of the last 150 years Egyptologists have settled on a acceptable numerical value for the 'royal cubit', the basic unit of measurement of the pyramid builders. One royal cubit is commonly accepted as being equivalent to 52.35cm in metric measure, although for reason that will become apparent later in this work, I have used a value of 52.3335cm for a number of years in my research work, the difference of 1.7 tenths of a milimeter being absolutely irrelevant to the analysis of the monuments being studied at the outset since the surveying data error margins are always larger than this value.

So having both the measuring rods which contain the system of units used in ancient Egypt and a conversion value derived from precision surveying of the ancient monuments at our disposal we are in a sound position from which to start any analysis of the measurement system that the ancients employed in the pyramid of Unas and beyond.

Looking at the cubit rod, one can see that it is divided into 28 section which are formed from seven groups of four divisions. These are the principle subdivisions of the cubit unit which were named the palm (seventh) and the digit (twenty eighth) since they

loosely corresponded to the width of a hand and the width of a finger, or digit. The illustration shows a digital reconstruction of an Ancient Egyptian measuring rod based loosely on the Maya rod which is preserved in the Louvre Museum in Paris.

The cubit, palm and digit can be seen marked along the top half of the bevelled edge of the wooden rod, and in the lower half of the bevel to the right are the hieroglyphic characters representing the fraction divisions of the digit - which are also marked with lines on the edge of the ruler. The top face of the rod contains the hieroglyphs for the names of the Gods that were associated with each of the digit measures. It has been noted by scholars previously that the choice of cubit subdivisions is somewhat unusual, since we are much more familiar with working in powers of 10 which one would consider to be a natural choice for humans, having 10 digits on the hand with which to count. Also unusual to the cubit system of the Ancient Egyptians is the subdivisions of the digit, which are divided through into fractions ranging from a half down to a sixteenth of a cubit. The smallest recorded measuring length on the cubit rods is therefore 1/448th of a cubit - in other words one 16th of one 28th of a cubit.

The additional markings on the rod which are not discussed in this text relate to other various subdivisions which are shown on the illustration and which comprise of all the known regular divisions of the cubit. Since there are numerous examples of these measuring rods which have survived the long duration of time since their creation, and which are displayed in various museums around the world, we can happily settle on the factual information uniformly contained upon them.

The measuring units of the pyramid builders is well known.

Ancient Egyptian Mathematics

The second area of knowledge we require in order to analyse the pyramids is an understanding of the capabilities of the ancient Egyptians when it came to mathematics. As one would expect, the subject has been studied and written about at length and I have no intention of replicating those works that have already been published. What will suffice for the content of this book is a brief overview of the depth of mathematical understanding known to the ancient Egyptians by reference to examples from some of the well known surviving mathematical papyrus manuscripts.

In particular there exist two papyrus manuscripts known as the 'Moscow' papyrus and the 'Rhind' papyrus, which contain between them 112 examples of Ancient Egyptian mathematical teachings. These scrolls have been studied in depth and from them a clear understanding of the principals of mathematical knowledge in ancient Egypt has been rediscovered by Egyptologists and historians.

The Moscow Papyrus is the smaller of the two scrolls, and obtains it's name from the fact that it can currently be found in the Museum of Fine Arts in Moscow, having been purchased by a Russian Egyptologist named Golenischev towards the end of the late 1800's. The 25 problems that can be found on the papyrus relate to the application of mathematics to the practical day to day living of the Egyptians, such as calculation of quantities of grain to be divided between people.

The Rhind papyrus gets it's name from a Scottish Egyptologist who reportedly purchased the document in Luxor Egypt in 1858. The papyrus is approximately 6 metres in length and a third of a metre wide and was written in 1650 B.C.E. by an ancient Egyptian scribe who signed his name as Ahmes, who states that he is transcribing a document which was written 200 years earlier. Whereas the date of the papyrus is at the beginning of what Egyptologist have labelled 'the New Kingdom', the original document dates from 1850 BCE and falls in what is known as 'the Middle Kingdom'. This is about 800 years after the commonly accepted date of construction of the Great Pyramid of Giza and 500 years after the supposed date of construction of the pyramid of Unas. In order to get an idea of the depth of mathematical knowledge in Egypt at the time it is worth noting an example that can be found on the Rhind or Ahmes papyrus as it is also known.

Problem or example 50 on the document (the numbering of the examples having been allocated in modern times) concerns calculating the area of a round field which has a diameter of 9 units. The solution to this problem today would be to multiply the square of the field's radius by Pi and the result would be immediately obtained. However the ancient Egyptians ran into two difficulties with this. Firstly they did not know an accurate value

of Pi, and so they used an estimate which one can deduce from example 50 as being 3.61 or more accurately 4 to the power of 8/9 squared. This shows that even one of the most fundamental of constants in the world of mathematics was not known to the ancient Egyptians around 1850 BCE, and also that the ancient Egyptians worked with fractions, and not in numbers containing decimal points.

The second problem that they came across was that they could not multiply numbers together, due partially to their system of numbering and secondly to the fact the conceptual idea of multiplication had yet to be developed. To explain this by way of a simple example, in our modern numbering system the numbers 11 and 99 can be written down using numbers of equal length (two digits), and we are so accustomed to this fact that it is hardly surprising to us. The Ancient Egyptians representation of numbers was largely pictorial, the number eleven was composed of two characters whereas the number 99 was composed of eighteen characters, nine of which represented the tens and nine of which represented the units. Addition and subtraction were easily achieved using firmly established principles, but multiplication and division were not, and so multiplication was achieved by successive addition, and division by successive subtraction clearly showing the level to which Ancient Egyptian mathematics had developed by the middle kingdom dynasties.

Probably the most important basic fundamental mathematical omission in their knowledge was that of rudimentary trigonometry. The Ancient Egyptians of 1850 B.C.E. would have had no theoretical idea regarding cosines, sines and tangents of angles, meaning that any building constructions which included angular measurements would have had to have been worked out pictorially rather than theoretically. Whereas we can specify the angle of a slope in degrees or radians, the Ancient Egyptians would have had to specify the slope in much the same way that we currently do in our modern road signs, for example one in 10, or 1 in 6. If one combines this knowledge with the measurements available in the cubit rod, it becomes clear that the builders would have been limited to a finite and relatively small collection of angular measurements from which to choose since the height and the length of the slope lines would have had to have been known subdivisions of a cubit.

the vanishing point, which is the name given to a point on a drawing, photograph of piece of artwork where lines which would be parallel in 3D space converge. The concept is not only an excellent manner in which to diagnose architectural elements within a building but is also a valid explanation as to how the human eye interprets three dimensional objects and thereby makes sense of the relative positioning of their elements.

The photograph shown on this page has had the perspective lines of the building superimposed upon the architectural features and, as can be seen, all of the parallel lines of the walls, roof and floor meet at a singular point on the back wall of the corridor. This is the point on the drawing known as the vanishing point, and a surprisingly large amount of information can be deduced from it, since the vanishing point is at the eye level of the observer, which in the case of this photograph was 169cm. We can draw a horizontal line across the photograph and from this determine the position of eye level on the pillar on the left of the photograph. This allows us to then perform a simple calculation to determine the width of the passageway on the same plane in the photograph as being 361cm, and from this we can work out where the center point of the corridor must be, allowing us to draw the center line of the whole corridor since it must connect to the vanishing point on the back wall.

We can see from the photograph that a series of lights are suspended in the gaps between the pillars, and so by projecting a line from the center of the floor up to the half way point between the first two lights we can reasonably deduce at what height the lights are positioned. The center of the circular light fittings is at approximately 278cm from the floor and the spherical light shades are about 20cm in radius, meaning the top of the light fittings is 298cm from the floor. If we combine this knowledge with our previous understanding of the architects use of units, we can see that the top of the lights are most certainly placed 3 meters from ground level and we have not only determined the lights' height but also that the person who designed their placement was almost certainly working in metric measurements. If one were to be in possession of other photographs of this corridor taken from other angles, then it would be possible to perform such an analysis on all of the images and by cross referencing all of the deduced data,

Cloisters in Egypt.

An example of the application of vanishing points and perspective lines to an architectural construction.

What is evident from these mathematical examples is that the Ancient Egyptians had the need and desire to use mathematics, but were lacking in knowledge and efficient systems. Their method of writing numbers was cumbersome, their knowledge of basic mathematical constants was rudimentary, but their ability to find solutions to the problems that they encountered was typical of human ingenuity.

Vanishing Points

The final piece of knowledge which will serve us well in our analysis of the architecture of the monuments is the principle of

come up with some very accurate estimations of distances, floor plans and wall sizes. It is in this manner that the chambers of the pyramid of Unas can be analysed, and when combined with accurate surveying data, provides a powerful method of resolving architectural anomalies.

There is only one exception to the validity of the use of this type of analysis, and that is when the architecture has been deliberately designed to abuse this very concept itself. We come across this technique in various degrees in ancient buildings, where pillars are made thinner at the top to give an apparent increase in visual height, or where building floors are slightly curved in profile so that a forced perspective is created. The technique of forced perspective is simply the clever use of the vanishing point phenomenon by an architect when designing a building. If architects can force the viewer to look at their work from a fixed location, then they can make use of the known perspective lines and vanishing point to trick the human eye, and one should be acutely aware that an architect who sets out to deceive us in this way will always succeed since the natural human instinct is to resolve visual clues into their most likely solution. So the technique of vanishing point analysis can be applied to the analysis of the pyramids, and in particular the underground chambers of the pyramid of Unas, but the cautions which go with the technique must always be kept in mind.

We are now armed with three very simple but powerful tools with which to tackle the pyramid of Unas. A small wooden ruler with which to understand the measurements of the architects; a limit to the mathematical knowledge that we should employ when looking at the architecture; and a universally accepted method of comparing and contrasting the walls, floors and ceilings. Most of all, the simplicity of these three tools guarantees that whatever the conclusion we come to regarding the architecture of the building, that it will be acceptable to both the architects and to us since there can be no debate whatsoever about the validity of their use.

Upon re-entering the pyramid of Unas's underground rooms we will make our way directly to the main chamber and use the wooden cubit rod to determine the width of the racks of hieroglyphs, since this is a highly logical place to start. The illustration below shows the ruler placed up alongside a random selection of racks from the main chamber's north wall and by viewing the divisions on the ruler we can see that the racks are exactly 1/7th of a cubit in width. Carrying out the same procedure at random locations on the north and south walls of the main chamber confirms that every one of the racks has the same width of one palm, except for the last few racks on the right side of north wall.

This repetitive use of the one seventh cubit measure shows us that the pyramid's internal architecture is based on a regular set of measurements, and it also links together the building with the ruler itself. We can be certain that the measurements on the ruler are the same measurements as those on the walls, and that despite the ruler in question having been designed from an example in the Louvre museum which is dated as having been constructed in 1330 BCE, the connection of the measuring rod to this building is correct and, as we suspected, the rod's design has been accurately passed down through the generations of ancient Egyptians. The one seventh of a cubit measurement from 2350 B.C.E. and that from one thousand years later are a perfect match. So having established the basic measurement unit which is reliable, let us try to resolve one of the principle anomalies that we came across in the main chamber, that being the construction of the west wall.

When we measure the racks of hieroglyphs on the west gable of this wall we find that their width is also 1/7th of a cubit, and since we know that there are 40 racks on the gable we can start to try to make some sense of the measurements in this section of the pyramid. The overall width of the west wall of the chamber was measured as being exactly 6 cubits, or 314cm in the modern survey work of Labrousse, and so by use of simple mathematics we can see that there must be two racks of blanks somewhere on the west gable (the gable should be 42/7ths of a cubit wide). At this point we need to resolve the parallax error that was encountered in the earlier chapter when looking at the west

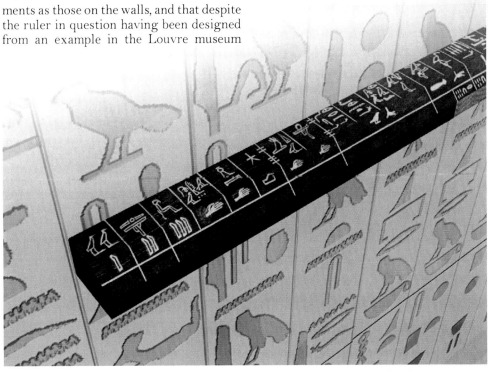

gable, and this can be done by examining as many photographs as possible of the region and in particular photographs which have been taken with the camera located very close to the north or south walls.

Whereas the two reconstructed photographs used in this part of the analysis are shown in the illustrations on this page, it is not possible to reproduce all of the analytical photography in this book that was used in subsequent analysis of the chambers, since there are well over 200 of such photographs which were necessary to conclusively determine the characteristics of the various architectural features. What will suffice in their place is a brief description of the technique that was repetitively used in the analysis. Since the close up photographs of the hieroglyphs were available from the work of Piankoff, and sufficient detail of the hieroglyphs was also visible on all the photographs that were in my possession, it was a simple yet time consuming task to overlay the Piankoff close ups of the hieroglyphs onto the larger photographs taken by other people. This allowed for highly accurate determination of the positions of the hieroglyph racks on each wall, after which the composite photographs were imported into a CAD system and photo editing software, and the vanishing points and line continuations applied to the images until the perplexing problems of the architecture were resolved.

When this method is used on the west gable in the main chamber we discover that the racks of hieroglyphs on the right side of the gable terminate exactly in line with a continuation of the north wall, and that on the left side there is one blank rack between the south wall continuation line and the last rack of carved hieroglyphs. as shown in the two illutrations left and right This gives a total of 41 racks along the gable which fits in with the systematic pattern that was postulated in the previous chapter where the east gable of the antechamber has 38 racks, the west 39, the east of the main chamber 40 and now the west of the main chamber 41. Logical as this may be it does provide us with a problem in that the west wall was measured as being exactly 6 cubits wide and we only have 41 racks of 1/7th of a cubit across the gable, *leaving us with a missing rack somewhere.* This is the first definitive proof that something in this building is wrong.

By further examining the photo-

The south side of the main chamber west gable.

The photograph shows the view down the south wall with Piankoff's original detailed photography overlaid onto the gable face to assist in the detection of the gable end in relation to the wall end.

graphs that were taken very close to the north and south walls of the chamber, the reason for the missing rack can be resolved since it is quite clear that the south wall of the chamber does not appear to be vertical on these photographs whereas the north wall does. It is by comparing the wall alignments with the vertical sides of the coffin that this distortion in the south wall can be clearly seen. If the south wall is leaning in at the top then the construction of the west wall of the chamber starts to make sense, since the width at the top of the wall must be less than that at the bottom. If the west wall of the chamber is constructed in this way then the artwork that is painted upon it must also be angled on the south side, since the lines of the artwork and the southwest corner of the wall are clearly parallel, as are the end racks at the left side of the gable. Have a close look at the illustration on the left and you will see this quite clearly in the back corner of the room. To confirm that this is indeed the case we can turn to the photography of Piankoff and examine the close-up that was published in his book of this section of the gable. When we do so we encounter something quite fascinating which will help us considerably when analysing the rest of the pyramid's walls.

There is a joint in the stonework in this section of the wall, and in the photograph from Piankoff's book this joint is not quite vertical, whereas the racks of hieroglyphs clearly are. Since it would be less than likely that the builders have inserted a stone joint at this location which was so slightly out from a true vertical we are left with the conclusion that *the photograph has been adjusted prior to publication in order to straighten up the racks.* Regardless of the distortions that are present in this photograph , the fact that the racks and the stone joint are not parallel confirms that the south wall of the chamber is angled and that the angular distortion has been copied into the gable racks and artwork on the wall. Since the same comparison can be carried out on the north side of the chamber which results in a deduction that the racks and artwork are vertical, we are left with the astonishing realisation that the decoration on the gable and west wall gradually changes from vertical to angled from north to south. The design requirements for such an undertaking would have been considerable and speak highly of the precision with which this building has been constructed.

Returning to our discovery of the layout of the racks on the west gable we can now see that there are 40 racks of carved hieroglyphs which are aligned with the north wall of the chamber and two blank racks at the left of the gable, one of which is inside the top of the south wall and the other of which is actually above the south wall itself. However, all 42 of the racks on the gable are vertically located above the 6 cubit long floor that was measured by the Egyptologists. We can also see from photography that the apex of the gable is located with 20 racks on the right side of it and 22 racks on the left meaning that *the apex of the room's ceiling is not in the center of the chamber*. The fact that it is offset by exactly 1/7th of a cubit is of vital interest to us since we can more than likely now calculate the exact angles of the roof stones on both sides of the chamber.

By referring to one of the illustrations in the 1987 survey work of Labrousse (dig. 16 in his book) we can see the general design of the cross section of the chamber, and then can convert the measurements from this drawing into the original cubit units of the builders. When we do so we see that the architects have employed a very basic system of measurements to the overall chamber cross section, with the principle

measurements being in whole cubit units as shown in the illustration below. From these measurements, combined with the knowledge that the apex is offset by 1/7th of a cubit to the north we can use trigonometry to calculate the roof angles as being 43.199° on the north side and 41.839° on the south. Unfortunately Labrousse failed to report the correct roof angles in his work and so we have no value to which we can compare our own. He did state that there was a difference between the angles on the two sides of the chamber which corresponds to the difference that we have just calculated with the angle of the north roof stones being greater that of the south.

The reason that these angles are of such great interest is that we can now draw lines at these angles on a CAD system and overlay them onto the photograph that Piankoff took of the chamber's west end. When we do so we find that the lines we have drawn *perfectly* match the angles of the roof that are visible at the far end of the chamber, *but only after the photograph has been rotated in a clockwise direction*. Since we can be certain of what has been worked out so far on the west wall we can now see that the angled design of the wall has clearly caused Piankoff's photographer or printer to rotate the photograph into a position

Piankoff's plate VII rotated.

The photograph has been rotated by an angle with a tangent 1/42 or -1.3639°. Notice how the coffin now looks much more realistically placed in comparison to its position in the unrotated photograph shown earlier.

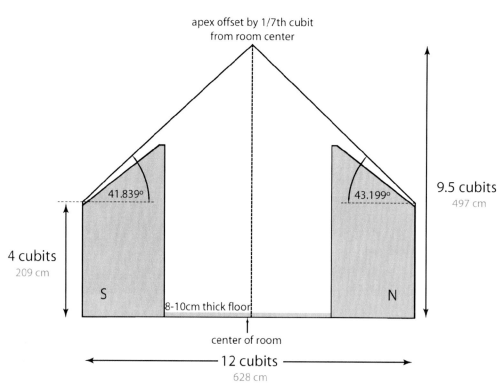

apex offset by 1/7th cubit
from room center

41.839°   43.199°

9.5 cubits
497 cm

4 cubits
209 cm

S   N

8-10cm thick floor

center of room

12 cubits
628 cm

The cross section of the chambers.

The dimensions for the diagram are taken from the technical drawings of Labrousse, with the 8cm floor thickness deduced from photography.

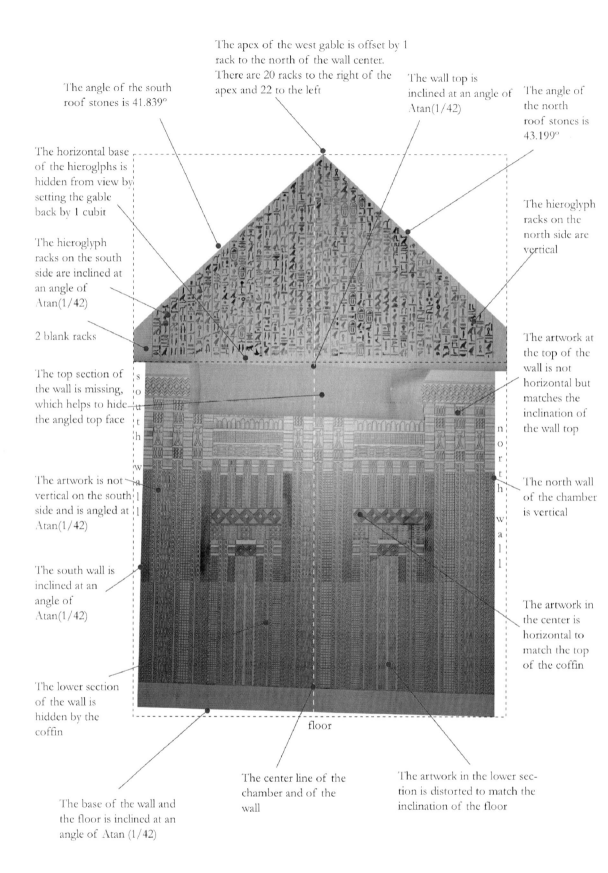

The apex of the west gable is offset by 1 rack to the north of the wall center. There are 20 racks to the right of the apex and 22 to the left

The angle of the south roof stones is 41.839°

The wall top is inclined at an angle of Atan(1/42)

The angle of the north roof stones is 43.199°

The horizontal base of the hieroglphs is hidden from view by setting the gable back by 1 cubit

The hieroglyph racks on the north side are vertical

The hieroglyph racks on the south side are inclined at an angle of Atan(1/42)

2 blank racks

The artwork at the top of the wall is not horizontal but matches the inclination of the wall top

The top section of the wall is missing, which helps to hide the angled top face

south wall

north wall

The artwork is not vertical on the south side and is angled at Atan(1/42)

The north wall of the chamber is vertical

The south wall is inclined at an angle of Atan(1/42)

The artwork in the center is horizontal to match the top of the coffin

The lower section of the wall is hidden by the coffin

floor

The artwork in the lower section is distorted to match the inclination of the floor

The base of the wall and the floor is inclined at an angle of Atan (1/42)

The center line of the chamber and of the wall

they considered to be horizontally aligned, presumably taking their cuing from the angled south wall.

Our deduction of the roof angles from the composition of the wall and the positioning of the apex has allowed us to determine an absolute reference system which is independent of the wall's architecture and from this we can start to analyse the photograph with much more confidence.

The first thing that becomes apparent is that the top of the wall is not horizontal, dipping down quite considerably on the right side. This solves one of the perplexing problems that we encountered earlier with the two photographs taken in the chamber, that with the students showing exactly this feature and Piankoff's photograph showing a horizontal top. Since we have just seen that Piankoff's photograph has been rotated then we can deduce that the photograph of the students was taken with the camera roughly horizontal and the wall does indeed dip to the right side.

We can see in the horizontally corrected photograph of Piankoff shown on the previous page that the top of the wall is perpendicular to the angled south wall of the chamber so we can easily now calculate the angle of the wall top since we know that the south wall comes in by 1/7th of a cubit over a height of 6 cubits, in other words an angle with a tangent of 1/42. Having established how the wall top, the south wall and the north wall are aligned it is a simple matter to then determine the floor alignment, since we have the measurements of the heights of the two corners of the wall in the survey work. They are stated as being 305cm on both sides, and we can conclude that the floor must have the same angular slope as the top of the wall. This answers another of the strange features in the pyramid, since we now have a thoroughly sensible explanation as to why the coffin is placed on two pieces of wood. With a need to keep the top of the coffin horizontal yet have it placed on a non horizontal floor, the architects have inserted two different thickness pieces of wood under the two ends of the coffin to compensate for the inclination in the floor.

A full summary of all of the architectural features of the wall is shown in the illustration opposite and there are several points of interest to be noted in the design. The most interesting is in the motif of the

paint work which is much clearer in this illustration than in the chamber since we are able to easily remove the coffin from our model to facilitate the photography. The artwork at the base of the wall is angled to coincide with the floor slope, the artwork in the wall center is aligned horizontally, and the artwork at the wall top is aligned once again to the slope. This horizontal distortion in the paint work has been combined with the vertical distortion required to conceal the angled south wall, and the combination of the two patterns must have taken considerable skill to achieve. Trying to reproduce those distortions for the illustrations in this book was particularly difficult even with the use of modern computer graphics packages and that they were produced by hand 4000 years ago is astonishing. A similar vertical distortion has been used in the alignment of the hieroglyph racks on the gable, and again the precision with which this has been measured is remarkable since the change from vertical to angled racks has been achieved gradually across the width of the gable.

The final part of the optical illusion, for that is quite certainly what we are looking at, is achieved by the small rotation which was put into the coffin when it was positioned in the chamber. If you look back at Piankoff's long shot of the chamber (in the second chapter) you can now see that the apparent horizontal rotation of the coffin is quite exaggerated. This is because by aligning the photograph to the west wall's non horizontal lines, an anticlockwise vertical rotation has been applied to the coffin in 2D which is translated in our minds to a horizontal rotation in our perception of the 3D space of the chamber. Since our minds know that the coffin is supposed to be angled, then we quite happily accept the fact that it has been over-rotated since it is the easiest solution for our minds to come to. Compare the Piankoff original to the illustration on the previous page with the angular rotation removed from the photograph and you will see the vast difference in the apparent rotation of the coffin. This optical illusion is just as much apparent when standing inside the chamber as it is on the photographs, and without doubt all the Egyptologists who have ever stood in this room and looked at the west wall have done so with their heads tilted slightly to one side. It is the visual clues that the eye picks up from the uneven roof angles, the sloping top of the west wall and the angled south wall that cause this tilting to occur, and the architects have quite deliberately transferred the resulting visual distortions into the coffin.

It is an interesting analogy to think of the visual distortions of the west wall having been transferred into the coffin 4000 years ago by the architects of this monument. What we have just done is taken them from the coffin and placed them back onto the west wall where they belong, in effect bringing the burial chambers of this pyramid back to life. It is also worth pausing at this stage to consider exactly what we are looking at in the west wall of the pyramid of Unas. It is supposed to be the back wall of a bronze age burial chamber, but is in fact an imaginatively designed and technically advanced optical illusion and the chasm between these two concepts cannot be ignored even at this early stage. We know without doubt from radiocarbon dating that the age of the pyramids is correct, yet what we have just investigated looks like it was built yesterday, such is the technical knowledge in the design.

ANOTHER BRICK
IN THE WALL

Of all the clues that were presented in the earlier chapter, the missing triangle of brickwork on the ante chamber's north wall is probably the most striking. As was mentioned when the missing stone was first described, by making a photo montage from the close up photographs of Piankoff on which the cracks between each individual stone are visible, it is evident that there simply is no triangle of stone on this section of the wall, but from the surveying data there quite clearly should be another brick in the wall. However, when examining these close up photographs, and in particular Piankoff's plate 3 which shows the top left corner of the wall, it is impossible not to notice that the hieroglyphs which are inscribed on the wall all appear to be leaning backwards as shown in the illustration. On other photographs of this section of the room the base lines of the hieroglyphs appear to be horizontal and the symbols are not leaning backwards, so we must conclude that the photograph in question has been distorted when published in order to make the photograph rectangular and the border lines between the racks vertical.

We know from the work of Labrousse that the central section of stone on this wall is trapezoidal, and by taking this into account when trying to determine the distortion on the photograph we can come to the only conclusion possible which is that the piece of stonework to the left side of the north wall cannot be vertically set into the construc-

Duplicate of Piankoff's plate 3.

The distortions in the hieroglyphs, particularly in the top right quadrant of the photograph indicate that the photograph has been distorted.

tion. If we thoroughly check through Labrousse's text we can see that he is quite specific about all of the trapezoidal stone's details and those on the right side of the wall, but is vague about the stone to the left which he describes simply as '37cm wide', neglecting to mention whether it is vertical or not. He also neglects to mention the angular details of the trapezoid that makes up the central section, and so we are left to make the assumption that it is regular and that the center of the top of the stone is directly above the center of the base. Although deeply offensive to any sense of regularity that one might have and the natural desire to want to make the wall rectangular, we are left with no other alternative for the architectural design in this area of the wall than that shown in the illustration overleaf. By constructing this arrangement on a CAD system using Labrousse's dimensions we find that the north wall of the antechamber must come in by 9cm at the top left corner, and consequently that the west wall of the antechamber has a quite pronounced overhang. There is however quite a problem

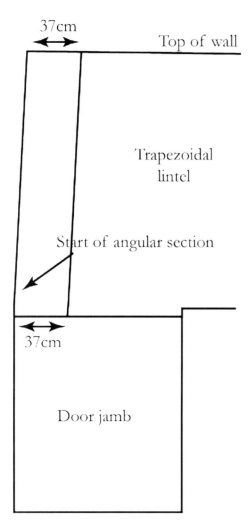

37cm

Top of wall

Trapezoidal
lintel

Start of angular section

37cm

Door jamb

into place and the 37cm long stone on the top left of the wall is positioned with the angle given to us by the architects. The second step is then to place the trapezoidal lintel of the passage into place using the measurements from Labrousse's survey of 309cm on the base of the lintel and 294cm on the top. The cross sectional shape of the lintel is still of a trapezoid, although now it is no longer symmetrical about its vertical axis. Lastly we can put into place the final stone on the top right corner of the wall and we can see that the right edge of the wall is no longer vertical, but set at an angle which is dictated by the architecture alone. If this method of construction is reproduced on a CAD system, the angle at the right side of the wall can be measured, and is as close to Atan 1/42 as could be imagined. The discrepancy in the angle is one tenth of one degree, and bearing in mind that the stonework has been measured to the nearest centimeter, the error margins allow us correctly state the angle at the two opposite ends of the wall is now the same.

This discovery brings us to a very important point in the analysis of this monument's chambers. We have taken the angle that was given to us in the main chamber and applied it to the west side of north wall of the antechamber, and the very same angle has appeared again at the east side. This confirms that our analysis of the main chamber was correct and that the architecture of the building conforms to a logical plan. We know for certain that the building's architecture was planned, that the optical deceptions that we have come across are intentional, and that the forced perspective that is apparent on the antechamber north wall is deliberate.

We can now further understand the layout of the racks of hieroglyphs within the chambers because, on the ends of many of the walls in the pyramid, one can find artwork racks which have been shown on the photographs in the previous chapter neatly aligned below the ends of the gables. On these racks the artwork pattern is semi-irregular in that it contains alternating quadrilaterals of dark and light coloured paint, but those squares and rectangles appear to have no consistent measurement pattern to them. Consequently, although the eye registers that a pattern exists, it pays no great attention to it, much as one disregards the picture frame that surrounds a piece of art. It is by using this rack of artwork that the

The first solution to the missing stone problem.

with this solution, since we have just created an angled piece of stonework on the wall which is positioned at a totally arbitrary angle, and there is perhaps a more sensible way of constructing this section of the north wall.

The architects have just gone to great lengths to make us work out the angle of the walls and floor on the west of the main chamber, and from this we found out that these walls have been built at an angle of Atan 1/42. If we apply this angle to the stone on the antechamber's north wall that we are working on, rather than setting it at an angle dictated by using a symetrical trapezoidal piece of stone in the center section, then we can look to see if there is a systematic pattern in the wall's design. The method for doing this is relatively simple and is shown in the illustration on the opposite page.

First the bottom level of stonework that makes up the door jambs is put

The construction system for the antechamber north wall.

The top diagram shows the top left stone being set at an angle of Atan 1/42 and the lower diagram shows how this angle is reflected into the other side of the wall when combined with the survey data.

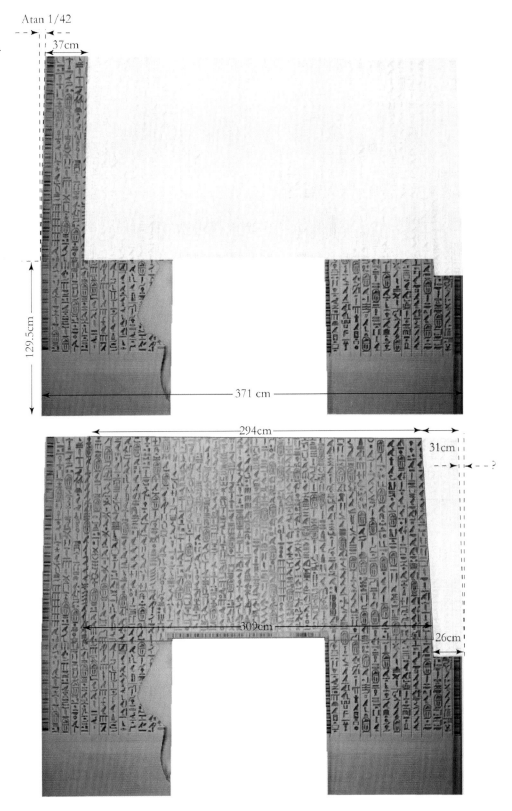

*The antechamber
north wall.*

*The illustration
shows planar
projections of
the north wall
and roof sections
directly above it..
The artwork on the
left and right sides
of the wall absorbs
some of the wall's
distortion.*

architects have managed to hide some of the distortion that is contained in the wall and in particular the fact that the racks of hieroglyphs are angled from top to bottom. If the architects had built the hieroglyph racks all the way up to the wall ends, neglecting to add the artwork racks, then any vertical distortions in the wall would have been considerably easier to detect.

This explains why the hieroglyphs in Piankoff's close up photograph are distorted, because the rack of artwork on the left has been omitted from the print. The original photograph's negative will be of a series of racks that are not vertical, yet the description that Piankoff gives of the north antechamber wall is that all of the racks *are* entirely vertical, and so the photographs have been adjusted accordingly. One can only imagine the fun that the book publisher, the photographer and the typesetter must have had trying to put the work together. The photographer will have insisted that the camera was horizontal when the photograph was taken, the typesetter will have insisted that it could not have been, Piankoff will have confirmed that the wall is indeed rectangular, and the publisher will have had to decide who is correct. Quite clearly the publisher incorrectly chose the view of Piankoff, and not that of the photographer as he should have done.

If we now have a look at the ceiling of the chamber and consider the roof stars on the north side, then we find that these have also been adjusted to fit the angled corners of the north wall. This arrangement is shown in the illustration opposite in which both the wall and roof are shown in planar projection. In the architectural design, the center of the roof stars and the center of the wall are aligned with each other but the center of the doorway is offset by 4cm to the left, a point which was noted by Labrousse in his survey work. What is so clever about this arrangement is that as a consequence, the rows of stars directly above the doorway are fractionally offset against the perpendicular to the chamber's central axis and in exactly the same direction as the entrance passage appears to be offset in the clues that we determined earlier.

So we now have a plausible explanation as to why the entrance passage and the antechamber appear to be perfectly aligned with each other when viewed from inside the antechamber. By overhanging the east and west walls of the room the architects have managed to distort the roof star grid. They have then offset the doorway to the left side of the wall and thereby visually aligned the distorted star grid and the entrance passage axis, making it appear as though the passage is perpendicular to the antechamber. This now confirms that the surveying measurements of the whole of the entrance passage are correct and that it does not meet the north wall of the antechamber perpendicularly.

This stunningly created illusion is further enhanced by the cross sectional design of the passage itself. From Labrousse's detailed measurements it is possible to determine that the doorway, and therefore the cross section of the passage when it emerges into the chamber, is 133cm wide at the top and 137cm at the bottom and that the sides of the doorway are not vertical. This feature assists in creating the illusion of forced perspective on the wall which is so subtle that it is almost impossible to detect, but which the human eye picks up immediately. A further addition to the illusion is created by the fact that, as Labrousse correctly notes, the north wall of the antechamber is higher on the left than on the right, giving the viewer the impression that they are probably standing slightly to the left of the chamber center line when viewing the wall, even though they are actually standing in the center. Consequently the fact that they can see more of the entrance passage's right wall than they can see of the left wall is perfectly acceptable.

The finished design of the antechamber north wall is shown in perspective on the following page, where Piankoff's original plate has been rotated so that the vertical section of the corner is now parallel to the sides of the page. All of the visual components come together to produce an optical illusion that has managed to deceive every Egyptologists who has ever entered this building.

If you look carefully at this illustrations you will see that there is one slight problem in that the non vertical side of the entrance door contrasts very strongly against the vertical lower portion of the corner on the left side of the wall. However, in the pyramid when it was uncovered by Maspero in 1881 both of the entrance door edges were discovered to have been damaged by the tomb robbers.

Another brick in the wall

The fact that the damage greatly enhances the optical illusion on the north wall adds yet further doubts as to the tomb robbers very existence. Every time that we come across a damaged section of the pyramid it perfectly coincides with a adjustment used to enhance the illusions that the architects have created. If this damage were to be deliberate by the architects, and the evidence points very strongly to this being a valid conclusion, then we would have a most remarkable situation on our hands. The design of the chambers would dictate that the hieroglyphs could be damaged to help hide the architecture, and this is a concept of such consequence that for it to be acceptable further evidence would be required that the hieroglyphs take second place to the architecture.

The south wall

If we now look at the stonework of the south wall in the antechamber, we can see that on the east side of the wall (the left) that there is a very similar pattern to the stones as we saw on the north wall. The top left stone is inset into the lower layer of the wall in an identical fashion, mirroring the design on the north wall. By analysing the south wall in the same manner that we analysed the north wall, searching Piankoff's close up photography for distortions to the hieroglyphs, and then looking at the survey data we can determine that the opposing walls have identical design.

The top section of either end of the south wall is angled at Atan 1/42 and consequently the east and west walls of the chamber both overhang the chamber floor, and the room incorporates a perfectly designed forced perspective. To get this forced perspective to work to its maximum effect, the architects have designed the room to be relatively small. It is just over 3 meters wide and the proximity of the

walls to the observer means that it is not possible to stand back an take an objective look at the wall's design when inside the pyramid. Whoever put this architecture together knew exactly what they were doing.

What is particularly interesting in the south wall's stonework is to see that the top stone on the left has been inset into the base level of the wall so that the overhang of the east wall could be easily

achieved. Because the height of the doorway that leads into the serdab is lower than that of all the other two doorways in the antechamber the stonework on the north and south walls has been adjusted to fit this feature. From a builders point of view it would have been considerably easier to have changed the height of the serdab door so that it was the same as the height as the others, and consequently the same height as the lower level of brickwork contained in the north and south walls. The fact that the architects have not adopted this simpler system, and have instead opted to indent the top stones into the lower layer of stonework leaves us in no doubt whatsoever that the disparity in the heights of the doors in this building must be an important feature in the design.

The joining passages

From what we have deduced so far we know for certain that the entrance passage and the antechamber north wall are not perpendicular to each other, and it is by referring to Labrousse's magnetic north measurements that we can determine which of the two, if either, is lined up to north. In his survey work, and shown clearly on his plan drawings, Labrousse states that the entrance passage axis is built 2 degrees west of magnetic north and to work out the bearing to true north we need to consult magnetic declination tables, since magnetic north wanders around over the course of the decades. At the time when Labrousse carried out his survey work these tables tell us that the magnetic declination at Saqarrah was just over 2° and so we can conclude that the entrance passage is aligned perfectly with true north. The deduction from this is that , since the passage and antechamber are set at an angle to each other, it must be the antechamber's central axis which is rotated in respect to north.

This fact then makes sense of the nature of all the passages in the pyramid, that which connects the antechamber with the main chamber on one side and that which connects to the serdab on the other. In the clues that we have come across, all three passages running off the antechamber appear to contain angular distortions, and by deducing that the antechamber itself contains the angular distortion, all three passageway's alignments can be understood from just one piece of architec-

tural information.

If we rotate the antechamber around by an angle of -Atan 1/42 on a CAD system we can then start to perform an analysis of the joining passageways and see if we can make sense of the wall length difference that we have come across. If the entrance passage meets the antechamber as we suspect, then one would expect to find that the east wall of the entrance is 3.26cm longer that the west wall. Since that is exactly the case that was reported by Labrousse we can provisionally be quite content that we have the rotation of the antechamber correct in relation to at least one of the passages.

The passage between the antechamber and the chamber contains a disparity in length between its opposing side walls as well, but the lengths themselves are of no significance when looked at using the cubit rod, being 156cm on the north and 154cm. on the south, and the difference between the two is only 2cm. However since we know that the walls of the antechamber are probably angled in relation to those of the main chamber, we can see that the distance between the west end of the antechamber north wall and the east end

The continuation of the north walls.

In the illustration the lintel of the door which joins the antechamber to the main chamber has been partially removed. Note that the section of stonework shown between the two north walls is part of the door lintel and continues northwards for several more meters

The first floor plan

The sections of the architecture that are aligned to north are shown in blue and the rotated sections in black

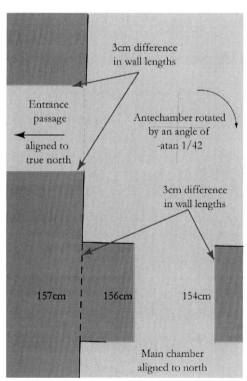

3cm difference in wall lengths

Entrance passage

aligned to true north

Antechamber rotated by an angle of -atan 1/42

3cm difference in wall lengths

157cm 156cm 154cm

Main chamber aligned to north

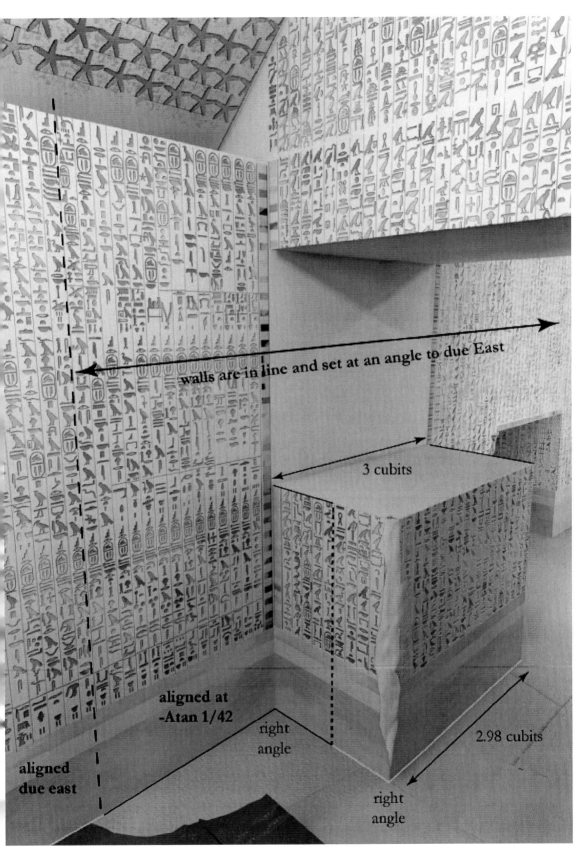

walls are in line and set at an angle to due East

3 cubits

aligned at
-Atan 1/42

right
angle

2.98 cubits

aligned
due east

right
angle

of the main chamber's north wall will be slightly longer than the distance measured down the passage. Although we do not yet have an accurate floor plan of the chambers to work from, it is evident that the distance in question is going to be about 157cm, and converting this back into cubits, exactly 3 cubits in length. This is a measurement which is entirely hidden from view, as shown on the illustration on the previous page, and only accessible after an understanding of the chambers' construction is achieved and some simple calculations have been performed.

Implicit within this design would be that the north walls of the two chambers are a continuation of each other, and here we have a link to one of the earliest clues that we looked at. The right side of the north wall in the main chamber was seen to be built coming in to the chamber ,and the architects, as you will recall, had adjusted the roof star lines to compensate visually for this feature. Could it be that this adjustment of the north wall in the main chamber is done to correctly align with the corresponding wall in the antechamber, and if so is there any way in which we can determine this.

The answer to this question is that we can and from the following information .We know that the west wall width of the main chamber behind the coffin is exactly 6 cubits; we also know from Labrousse that the length of the east wall is 2cm shorter; we can calculate the length of the section north wall that is distorted since we have a photograph of it and also know the width of each of the racks; we have a very plausible value for the angular rotation of the antechamber, which we can assume may well be the same as the angular change in the north wall of the main chamber. From these calculations it can be deduced that the length of the east wall of the main chamber is indeed 1.85cm shorter than that of the west wall. In addition it is possible to determine from extensive vanishing point analyses of the photography from inside the chamber, that this is the exact design of these sections of walls, and that the 3 cubit measurement that separates the two ends of the north walls of the two chambers is a deliberate architectural feature.

In order for this arrangement to correctly match all of the surveying data we find that the section of the main chamber's west wall on the left of the doorway

must be built at two different angles, as shown in the detail on the diagram. This arrangement may look unusual until one considers that as a consequence both the corner of the room and the angle of the west wall/passage will both be right angles, deftly concealing the architectural distortions from revealing themselves during an analysis.

Since we have now successfully worked out the remarkable arrangement of the entrance passage, part of the north wall of the antechamber and part of the north wall of the main chamber, and the connection between the two chambers, and in the previous chapter correctly worked out the arrangement of the main chamber's west wall, then we are in a good position to now have a look at the east section of the north wall of the main chamber onto which the hieroglyphs are carved. If we can correctly diagnose the architectural features of this section of wall, then we will be able to connect up the construction from the west end of the main chamber all the way through to the east end of the antechamber's north wall and then use this structure as a fixed reference system from which to complete the analysis of the rest of the pyramids design.

Before leaving this chapter there are two significant points to note about what we have just seen. The existence of the 3 cubit measurement hidden behind the joining-passage's north wall gives us absolute proof that this building has not just been built - it has been very carefully designed. And secondly we have just seen the use of a very devious piece of architecture with the creation of two right angles on two pieces of the same wall, specifically designed to confuse us. The deduction from both of these pieces of information is that when planning the building's design, the architects must have expected the chambers to be fully analysed at some point in the future, making a mockery of the current deduction that this building is nothing more than a simple burial chamber that was sealed for internity.

A LONG LINE OF PHARAOHS

The north wall of the main chamber contains the most fascinating of all the collections of carved symbols within the pyramid, with 56 racks of hieroglyphs bordered on the right side by one rack of artwork. These 57 racks are divided into three rows, or 'registers' as they are called by Egyptologists, and a reconstructed photograph of the wall is shown in the illustration below.

There are several pieces of information regarding the architectural features of this wall that we know either from our previous work, or from the survey work of Labrousse. The height of the right side of the wall is known from Labrousse and was measured at 308cm from the floor level at that point ; the height of the floor in absolute terms is known and contains a rise from right to left of 4cm, taken from the spot heights in Labrousse's technical drawings; the plinth at the base of the wall which separates the floor from the hieroglyphs is 51cm high at both ends of the wall and its top and bottom are parallel; and the dimensions of all of the individual pieces of brickwork from which the wall is constructed is also provided in the survey work. Taking all of these pieces of information into account, and comparing them at length to photography from within the chamber, it is possible to deduce that the bottom line of the hieroglyphs cannot be horizontal and must also rise by 4cm from right to left, since its base line is parallel to the floor. This deduction is based on the height of the plinth being consistent from one end of the wall to the other, a fact which can be easily confirmed from close up photography since we know that the width of the racks is 1/7th of a cubit and the vertical distances on the photographs can be compared to these values.

What we do not know about this wall is the design of its top line, and this is the piece of information that we need to establish from all the other evidence that we have. There is a quite simple technique that we can use to determine where the top of the wall lies, and this involves constructing the wall from the individual brick dimensions given in the survey, but leaving the height of the top most layer as an unknown. We can then take the detailed photography from Piankoff and, since we know that many of these close ups have been distorted in the printing process,

Main chamber north wall.

A perspective view of the north wall of the main chamber showing the corner of the coffin lid in the foreground.

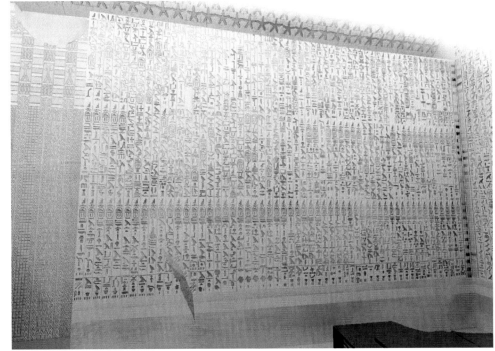

re-align them on top of the CAD drawing so that the tiny cracks between the bricks on the photographs line up with the corresponding lines on the CAD drawing. There is a further benefit in using this technique in that the photographs of Piankoff overlap each other by a couple of racks and so as well as lining them up with the wall bricks we can also unsure that the hieroglyphs themselves line up perfectly with those from the adjacent photograph. By starting this process in the bottom right corner of the wall, where the blocks of limestone from which the wall is built are the smallest, measuring approximately 70cm square, and continuing along the lower section of the wall before overlaying the upper layer photographs, we can be quite sure that the top of the wall will be very close indeed to its actual position on the finished mosaic. There are two more pieces of information that we can use to verify that the mosaic is correct, the first being that when finished, all of the hieroglyphs must have horizontal bases and show no signs of distortion. The second is that, from the use of other

A plan view of the north wall.

The whole of the north wall is shown in planar projection the illustration. The positioning of the coffin in the chamber ensures that the visitor

Wall height of 305cm Damaged section of wall Apex in ce

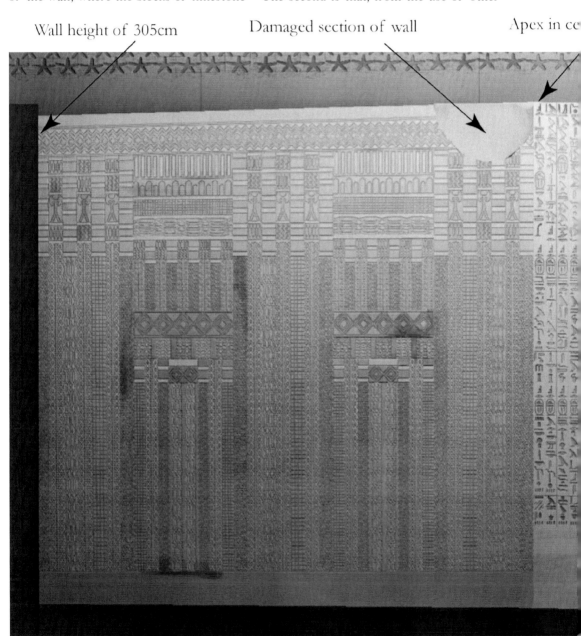

to the chamber will always stand in front of the apex of the wall an hence never see the correct construction of this wall.

photographs, it is possible to see that the 3 registers of hieroglyphs from which the wall is comprised each contribute exactly one third to the overall height of the wall section above the plinth, even if this one third distance is different at each end of the wall.

When we carry out this procedure we find that the height of the wall on the left hand side, where it meets up with the artwork section, must be 314cm high, or exactly 6 cubits. This is a highly significant distance and confirms our earlier

deduction regarding the artwork end of the wall which must also have contained a rise from left to right in order for the forced perspective of the north west corner of the room to work correctly. The final construction of the whole of the north wall is shown in the illustration below and is a thoroughly impressive piece of work, since the wall appears absolutely level when viewed inside the chamber, yet contains a quite obvious apex at the point where the hieroglyphs meet the artwork. If you now refer back to the perspective

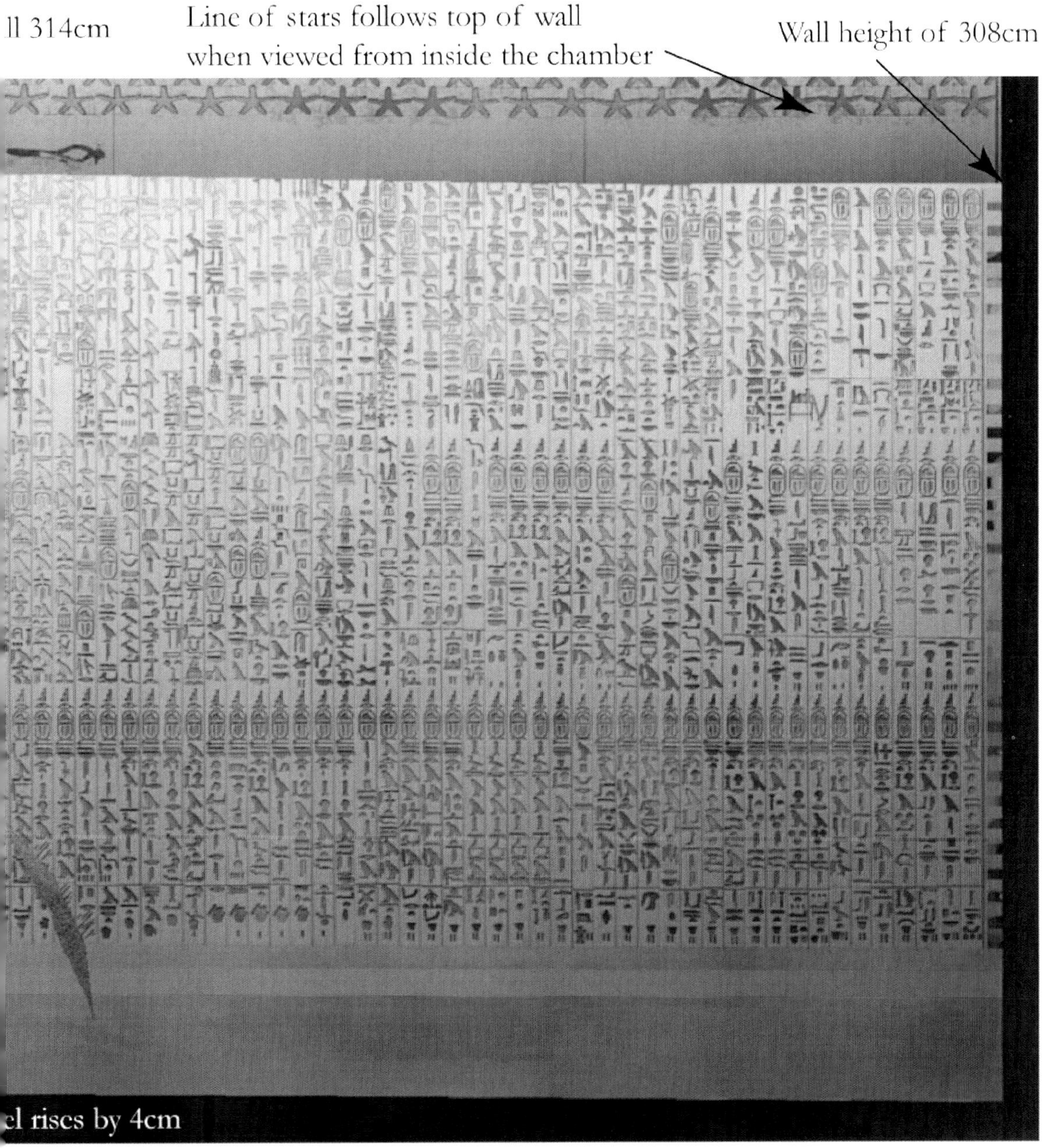

ll 314cm

Line of stars follows top of wall when viewed from inside the chamber

Wall height of 308cm

el rises by 4cm

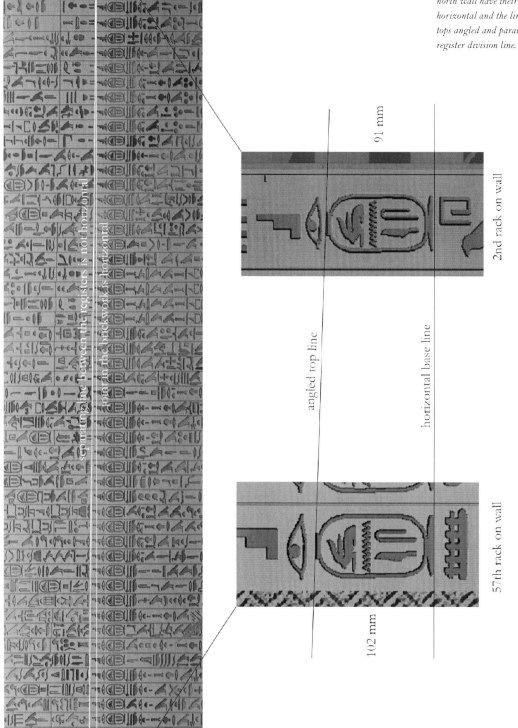

The cartouches of Unas on the north wall have their base lines horizontal and the line of their tops angled and parallel to the register division line.

91 mm

2nd rack on wall

angled top line

horizontal base line

57th rack on wall

102 mm

separating line between the registers is not horizontal

a column in the backwork is not horizontal

photograph on page 23 you will see that once again there is a damaged section of wall which perfectly removes this apex and the question as to whether the damage in the chambers was created by the tomb robbers or the architects is resolved. Since *every* piece of damage that we have come across has an architectural purpose we are fully justified in deducing that the damaged sections of the chambers of Unas are deliberate architectural features, with all of the implications that that entails.

There are three other features that have been used to hide the rise in the center of the north wall, the first being that the hieroglyphs themselves stop at this point and the high contrast edge between them and the artwork serves as a natural break to the eye. The second is that, because the north wall has been built coming in to the chamber on the right side, then it appears to rise when viewed from a standing position at the chamber's door, as was shown earlier. Although entirely imaginary, this rise in the wall height on the right helps to balance out the rise on the left side since the eye sees the two ends of the wall as being approximately at the same height, a feature which is quite apparent on the perspective photograph on the earlier page. And the third feature is that the positioning of the coffin, and the fact that it is virtually as wide as the chamber itself which prohibits access to the space behind it, forces the visitor to the chamber to stand in front of the coffin when looking back down towards the doorway. From this point the only thing that can be seen is the hieroglyph sections of the walls, and the apex and descending artwork is totally out of sight.

Remarkable as all this is, there is something even more significant about the details contained on the north wall of the main chamber. The illustration opposite shows a more detailed view of the line of hieroglyphs which make up the lower section of the wall. On this diagram the horizontal join of the blocks of stone is shown as well as the slanting dividing lines of the registers of hieroglyphs. Look carefully at the line of identical symbols which mark out the pharaoh's name Unas, this symbol being known as a 'cartouche' or royal name. Notice that the bottom lines of the cartouche's are perfectly horizontal yet the tops of the cartouches are perfectly parallel to the dividing line between the registers, and not the horizontal line which divides the brick-

work. This means that these cartouches are of different sizes, reducing from left to right, and that the architects have used them to present a false horizontal line with which to distract the eye from the anomalies in the wall's design. The cartouches on the left side are 102mm high and those on the right are 91mm high and there is no perceptible error in the way that they have been carved from one end of the wall to the other, producing a perfect straight line along their tops. This means that, with 56 cartouches from end to end and a difference of 11mm between the heights of the cartouches at the two extremities, that each subsequent carving is two tenths of a millimeter different from the previous one. The cartouche of the Pharaoh has been carved along 56 racks to an accuracy of two tenths of a millimeter, with the sole intention of hiding the wall's construction, meaning that the hieroglyphs are secondary to the architecture without any doubt whatsoever.

I cannot put enough emphasis on the significance of this statement, since the whole of Egypt is full of monuments dating back to the same period in time, and we have just determined that the hieroglyphs are nothing more than secondary decorations, subservient entirely to the architectural design. It is from the hieroglyphs themselves that Egyptologists have put together the story of the architecture of these ancient monuments, designating who built them and why from what they have read on the walls. Yet it is clear, as we make our way through the pyramid of Unas, that who built them and why is contained not in the writing on the walls, which simply serves to add to a deliberately created illusion, but in the masonry itself which tells us a completely different story.

The south wall

We can now look at the south wall of the main chamber, since we have just developed a technique on the north wall which has served us perfectly in analysing the construction of the wall top. If we apply this same technique to the south wall and overlay Piankoff's detailed photography onto the CAD drawing of the wall stones, something strange happens. The finished drawing contains hiero-

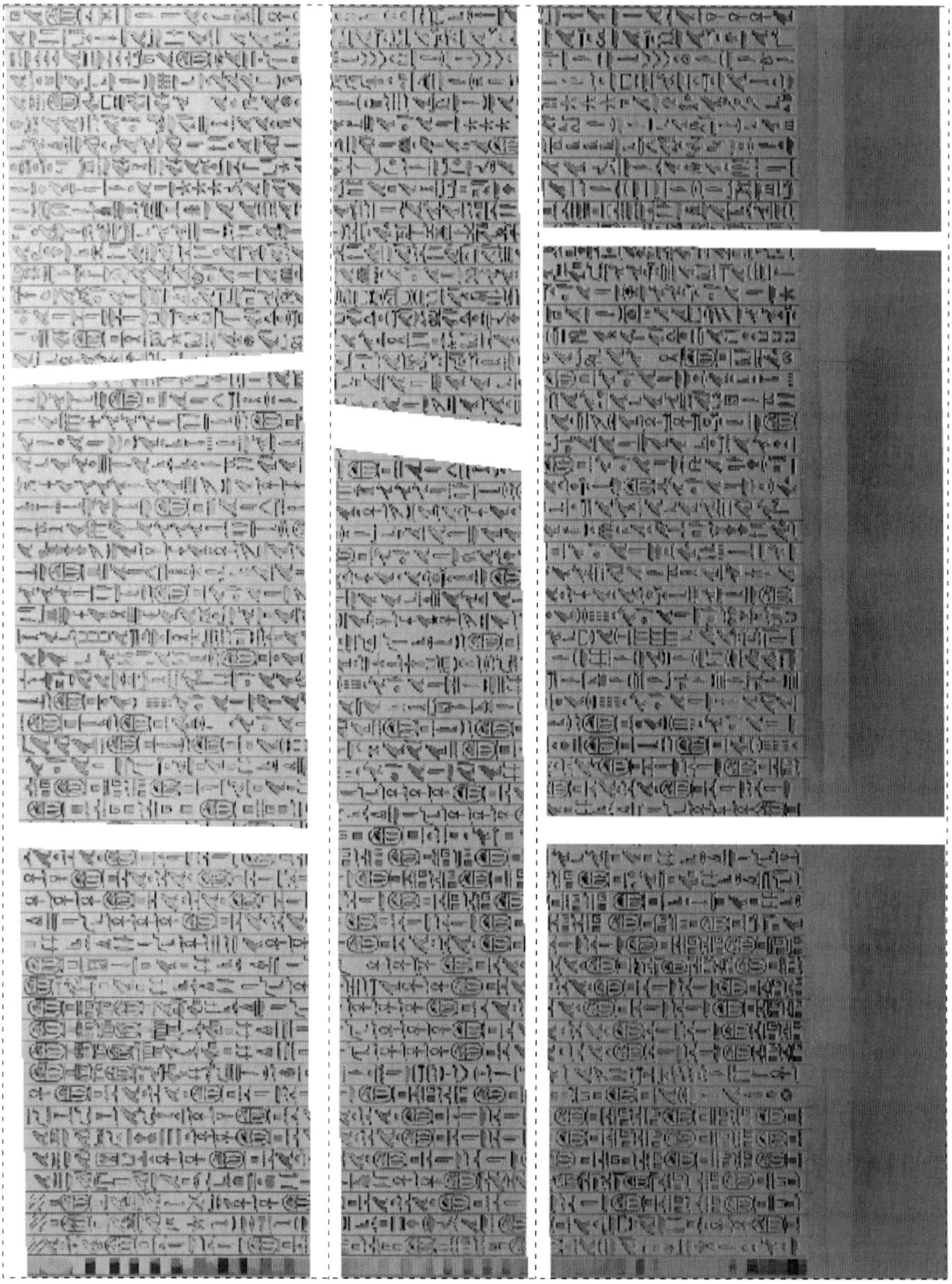

All of the joints between the stone-work of the south wall are iregular. The non horizontal joints that run along the length of the wall help to create the forced perspective illusion within the chamber

glyphs which are distorted, showing obvious signs of angular skewing towards the top right section of the wall. Furthermore, on trying to determine the source of the error in the mosaic composition by referring to the vast quantities of photographs that show this section of the pyramid, we can see something quite significant in the correctly aligned photograph of Piankoff which we rotated earlier Because we know the exact composition of the west wall of the chamber behind the coffin and have rotated Piankoff's photograph so that the horizontal is true, we can use the photograph to compare the heights of the north and south walls of the chamber. By running a horizontal line across the corrected photograph it is apparent that the heights of the south wall and north wall at the join between the hieroglyph section and the artwork section are identical, within the errors of our ability to rotate the photograph correctly. If we look at the survey work of Labrousse, he specifies that the three sections of stonework that make up this wall are 140, 65 and 101 cm from bottom to top, giving a total height of 306cm. If we allow for the rise in the floor level between the entrance door wall and the coffin area of 4cm, then we have a discrepancy between what was measured and what we can see of 4cm.

It appears that every wall in this pyramid has its own architectural riddle, and with the south wall in the main chamber it is one which is particularly difficult to resolve. When you try to determine the source of the problem, you end up going around in circles. The measurements of Labrousse can be checked as best as possible using vanishing point analysis and close up photography in which the rack widths can be used as measurement standards. The CAD drawing can be checked and checked again to ensure that there are no mistakes in it, and the photography overlays can be examined in great detail, looking at all of the hieroglyphs to try to determine angular distortions which might lead to the source of the problem. Every time this is done the whole system looks perfect, and yet there is still a significant error in the height of the right side of the wall. The question that needed to be asked was 'Are there any clues in the construction of the wall that might help us and if we carefully consider everything that we have done in the construction process, are there any assumptions that we

have made that are so obvious that we have overlooked their validity?' The answer to both of these questions is 'yes'.

If we refer to the technical drawings in the work of Labrousse we can see that the joins between the stones on the horizontal layers of the wall are not all vertical. The two on the right in the second and third layers are angled in opposite directions leading on to the conclusion that perhaps the stonework contains some feature that we have not spotted. The last time that we saw an angled join between two stones was above the entrance door of the antechamber which turned out to have a significant distortion in the blocks.

If we look through the methods that we have employed in trying to recreate the south wall there is only one assumption that can be found, and that is that the blocks of stone are, of course, horizontal. This is a perfectly sensible assumption since builders would always use horizontal joint between bricks in walls, as we have seen throughout this pyramid and in particular on the north wall that we have just studied. However, since it is an assumption, it is necessary to reconstruct the wall using non horizontally joined blocks of stone just to check that this is not the source of the error, and when we do we find that the whole of the wall can be perfectly recreated. If we start the reconstruction using the known height of the join between the hieroglyphs and the artwork as being 314cm, use Labrousse's block heights on the left side of the wall only, and then draw all of the longditudinal block joints at an angle parallel to the floor we end up with the construction shown in illustration opposite. Upon overlaying the photography from Piankoff onto this wall, aligning all of the stone joints with those that we have just drawn, we find that all of the distortions that were previously evident have now all disappeared. Additionally, the construction now makes full architectural sense, and when standing in front of the coffin and looking back down the chamber one can see a perfect forced perspective design - or more to the point, one cannot see it. This non horizontal nature of these stone joints is particularly clear in the photograph on page 32 of Mark Lehner's reference book "The complete pyramids" where, due to the lighting employed in the photograph, the stone joints on the north and south walls are clearly defined and can be compared against each other.

So we can conclude that the south wall of the main chamber conceals its true architectural shape by employing non horizontal longditudinal stone joints. The architects have managed to create exactly the same effect on the two opposing sides of the chamber, but have used a different technique on either side. On the north side they have used three sections of hieroglyphs to define the false perspective lines that the eye will follow, and on the south side they have used continuous racks of hieroglyphs from top to bottom, but carved them onto distorted brickwork with non horizontal joints. This difference between the two sides leads us to the firm conclusion that this building has been designed at great length to completely confuse anyone who looks at it.

The only thing left for us to do is to connect the section of the south wall containing the hieroglyphs that we have just constructed to the south west corner of the chamber at the far end of the artwork section. One would assume that this would be a quite straight forward task,

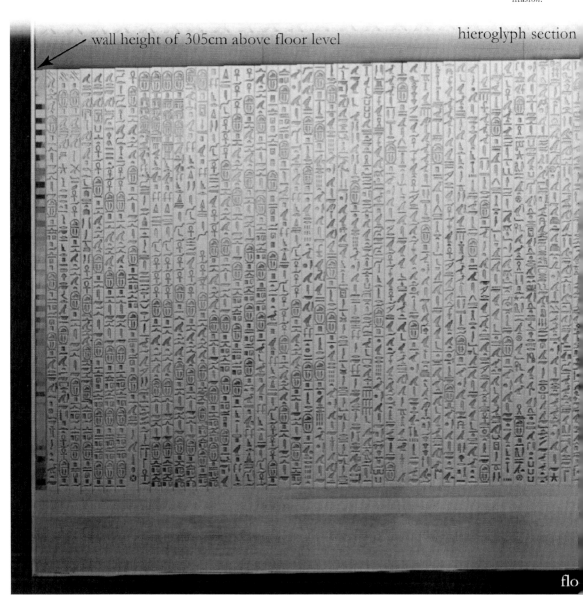

wall height of 305cm above floor level   hieroglyph section

flo

since we know the height of this section of wall at both end, one from our analysis and the other from the work of Labrousse. But upon trying to reconcile the dimensions in this section of the pyramid we find that the two ends of the wall cannot be easily connected. Labrousse states quite clearly that the height of the artwork sections of walls which surround the coffin, and which are made from the stone type alabaster, are all of the same height, that being 305cm with measurements as always rounded to the nearest centimeter. We also know from reading his work in conjunction with the evidence that we have found so far that he did not measure the north or south walls of the main chamber in their middle sections. So what we know about these height measurements of the alabaster sections is that they must be the measurements taken in the corners of the west wall where the alabaster meets up. There is no problem on the right side of the west wall, since we know that the wall dips down on this side, and the measurement of 305cm corresponds perfectly with what we have deduced about this wall's construction. However, on the left side of the wall if the

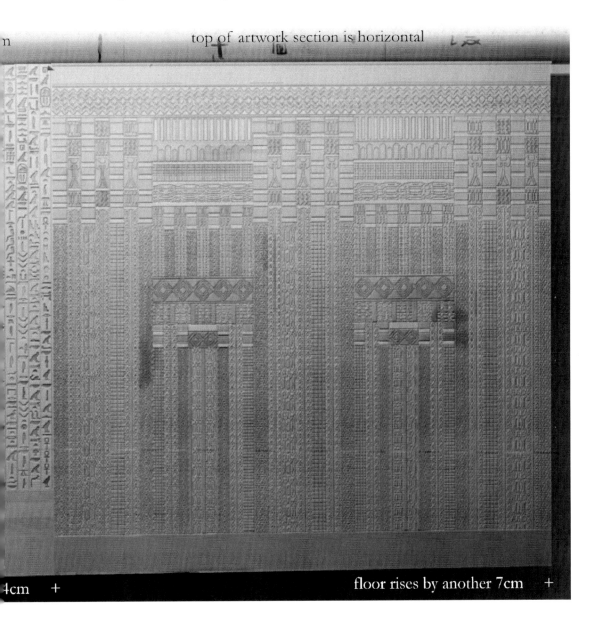

top of artwork section is horizontal

n

4cm   +

floor rises by another 7cm   +

height above the floor level is also 305cm, then we are left with the conclusion that the floor must be higher in the back left corner of the room (when viewed from the door). This is exactly the same conclusion that we came to when analysing the west wall of the chamber and confirms what we already know about this section of the chamber.

The whole arrangement of the south wall can be seen in the illustration on the previous page. Note in the diagram that the south wall section of the chamber which contains the artwork is perfectly horizontal along its top section, which is the final feature that causes the beautiful optical illusion of the west wall to work so efficiently.

With the full floor plan of the chamber and that of its walls fully diagnosed, we are going to make our way back down to the other end of the pyramid's underground rooms and look at the serdab - the strangely shaped room which contains no hieroglyphs and appears to serve no purpose whatsoever. Knowing what we do about the architects of this building we can probably already assume that if the serdab looks like it serves no real purpose, then it may well contain the greatest interest of all, such is the nature of the illusions that we have detected so far.

THE FORGOTTEN CHAMBER

The smallest of the three underground rooms in the pyramid of Unas is known by Egyptologists as "the serdab", which, loosely defined, is a hidden chamber inside of which a statue of the deceased Pharaoh would have been placed. In the Unas pyramid this room is tiny with a total floor space of only 3 square meters and with walls that are un-decorated throughout. It is due to these constrained proportions and the lack of hieroglyphs on the walls that there are no photographs of the inside of the room available for inspection, and that archaeologists investigating the chamber complex have paid much less attention to the serdab's construction than they have to the other two rooms, which are quite magnificent in comparison.

However the room does lend itself to architectural investigation in a much better manner than the two other chambers, since the slabs of stone which make up the roof of the room also serve as the upper section of the antechamber's east wall. This is a unique configuration in the stonework of the building in that we have a system of stones which lock together two sections of the building, and from this fact we can perform an accurate analysis of the room's construction relative to that of the antechamber. Even though Labrousse has neglected to specify the lengths of all the stones which make up the serdab walls, he has included their details in the technical drawings which accompany the text, and combined with the numerical data of wall heights and passage lengths, an accurate model of this room can be constructed. From the plan views of the east and west walls of the serdab which Labrousse presents it can be seen that the join between the second and third roof stones (counting from north to south) is perfectly aligned with one end of the central alcove in the serdab, as was shown in the diagram in the earlier chapter. Yet if we carefully follow Labrousse's details of the construction of the antechamber's east wall, the joining

passage between the antechamber and serdab, and the serdab itself we find that the join in the roof blocks is 5cm further north than is shown on his diagrams. This is not a particularly perplexing situation, since we already know that the antechamber is rotated in relation to the main chamber and entrance passage, and so it is a simple matter to deduce that the serdab center line is aligned with the north south axis of the entrance passage and not with that of the antechamber. When the CAD drawing is adjusted to take this fact into account then the join in the roof stones and the alcove in the room perfectly match up and the generalised positioning of the serdab is complete.

The question now arises as to the construction of the passageway which joins the serdab to the antechamber and it is at this point that we come across a problem. Labrousse states that the passage, unlike the other passages in the building, has walls of equal length at 153cm on both the north and south sides of the passage. But we have just concluded that the serdab is aligned along a true north south axis and we know that the antechamber has a rotation in it, so it should be impossible for the passage to have equal length sides. By carefully checking once again the stonework measurements of Labrousse and adjusting the passage drawing in various manners, such as offsetting the two passageway sides so that they are the same length as each other but forming a parallelogram rather than a rectangle, we can see that this is not a viable solution to the problem. The only clue that we have about the passageway wall lengths is from the shape of the antechamber floor that we have deduced in which the north east corner is aligned to true north. But since the south east corner walls are aligned to the rotated angle of the antechamber we are left with little alternative but to move into the serdab itself and see if the dimensions contained within it shed any light on this problem.

Labrousse has the perimeter shape of this room (ie excluding the walls between the alcoves) as being perfectly rectangular, with a length of 6.76m and a width of 2.12m with the measurements, as always, expressed to the nearest centimeter. Yet in the work of Maspero, where the measurements are expressed to the nearest half centimeter, he has

Gaston Maspero 1881

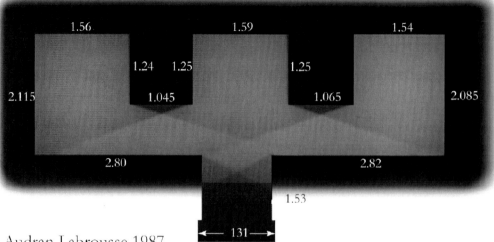

Audran Labrousse 1987

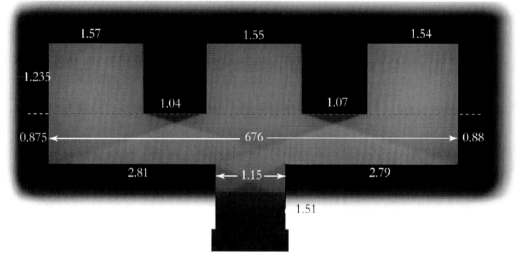

Correct floor plans

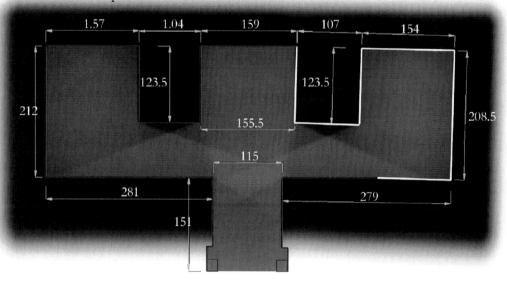

The forgotten chamber

The serdab floor
plans

The illustration
shows a compari-
son of the floor
plans of the first
and last surveys
to be carried out
on the building
alongside the cor-
rect floor plans

the length of the back wall (calculated by adding up the alcove lengths and alcove dividing wall lengths) as being 6.80m. Since Maspero seems to have measured these sections of wall with some accuracy, it would be foolish to dismiss his measurements as being incorrect simply because they were carried out way back in 1881. Upon analysing the individual pieces of data we can see that Maspero has the width of the central alcove as being 159cm, whereas Labrousse has it at 155cm and the 4cm error in the overall wall length is contained in just this one measurement. If we try to check the length of the room by looking at the opposite wall, the west wall, we find that we have another apparent error as Maspero has the door width, and hence the joining passage width, as being 131cm and Labrousse has it at only 115cm. This massive difference can be quite easily understood when one looks at the antechamber end of the passage, which contains the strange feature that we remarked upon in the 'clues' chapter where it was noted that the walls at the start of the passage have been carved back from their original position seemingly to take a door frame of some sorts. Maspero has clearly measured the passage width at the antechamber end, and Labrousse has measured the width on the serdab end, leading to the massive disparity in the values. The length of the serdab's west wall is therefore 675cm based on Labrousse's measurements and about 5 cm shorter than the serdab's east wall. We can see that both Maspero's and Labrousse's measurements of the passage width are correct and we also now know for certain the measured width of the cutaway section on the joining passage doorway to the antechamber.

What we have also just noticed is that a discrepancy between two people's sets of measurements was down to them having measured the same object in two different locations, and of course this could also be a possibility in the central alcove of the serdab. The alcove may not be regular in shape and the two different measurements that they report have been taken in different places, one measuring the back wall of the alcove, and the other measuring the width at the front. If we conclude our comparison of the two sets of measurements, we find that there is one more disparity contained within them, that being the width of the serdab. Labrousse has the measurement as being 212cm on either end, whereas Maspe-

ro has a measurement of 211.5cm on the north end and 208.5cm on the south end. Bearing in mind that Maspero is working to a better accuracy than Labrousse and that it is quite clear that he has measured both ends of the serdab, whereas Labrousse appears to have calculated the south end rather than measured it, the 3.5cm disparity looks to be a genuine error and is most perplexing. If we take an overview of the two men's work we can see that all of the measurements on the north side of the serdab, to the left as you walk down the passage from the antechamber, are the same (+/- 0.5cm) in the two sets of work, and the only errors occur in the measurements on the right side of the room. The easiest way to resolve this problem is to make a detailed CAD drawing and adjust the walls in various sections of the serdab on the right side by the small angle which we know as the architects reference angle of Atan 1/42, to see if any sensible construction can be arrived at which both fits the known design of the pyramid so far and the combined measurement data of Maspero and Labrousse.

In this manner it is possible to come to a satisfactory conclusion regarding the shape of the serdab, and the final floor plan is shown in the illustration opposite. The north half of the serdab is perfectly aligned to north and the south half is aligned to the central axis of the antechamber. The only exception to this arrangement is that the west wall is built at the architects angle at one end so that a right angle is formed in the corner, and at the other end of the wall it is aligned to true north and so produces a right angle on the passage corner, the passage being aligned to true north. This construction method on the west wall is precisely the same as that which was seen earlier in the main chamber, and it is this feature that makes the serdab so difficult to measure with accuracy. The one feature which gives this construction plan away when viewing the room from the antechamber is that the south wall of the passage and the south wall of the central alcove are not parallel to each other. This feature is clearly visible on the photograph shown overleaf.

Whilst neither Maspero or Labrousse has done a satisfactory job of correctly measuring the shape of the serdab, between them they have supplied sufficient information for the precise de-

Antechamber floor plan

The alignment of the serdab.

(left) The non parallel nature of the serdab passageway and the south wall of the serdab alcove can be seen in this illustration

We can now turn our attention to the east wall of the antechamber since it is more than likely to conform to a very similar construction method as the west wall of the serdab. What we know about the antechamber so far is that it is rotated clockwise when viewed from above in relation to the true north of the entrance passage. This rotation is applied to the north, south and west walls (the only ones we have so far put together) and causes the entrance passage and the chamber-antechamber passage to be slightly longer on one side than on the opposing one. In his survey work, Labrousse states that the lengths of the four sides of the antechamber are as follows: the north is 371cm, the south 375cm, the west 306cm and the east 309cm. Since we know that the north doorway and wall section to its left, and the west doorway and wall section to its right are already solved, then it is again a matter of placing all of the relevant data into a CAD system and finding out how the rest of the walls must be positioned. The resulting floor plan is shown in the diagram opposite on which there is also a guide drawing with the angular distortions exaggerated in order to better explain how the room has been constructed. All of the angles used in this construction are the same as that previously deduced being 1 part in 42 (ie an angle with tangent of 1/42). All of the lengths of the walls correspond exactly to the measurements of Labrousse when the room is put together in this manner and it can be seen that the east wall of the antechamber is a duplicate of the west wall of the serdab in design concept.

The floor plans of the pyramid's chambers.

(right) The floor plan of the pyramid is shown in the diagram along with a schematic illustration of each room on which the angular scale has been increased to emphasise the construction principles.

Main chamber floor plan

So we are now in a position to draw out the whole of the floor plan of the pyramid chambers, and this is also shown in the illustration with the corresponding angular distortion guide drawing accompanying it. You can clearly see on these drawings that the two main chambers contain one corner which has be adjusted out of line with the rest of the room and that the serdab is simply constructed using the half of the design borrowed from the main chamber and half from the antechamber. You may well want to cast your mind back now to the de-

tails of the room's shape to be determined. The contrast between Labrousse's highly detailed block by block description of the rest of the pyramid, and his casual measurements in this area is striking, and can be put down to one simple reason : the architects. They have employed optical illusions in the construction of the pyramid throughout, and the unfinished walls and small size of the serdab appear to be just another in a series of 'tricks'. Had the serdab also been covered in a breathtaking array of hieroglyphs, then no doubt we would have had equally precise measurements of this section of the building from the Egyptologists. The architects have disguised all of the details of the walls in this section of the pyramid by making them seem unimportant, and once again they succeeded admirably in their objectives, hiding the information from the inquisitive minds of both Maspero and Labrousse.

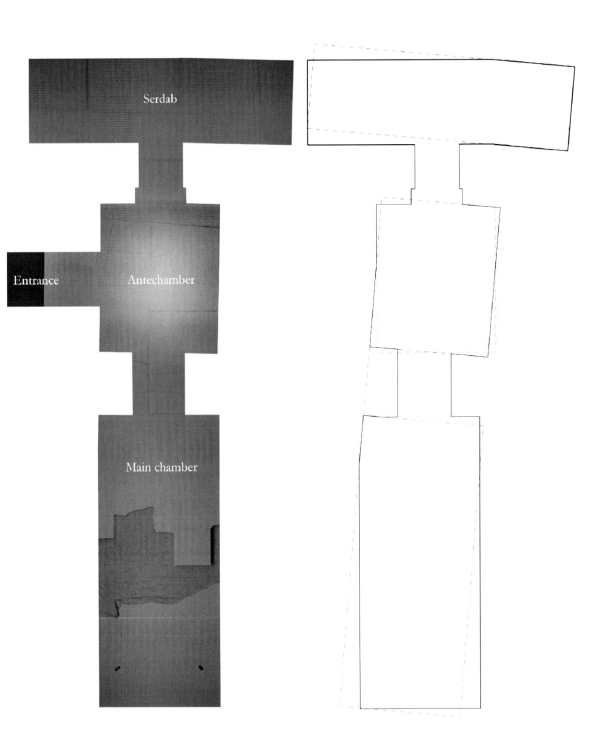

sign of the coffin which was shown in the earlier chapter and note that the chamfered corner of the coffin mimics the design of the rooms in the pyramid, a fact which further enhances the uniform design that the architects have presented to us, all be it in a particularly clandestine fashion.

We have nearly finished the analysis of whole of the inside structure of the pyramid, but have yet to determine *a purpose* for all of the remarkable architectural design that we have come across. For sure we are looking at a highly sophisticated system and it is difficult to believe that work of such quality could have been put together by people with such a rudimentary knowledge of mathematics. If you recall, when we re-entered the pyramid armed with our wooden ruler and vanishing point analysis, we also took in with us the limits of mathematical knowledge that we *assumed* that the builders would have had, based entirely on the papyrus that we looked at. This papyrus was dated some 1000 years after the pyramid of Unas was built, and having seen the astonishing detail within the underground chambers we would be well advised to confirm, before we proceed much further, that we really can backdate the limits of the mathematics on this papyrus to the time of the Unas construction. Everything that we have seen so far speaks of a highly knowledgeable grasp of engineering, and fundamental to high quality engineering is mathematical knowledge.

The obvious place in which to check the limits of mathematical knowledge possessed by the architects of the pyramid of Unas in the descending part of the entrance passage that leads to the underground chambers, since it is angular in nature and we know that the ancient Egyptians of our papyrus had no easy way of expressing angles. We should therefore be able to find a triangular construction in the descending section of the passage which uses fixed lengths sides, since they had no other way of expressing angular measure.

A VERY PRIMITIVE TRIANGLE

The start of the descending section of the entrance passage is shown in the illustration below in which the rather unusual step is clearly visible at the start of the sloping passage. Since we know that all of the angular rotations that we have come across so far in the pyramid can be represented by a right angled, or Pythagorean, triangle with perpendicular sides of 1 unit and 42 units in length, then what we are looking for in the entrance passage is a similar style of angular construction, where angles are specified using triangles of whole unit lengthed sides.

To do this we need to determine the measurement details from the various survey work that we have in our possession, and then convert these measurements into builder's units which we know must comply with the divisions on the cubit rod. The principle unit of measurement inside the chambers is 1/7th of a cubit, since the majority of the hieroglyph racks in the main chamber are of this width and especially those of the west gable above the coffin, so it is this unit that we will use at the outset when looking at the entrance passage's measurements in the cubit system.

From the survey work of Labrousse we find that the length of the slope of the descending section of the passage is 15.80m. The height of this section is 6.07m, a value which can be deduced from the elevation heights above sea level that are shown on the plan drawings in his work. The pavement is at 55.28m above sea level and the floor of the vestibule at the bottom of the slope at 49.21m above sea level. By simple deduction we know that the horizontal length of this section must be 14.58m in order to complete the right angled triangle. We can now convert the measurements of this triangle into the cubit system and find that the triangle has side lengths of 195, 81.25 and 211.25 1/7ths of a cubit. Since we need to express the side lengths in whole numbers in the same way that the builders would have done, then we will need to change units by a factor of 4 to get rid of the decimal part of the numbers.

It would appear therefore that the units that builders were using in this section of the pyramid must have been 1/28th of a cubit, which is the smallest of the divisions on the top of the cubit rod and known as a digit. The triangle of the entrance passage, when expressed in dig-

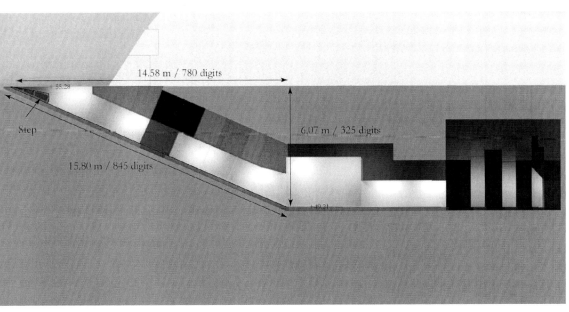

its has sides of length 780, 325 and 845 and the average error across the three sides of the triangle from the conversion from meters to cubit measure is 3mm, which falls well within the tolerances of the survey data.

If we now look at the ratio of the lengths of the sides of this triangle we find something quite remarkable. The triangle sides are in the proportions 5,12,13, which is an instantly recognisable triangle to anyone with a good grasp of mathematics. It is the second triangle in a series known as Pythagorean primitives, or Pythagorean triples as they are also known, and which are very easy to explain and understand. The simplest of all right angled triangles with sides comprised of integers is the well known 3,4,5 triangle taught to just about every school student on our planet. The 5,12,13 triangle is the next one in the series i.e. the second smallest of all right angled triangles that can be formed from integer lengthed sides. The use of these triangle proportions as the principle triangle of the entrance passage should make us immediately sit up and take note, and it achieves exactly that aim, switching us on immediately to the incongruous appearance of a piece of mathematics that is historically out of place. However, the use of the triangle is even more complex than first appears.

If we look at the stone step at the start of the passage it is evident from the technical drawings of Labrousse that the top line of the step is actually a bisector line of the entrance passage triangle, as shown in the diagram opposite. This construction detail forces us to change our builders units from digits to 1/56ths of a cubit, since by dividing the vertical face of the triangle into two parts, each of the two halves of this face no longer contains integer values in digit units, making the construction of the angular face of the step impossible in digit measure. By forcing us to use 1/56th of a cubit as our base measure we now have the lengths of the sides of the entrance triangle as **1560,1690** and **650** units of 1/56th of a cubit. This seemingly random series of lengths is not recognisable as anything in particular upon casual inspection, but is in fact an utterly astonishing set of data to find in a building of this age. To explain the theoretical significance of these series of measurements is somewhat complicated, but by referring to the diagram opposite the explanation should be comprehensible.

We have already seen how the first two triangles in the series of Pythagorean primitives are formed, and these are shown in the top row of the illustration. In the second row we are forming a compound shape from the Pythagorean triangles from the row above by extending two of the lines of the triangle in the manner shown. The lengths of the resulting triangle are shown and clearly are not integer values. This is where the third row of the diagram comes into play, where the resulting compound shapes shown in row two have had their sides recalculated so that they are expressed in the smallest integer values possible. This third row is therefore the series of compound Pythagorean primitives and whilst the values of the triangles sides are not as easily recognisable, the second of them certainly stands out clearly when compared to the triangle of the entrance passage of the pyramid of Unas.

The entrance triangle is a perfect representation of the second of the series, and by including the small step at the start of the passage, which forced us into the correct builders units, the architects have done their utmost to help us recognise the triangle that is at the heart of the construction. It is beyond doubt that this is a deliberately planned and executed mathematical construction but there is one point to note which adds a small amount of doubt. You would have expected to have found a significant architectural feature at the intersection of the perpendicular, shown in the illustration as the 'perpendicular join point', and what you actually come across in the pyramid is a complete lack of any features at all at this location. There are no roof, floor or wall joints at this place and knowing that the architects have hidden much of the previous design so carefully inside the chambers of the pyramid, then it would be more than plausible to wonder at this juncture whether the architects have just set us another puzzle to solve. The question that we are being asked is "Can we prove that the use of the compound Pythagorean triangle is deliberate by showing that the point in the diagram is a significant point in the entrance passage architecture, but one which has not been explicitly marked out ?". The architects clearly want us to investigate the design of the entrance passage, at which point we turn once again to Labrousse's survey and our rather useful cubit measuring rod.

Pythagorean primitives

The series of pythagorean traingles from which the entrance passage has been created.

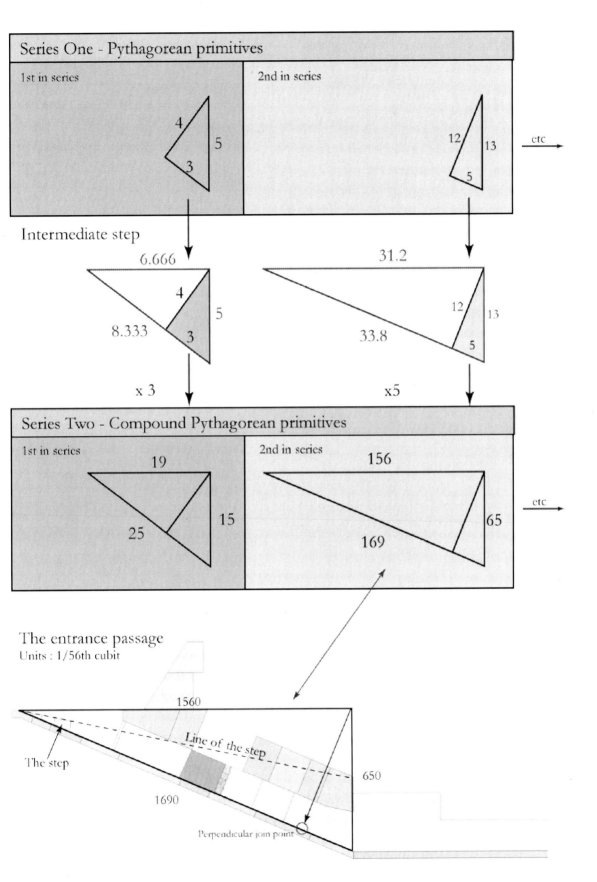

Series One - Pythagorean primitives

1st in series

4
5
3

2nd in series

12
13
5

etc →

Intermediate step

6.666
4
5
8.333
3

x 3

31.2
12
13
33.8
5

x5

Series Two - Compound Pythagorean primitives

1st in series

19
15
25

2nd in series

156
65
169

etc →

The entrance passage
Units : 1/56th cubit

1560
Line of the step
The step
1690
650
Perpendicular join point

A very primitive triangle   83

One would expect that all of the stones that were used in the entrance passage on the walls, floor and roof, would display regular cubit based values, but as can be seen in the diagram below that is simply not the case. The diagram shows the metric lengths of the stones that were reported by Labrousse and the cubit equivalent lengths, shown as whole cubits, palms and digits, with the digit fractions rounded off. Of all the stones which one comes across in the first section of the pyramid, the only one which shows any conformity whatsoever to the standard builder's measure is the height of the first layer of the pyramid's casing stones, shown as 'α' on the illustration, which is 3 cubits in height. There appears to be no logical pattern to the roof, floor or walls of the structure, yet these massive blocks of stone have been cut with precision so that they all butt together perfectly. It is worth considering the practical aspects of what is on show, since at some point in the construction of this pyramid, a stone mason must have taken instructions from the architects to cut each of the stones to their measured lengths, and those lengths

must have been passed to that stone mason in cubit measures. The list of numbers on the illustration must therefore have been the same list of lengths that was passed to the stone mason 4300 years ago.

In order to pursue the apparent random nature of the stonework lengths we need to study all of the intricacies of the passageway's design from the archaeological evidence that remains and look to see if there is anything within that evidence which points to a further depth in the design of the architecture. This is very similar to the approach taken at the outset of the book - we are looking for the clues that might help us on our way. The illustration opposite shows the same cross section of the passageway as shown previously, but with all of the structural anomalies highlighted and explained. The first point of note is the two post holes which are cut into the passageway floor just after the small step. They are, as their description implies, designed to take some sort of posts and so it would be sensible idea to insert a theoretical post into the holes to see if any information can be gleaned from doing so.

Architectutal anomalies in the entrance

(right) The architectural features in the entrance passage which serve as clues as to the design of the masonry

Random stone lengths.

(below) All of the lengths of stone from which the entrance is constructed appear to have no logical pattern to them

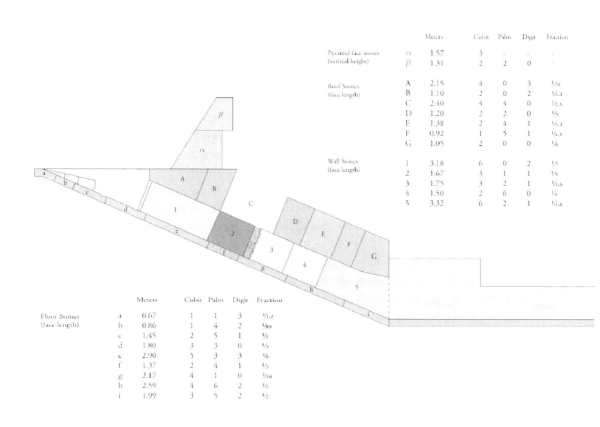

		Meters	Cubit	Palm	Digit	Fraction
Pyramid face stones (vertical height)	α	1.57	3	-	-	-
	β	1.31	2	2	0	-
Roof Stones (face length)	A	2.15	4	0	3	1/32
	B	1.10	2	0	2	1/1.2
	C	2.40	4	4	0	1/2.5
	D	1.20	2	2	0	1/5
	E	1.38	2	4	1	1/1.2
	F	0.92	1	5	1	1/4.5
	G	1.05	2	0	0	1/6
Wall Stones (face length)	1	3.18	6	0	2	1/2
	2	1.67	3	1	1	1/3
	3	1.75	3	2	1	1/1.6
	4	1.50	2	6	0	1/4
	5	3.32	6	2	1	1/1.6

		Meters	Cubit	Palm	Digit	Fraction
Floor Stones (face length)	a	0.67	1	1	3	1/1.2
	b	0.86	1	4	2	1/80
	c	1.45	2	5	1	1/2
	d	1.80	3	3	0	1/3
	e	2.90	5	3	3	1/6
	f	1.37	2	4	1	1/3
	g	2.17	4	1	0	1/10
	h	2.59	4	6	2	1/2
	i	1.99	3	5	2	1/2

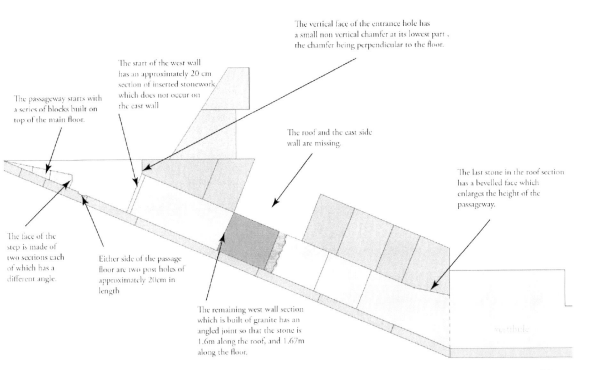

The vertical face of the entrance hole has a small non vertical chamfer at its lowest part , the chamfer being perpendicular to the floor.

The start of the west wall has an approximately 20 cm section of inserted stonework, which does not occur on the east wall

The passageway starts with a series of blocks built on top of the main floor.

The roof and the east side wall are missing.

The last stone in the roof section has a bevelled face which enlarges the height of the passageway.

The face of the step is made of two sections each of which has a different angle.

Either side of the passage floor are two post holes of approximately 20cm in length

The remaining west wall section which is built of granite has an angled joint so that the stone is 1.6m along the roof, and 1.67m along the floor.

vestibule

As can be seen in next diagram, the posts highlight a 6 cubit long measurement along the ground level horizontal, a measurement which if deliberate would be clearly significant as it is the same measurement that appears along the main chamber west wall, and is the first whole cubit measurement that we have come across in the structure of the descending passage.

The passage floor

If the post hole positioning is intentional, and the 6 cubit measure has been designed into the monument's architecture, then the next logical step would to be to produce a line from each of the floor joints perpendicular to the sloping face of the floor, in exactly the same manner as we have just done with the imaginary post. When this is done one finds that the distances between the line projections along the horizontal ground level have no significant values whatsoever, producing the same type of distribution of random measurements as was seen in the original tabulation of the stone lengths. However, doing so is not strictly a correct manner in interpolating the design, since the post hole is found on the passageway floor, and prior to this point the passageway floor is raised up and at a shallower angle due to the presence of the step. So it is an entirely logical step to check a similar construction method using lines which are perpendicular to the top of the step. It is when this is done that one can immediately see that the lengths of the stone on the main floor slope have been designed from rational cubit measurement lengths along the horizontal ground line when a perpendicular line is projected from the top of the step, exactly as was suggested by the post hole placement.

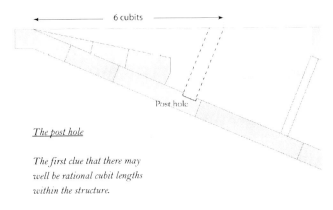

6 cubits

Post hole

The post hole

The first clue that there may well be rational cubit lengths within the structure.

This arrangement is shown in the illustration below and holds true for the first three stone joints on the main passageway floor. (If you are wondering how these joints are visible, since the first two have the step on top of them, it is due to the fact that the stonework which makes up the step is both cracked and incomplete, allowing inspection of the lower level.) The lengths of the floor stones in the passageway can be deduced from the geometry and contain a deviation from the surveying measurements of 3mm on the third stone, which is the only one of the three that Labrousse specifies in the text of his book. The lengths of the other two stones can be taken from the technical drawings which he published and are visually exact on an enlargement of that drawing with an estimated error of just a few millimeters. I have chosen to leave the drawing's units in 1/7ths of a cubit since the numbers are much simpler to view than the builders base unit of 1/56th of a cubit.

The next floor joint, the fourth from the top of the slope, is created from a vertical projection of a regular palm measurement along the horizontal ground level, as shown in the next diagram. Clearly, without an understanding of the first three stone joints, the fourth would make very little sense since it is a requirement that the construction line from joint 3 is first projected onto ground level. When a CAD drawing of this system is produced the length of the fourth stone can be calculated and comes out at 179.8cm, a value which is out by 2mm from the value reported in the Labrousse survey.

The fifth floor stone in the sequence is massive at nearly 3m in length and with an estimated thickness of 40cm would have a weight of about 4 tonnes (4,000kg) based on an approximate density of limestone of 2.5 tonnes per cubic meter. It would have taken a considerable effort to manipulate into place, and one would therefore conclude that the architect had a particularly good reason for wanting to use such a cumbersome item at this point in the pyramid's construction and thereby avoid any stone joints in this section of the floor. Since we can already see that the floor joints are not arbitrarily placed it would make sense that this stone may well play a significant part in the overall design of the descending passage.

To understand what is going on here we will have to look at a sequence of design elements in succession, during which time the validity of the calculations and system may well appear as conjecture

The construction of the first three stones which make up the floor is shown in this illustration

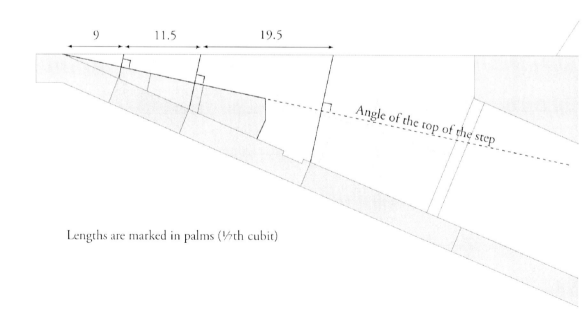

9   11.5   19.5

Angle of the top of the step

Lengths are marked in palms (1/7th cubit)

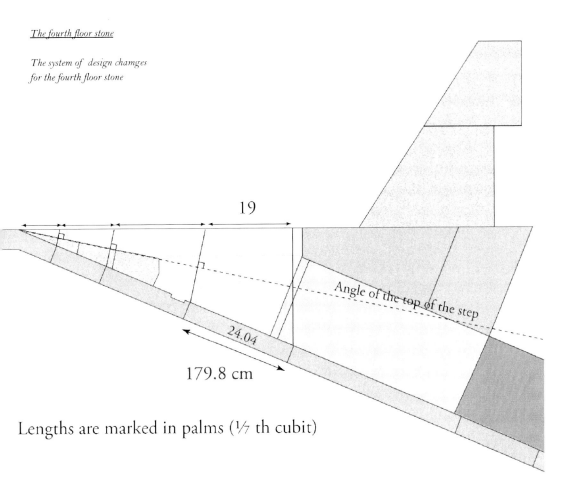

19

Angle of the top of the step

24.04

179.8 cm

Lengths are marked in palms (⅟₇ th cubit)

on my part. However, when the whole sequence is completed it will be abundantly obvious that the each step that we are about to take is a correct interpretation of the architectural design.

The illustration overleaf shows that from the vertical projection of the fourth joint on the ground level, the distance to the start of the pyramid's face is exactly 14 palms and that the face line projects down onto the passage floor at an apparently random point, which I have marked with a question mark. What we then can notice is that the horizontal joint which defines the top of the first layer of stones from which the pyramid is built is the same distance, 14 palms, from the pyramid's base when projected onto the ground level. I have continued this line down to the floor level of the entrance passage in a similar manner as before and marked off the point as 'X'.

This very tidy system of construction is highly significant, since we know from the work of Labrousse that the first layer of the pyramid's face stones are exactly 3 cubits, or 21 palms high. This means that we now know the angle of the pyramid's face mathematically since its gradient must be 21/14 or 1.5 giving the pyramid a face angle of 56.31° or 0.9828 radians, a value which corresponds perfectly to the surveyed angle shown on the technical drawings of Labrousse (although the written value is incorrectly displayed). The value can be confirmed with reference to Mark Lehner's reference book, "The Complete Pyramids" page 155 where he also shows in his illustration a face angle of 56°. So the point that we have marked on the floor of the passageway as point X defines the angle of the pyramid - which is about the most significant purpose that any point on an Egyptian monument could possibly serve. It would therefore be reasonable to expect it to have been clearly marked on the floor, but as the illustration shows, this is not the case as there is no floor joint at this

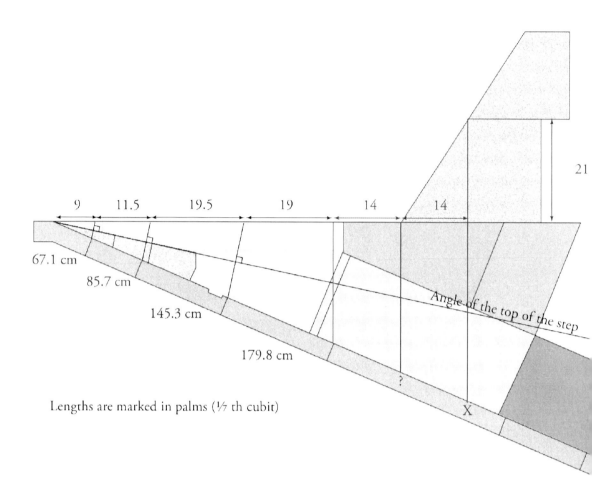

9   11.5   19.5   19   14   14   21

67.1 cm

85.7 cm

145.3 cm

179.8 cm

Angle of the top of the step

?

X

Lengths are marked in palms (1/7 th cubit)

point. Naturally, when studying the construction of the passageway this point is one which warrants large amounts of attention, and by systematic analysis of the inherent geometry that we have already discovered compared to the accurate CAD drawing of Labrousse's work, it is not long before the point on the floor gives up its secrets.

The illustration opposite takes us forward a large step in our understanding of this pyramid's entrance passage, as it can be seen that the chamfer that is cut on the southern most roof stone has been carved from a geometric construction in the following highly logical manner. The point X on the floor is located 87 palms horizontally from the start of the entrance passage and therefore 108 palms from the lower end of the entrance passage, since the master triangle is 195 palms in length along its long side. If we then measure 108 palms along the horizontal passage (to the right on the drawing) and mark off a point Y, then the geometric line XY

perfectly defines the chamfered roof section. Since the whole of the construction is mathematical in origin, the height of the doorway at the bottom of the entrance passage can be determined with precision and is exactly 22.5 palms high or 168.2 cm. The same height in the Labrousse work is given as 169cm showing a variation of 8mm from the calculated figure. Now this is obviously a quite complex construction system, and it is based around the point X, which is not marked in any obvious way on the passage floor, so it would be useful if we could now find the next piece in the puzzle which confirmed that what we have just seen is correct.

The floor stone joints at the start of the passage were formed from lines which were perpendicular to the preliminary passage bisector line as was first shown in a previous illustration. If you look carefully at the last diagram you will notice that the geometric line which defines the roof chamfer is parallel to this bisector line This is a mathematical

Top section of the entrance

The point 'X', which is not marked on the floor in the design, defines the angular slope of the pyramid's face.

The bevelled roof section

The geometric design of the
bevelled roof section of the
entrance passage

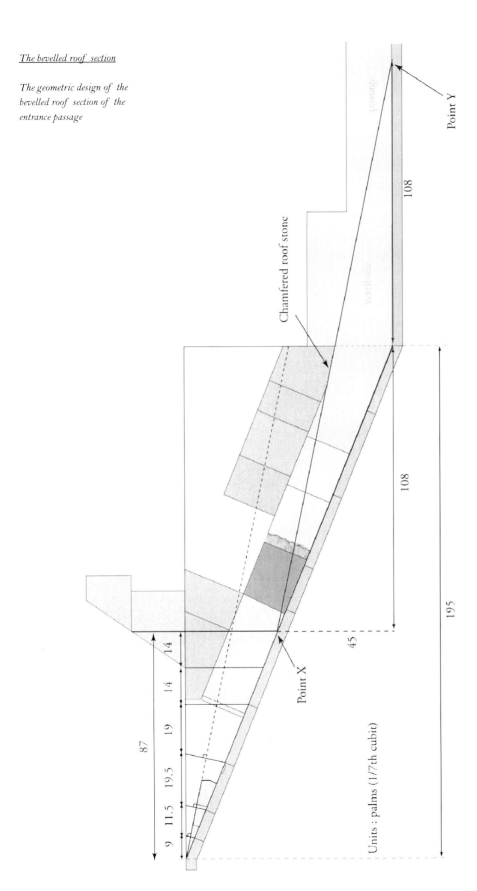

Point Y

Point X

Chamfered roof stone

passage

vestibule

108

108

195

45

87

14

14

19

19.5

11.5

9

Units : palms (1/7th cubit)

statement rather than an observation, since the formation of the geometry dictates that they two lines must be parallel. It would be entirely reasonable to use the same system on the floor joints at the bottom of the passage as we used on those at the top, and the illustration below shows the results of such an application of the previous system.

Once again it is possible to mark of rational divisions of palm lengths (18, 28.5, 34 and 21.5 from top to bottom) along this line and project the perpendiculars down to the floor to form the floor joints. The correspondence with the surveyed measurements from Labrousse is as follows :

	Geometry	Survey
First floor stone	137.0 cm	137 cm
Second stone	217.0 cm	217 cm
Third stone	258.8 cm	259 cm
Fourth stone	198.6 cm	199 cm

The above list requires no observations adding to it, since the accuracy of the geometry to the surveying is immediately apparent. This confirms that the sequence of constructional geometry that we have just performed is quite certainly correct and that we have successfully defined all of the joints on the floor of the descending passage and that the point X is a real point in the pyramid's

architecture.

Having defined the floor joints from geometry, it is quite likely that the roof and wall joints will also have been designed with respect to the same geometric system, and so it is to these that we should now turn our attention.

The passage roof and walls

You may have noticed a feature of the geometry that has already been described that is clearly another design feature of the pyramid, and one which we have so far not used. The bisector line that forms the top of the preliminary step angle and the line marked as XY on the previous diagrams are not only parallel, but are spaced apart by the same distance as the passageway height. They make up what is in effect a virtual passageway which is out of line with the real passage and is waiting to be rotated into place. It is at this stage that we have to be particularly careful and pedantic about the manner in which we proceed since the geometric construction is about to get significantly more detailed and complex.

Let us start with all of the currently known geometric definition lines clearly marked on the drawing with each one in a different colour, so that we can easily see which lines are which once they have been rotated. The illustration below shows this set up,

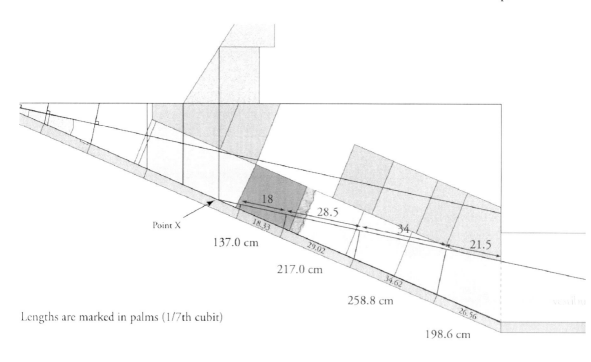

Point X

18

28.5

18.33

137.0 cm

34

21.5

29.02

217.0 cm

34.62

258.8 cm

26.56

198.6 cm

Lengths are marked in palms (1/7th cubit)

Creating the passage roof

The remarkable construction of the entrance passage roof, relying upon the rotation of the geometry around the unmarked point 'X'

along with the position of the lines once they have been rotated in the second part of the diagram. The rotation has been carried out around the point X on the passageway floor, and what was the preliminary step line which bisected the master triangle (green) is now perfectly superimposed upon the surveyed line of the passage roof giving the roof a geometric height of 132.66cm above the floor line. This value is reported by Labrousse as 132cm and once again we have determined a principal feature of the pyramid with an excellent degree of coherence to the surveying by using the same overall geometric system.

By rotating the step line in this way we have solved one problem but created another, because if you consider the start of the entrance passage where it first starts to descend from the ground level, we have created an ambiguous start to the passage. When the blue line, which was originally the floor line, is rotated around the point X it s end point does not fall on the perpendicular that can be extended from the original passage start point. Consequently we do not know if the roof length of the passage or the floor length of the passage is the intended reference line. If it is to be the roof line, then the passageway will be slightly shorter than if the floor line is taken as the reference, and since the architects have been utterly precise in the design work so far, this is an ambiguity that needs resolving.

Both the problem and the solution are shown in the illustration below where it can be seen that the geometric solution's validity at the passage end has been demonstrated to us by the builders of the pyramid

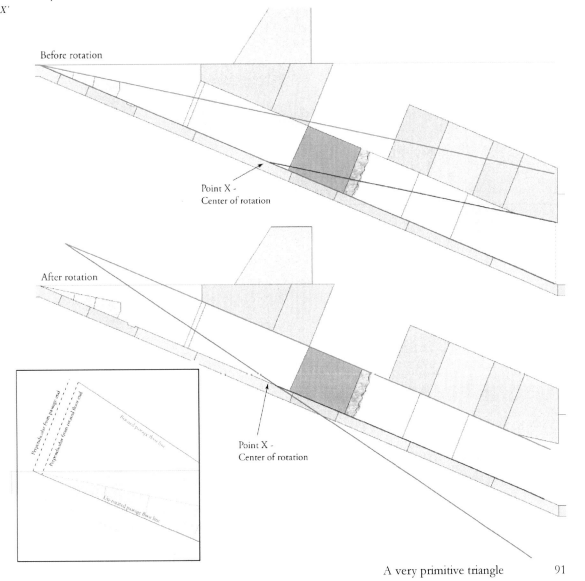

Before rotation

Point X -
Center of rotation

After rotation

Point X -
Center of rotation

by inserting the narrow band of stonework at the start of the passageway's west wall, along with a very small bevelled edge prior to the vertical face of the entrance hole. This small section of stone insert, which has always been assumed to be repair work in previous studies of this pyramid, is in fact a perfect duplication of the entrance passage start geometry, and has been built at this location since it is not possible to build it at its correct position in space. From the CAD system it is possible to extract the values of the dimensions of this rock insert, and it is 132.66 cm in height perpendicular to the floor up to the roof level, and 12.7 cm in length when measured along the floor slope. The difference in the height between the passage roof and the extended passage roof which was formed from the geometric construction is 2.4cm, and this extended roof line is shown on the illustrations as a dotted green line and will turn out to be highly important at a later stage in the analysis.

It is interesting that the stone insert at the start of the passage wall only appears on the west wall of the passage, and the east wall is constructed of one complete block, implying that the geometric design should be aligned in space with the west side of the passage and not with the center line. If you return to the diagram of the architectural anomalies in the passage it can be seen that west wall is also the only complete wall - the east wall having a section missing in the area of the granite stone flooring block. Whilst this is of no consequence at this stage in the analysis since we are working on a flat two dimensional plane, we will obviously have to look at the system in plan view at some time later if we are to understand the widths as well as the lengths and heights of the construction and we should not forget the west wall alignment when doing so. Additionally, whilst the stone insert at the start of the wall is clearly formed from the geometry, we have no justification yet for determining a place for the start of the wall in our overall geometric plan. In other words, it is clear that the geometric construction should be placed at the wall start, but we have yet to determine in a logical manner where that wall start is located in the system. The vertical face of the first roof stone which forms the back of the entrance hole is located at an irregular position on the ground level in respect to the passage floor start and shows no desire to give up its formation geometry when analysed on the CAD system

The end of the entrance passage

The geometry of the start of the entrance can be duplicated at the bottom of the passage

The ambiguous passage start

(left) Due to the rotation used to define the passage roof, the start of the entrance becomes ambiguously defined

The flow of design logic

(right) The creation of the floor of the passage has followed a linear sequence from start to finish.

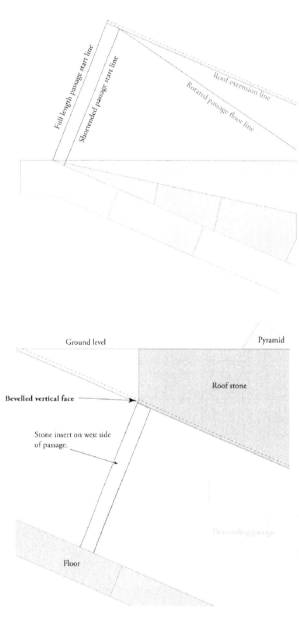

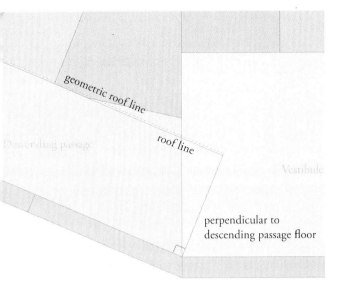

geometric roof line

Descending passage

roof line

Vestibule

perpendicular to
descending passage floor

which emanates from the end of the passage floor as shown above. We have no real use for this construction at present, but it has to be drawn at this stage for a reason.

Not only has the geometry so far been perfect, but the systematic way in which it has been presented excluded the possibility for us to jump around in the analysis and pick out pieces of geometry at random. The system is what is known as a linear system, in that you have to complete the geometric analysis in a step by step manner, and if you were to miss out a step, then the analysis would fall apart. Consider what we have done so far by reference to the diagram below and you will see that it is possible to draw a logical path through the geometry of the floor stones. Once we have concluded the study of the wall and roof stones, we should be able to construct a similar path diagram which flows just as easily, and so it is important to note how we have progressed since the rotation around the unmarked floor point. Having rotated the floor geometry around the point X, we have recommenced at the passage start point, constructed the passage start perpendiculars from floor to roof, slid down the passage roof to the bottom end of the passage and we currently find ourselves at the floor point at the bottom of the passage.

We cannot leave this point other

: perpendiculars to the floor or to the rotated floor lines yield no results.

Despite this fact we can still continue with the geometric construction, since the rather elegant piece of geometry that forms the passage start can now be logically duplicated at the bottom of the descending passage where the passage emerges into the first room of the pyramid, known as the vestibule. This can be done by extending the roof line and the geometric line which is above it down until they intersect with the perpendicular line

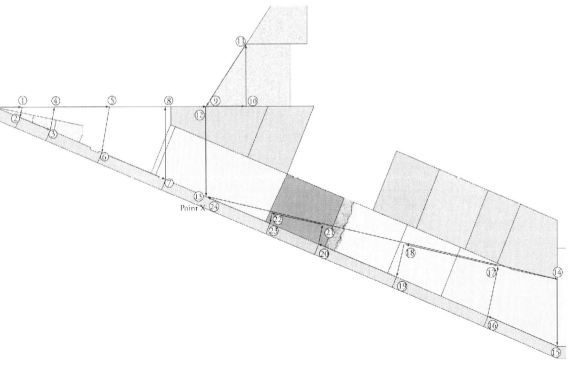

than by logical geometric means and the key to understanding how to do this can be found in the granite wall stone in the center of the passage. If you check back to the architectural anomalies diagram at the start of the chapter you will see that the left face of this stone (as viewed on the diagram) is not perpendicular to the floor slope. Where this face meets the floor it was measure by Labrousse as being 7cm higher up the passage than the corresponding point at roof level - in relation to the other wall joints it is slightly diagonally aligned. On its own this gives us little information to work with, but if you look now at the geometric construction that forms the stone insert at the start of the wall, this also could contain a diagonal element which would be aligned at about twice the inclination of the granite wall face joint just mentioned. In fact, the existence of such a diagonal line would make complete sense, since it would have the mathematical property of being perpendicular to the line which bisect the triangle from which it is formed - the exact same system that was used to form the preliminary step in the passage from the master triangle

This is somewhat difficult to understand from a description in words, but much more simple when seen on the illustration below in which lines with the same colour are perpendicular to each other. One can immediately see that this construction is correct, because not only does it fit with the logic used in the master triangle (the splitting of the triangle using a bisector) but also perfectly explains why the preliminary step was terminated at the point that it was, and also why the face of that step contains two angled faces. It is the red and green lines on the diagram which define these points and the angles at which the face of the step has been cut. Since we know the geometric definition of the step's top angle, and the lines we have just drawn are also geometric in origin, it is obviously possible to calculate all of the lengths and angles involved in the step's construction.

It is highly likely that the post holes which are cut into the floor and which have been described earlier in this chapter also fit into this system, since it would appear from the illustration that the '75% bisector line" is missing and would perfectly account for the width of the post holes at about 20cm. However, this detail is too small to measure on the technical drawings of Labrousse, and so I have chosen to leave it out from this description.

Since we have formed these angled lines at the top of the entrance passage, and

Entrance passage verticals

The vertical sections of the start of the entrance are in fact designed around the point 'X' and angular bisectors which eminate from this point

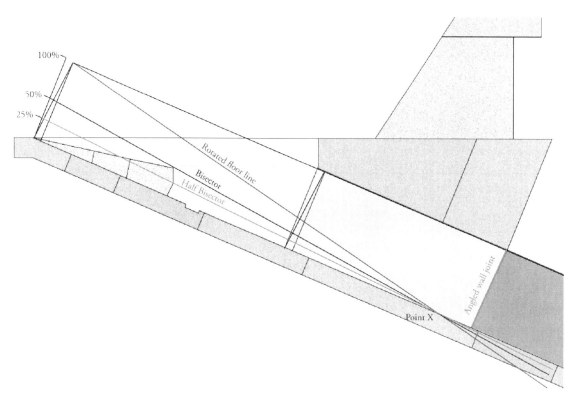

they all pass through the point X and emerge again on the other side of this point, then we now have a complete new set of construction lines to work with at the bottom of the passage where we left our analysis a few paragraphs ago. These angled lines can be extended on the CAD drawing and the system of roof and floor joints can be established. It is quite unsurprising that the point that we marked on the passage floor as the 'perpendicular join point" earlier in the chapter now comes into play since it has been clearly marked out by the architects as being significant. It is the first defining point in the roof and floor joint geometry and shows us the system that needs to be followed as we progress up the passage. Each of the roof joints matches each of the wall joints when a perpendicular line is drawn to the angled construction lines that we have just formed at the top of the passage. This is by far the most elegant of all of the geometry that has been presented so far, and its complexity does not detract one bit from the precision with which it conforms to the surveying data.

The layout of this construction is shown in the adjoining illustration, where it can be seen that the geometric system continues past the point X in the passage and forms the diagonal face of the granite wall stone and the positioning of the stone insert at the start of the passage. It is worth having a good look at this illustration since the geometry is quite simple, yet when presented as a whole looks quite complex. You will notice that there is now just one roof joint that is not defined, and that is the very first joint that one comes across after entering the roofed section of the passage, and it is by strict application of the geometric principles (that the wall and roof joints must be joined up) that it is possible to deduce that this roof joint is formed by connecting the covered passage start point at floor level to the primary triangles right angled corner - a construction shown on the diagram by a dotted grey line.

This final piece of geometry very nicely returns us to where we

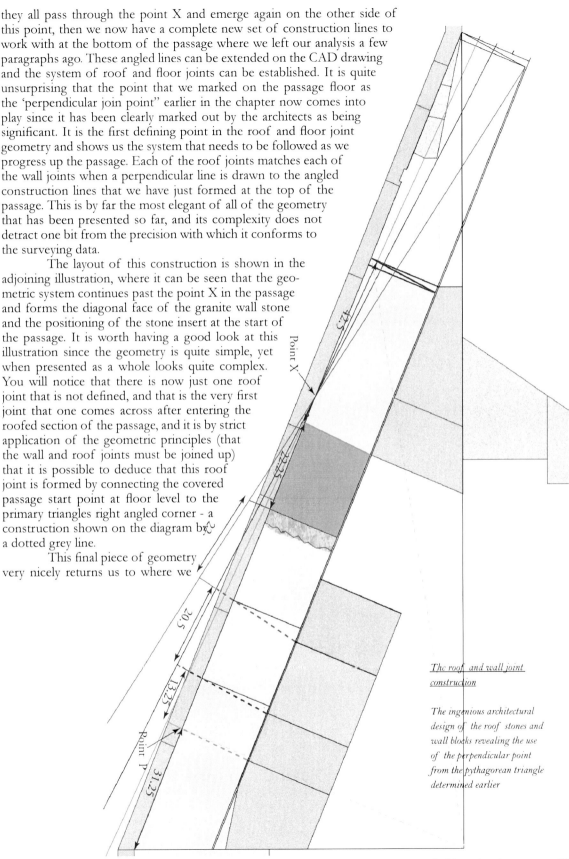

The roof and wall joint construction

The ingenious architectural design of the roof stones and wall blocks revealing the use of the perpendicular point from the pythagorean triangle determined earlier

A very primitive triangle   95

started the geometry, since the 'perpendicular join point' was the starting place for the roof-wall system, and this commenced in the right angled corner of the master triangle. It also explicitly defines the master triangle, rather than implicitly defines it as has been the case up to this point, and serves one other very useful purpose. It makes the length of the first roof stones appear totally arbitrary, and means that the very first thing that you come across when analysing the covered section of the passage is the very last part that you will be able to understand.

So we now have the whole of the entrance passage quantified in a geometric manner, which leads us on to a very useful cross check that can be performed. From the CAD drawing it is evident that the accuracy of fit of the geometry to the surveying is very close indeed. For example, the last two roof stones that we formed measure 215.0 cm and 110.1 cm on the geometry and were reported by Labrousse as being 215 cm and 110 cm long in his surveying. We can therefore now make a table of all the surveying measurements from Labrousse that are specified in the text (rather than the ones having been extracted from the technical drawings), tabulate the corresponding measurements in palms from the geometric construction, and calculate the length of the cubit in centimeters.

Table of measurements

	A	B	C
Floor length	1580	211,25	52,36
1st floor stone	145	19,44	52,22
2nd floor stone	180	24,04	52,40
3rd floor stone	290	38,80	52,31
4th floor stone	137	18,33	52,33
5th floor stone	217	29,02	52,35
6th floor stone	259	34,62	52,37
7th floor stone	199	26,56	52,44
1st roof stone	215	28,69	52,46
2nd roof stone	110	14,77	52,14
Granite wall bottom	167	22,25	52,54
Granite wall top	160	21,40	52,33
Lower wall length	658	87,94	52,38
Column totals	4317	577,11	680,61
Cubit value			52,35

Column A - Labrousse measurement in cm
Column B - Length from CAD drawing in palms
Column C - Calculated value of cubit in cm

The result is that the average cubit measure comes out at 52.35cm, perfectly matching the commonly accepted value of the cubit down to one tenth of a millimeter. Indeed it does more than just match existing values - it defines them.

Additionally this perfect conformity to the known cubit length establishes the fact that the published values of the stone lengths in Labrousse's book must, on average, be perfect and that the rest of his work should be taken as being equally well researched and presented. The small number of errors which do appear in his publication, and of which we still need to be aware, derive not from errors in his measurements, but in errors in interpreting those measurements when the analysis of the structure was performed at a later date.

With the roof and wall joints firmly in position we can now construct a diagram to illustrate the flow of the geometry's logic for this section of the analysis, and also a similar diagram showing the logic flow on a stone by stone basis, numbering each of the stones in order as they are defined. These two diagrams are shown in the illustration opposite with the numbering of the logical steps in the first part of the diagram continuing from those of the similar previous illustration for the logic of the floor stone construction. There is one important point to note in the passageway's construction which is that **the central section of the roof is excluded from the logical definition process - and this roof section is of course missing from the pyramid.**

It has always been suggested by Egyptologists that this missing stone was removed by un-named 'tomb robbers' at some point in the pyramids history. We therefore have more than reasonable grounds once again to question the 'tomb robber' theory as an explanation for this missing section of stonework.

We are left with just one piece of the geometric construction to explain, that being the extended roof lines that we terminated inside the start of the vestibule. You will recall that there are two geometric lines which appear in the vestibule formed from the ambiguous start to the entrance slope, and the way in which these have been incorporated into the building's architecture is quite magnificent. At the far end of the entrance passage where it meets the antechamber there is an anomaly in the architecture which is very difficult to understand. The lintel of the doorway from the antechamber to the entrance passage in

This diagram follows on from
the earlier logic map, and
shows how there is a linear
path of logic which flows
through the design

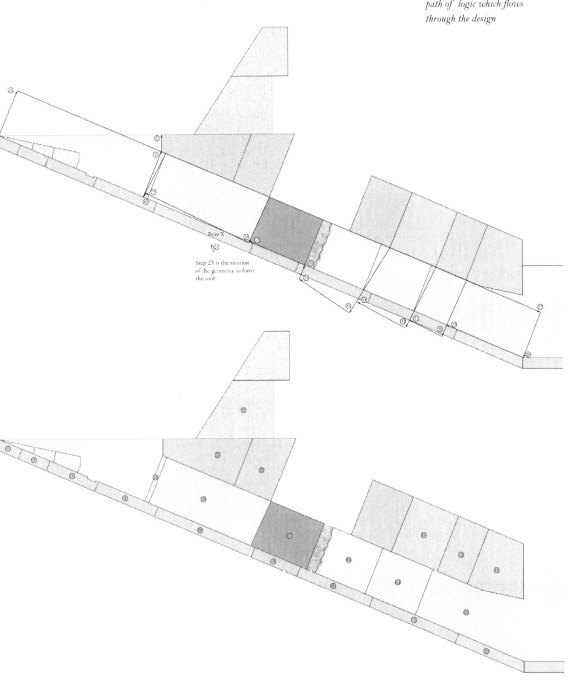

Point X

Step 25 is the rotation
of the geometry to form
the roof

inset by 2.5cm meaning that the door jambs are 129.5cm high and the passage is 132cm high. This architectural feature is shown in the photographic illustration below and one can immediately appreciate the amount of extra work that this would have given the builders as opposed to having set the door lintels to the passage height. The reason for this unusual construction is that the architects have given us a physical representation of the entrance passage geometry at this point.

In the illustration on the facing page you can see all of the measurements that were taken from the survey work of Labrousse (the 7.6cm floor drop being a calculated value since Labrousse details only the 6cm drop along the section of the passage after the vestibule). The whole of the architecture of the entrance passageway is consistent down the full 27m length and has clearly been surveyed **by the architects and builders** since it is possible for us to appreciate their work from our surveying measurements. There is no discrepancy at all in the details that are on show in the stonework and those derived from the geometry and this is a fact with far reaching consequences.

The alignment of the stonework by the architects is perfect *but it is aligned to a theoretical geometric point* at the base of the sloping entrance passage. This means that geometry of the whole of the entrance passage analysis that is set out in this chapter is correct and that, more importantly, the architects were capable of doing the following two things. First, they could survey to what appears to be 1mm accuracy from a theoretical point in space along a length of 27m, suggesting the use of quite sophisticated equipment. Secondly, **they must have been able to carry out trigonometric calculations to perform such a task.** Since we know for certain that the Ancient Egyptians that the Egyptologists tell us about quite certainly could not do such calculations in 1350 BCE then we are left with the conclusion that currently we do not know who built this building. And if we do not know who built this building, then we

The antechamber door

The lintel of the door is unusually shaped with the roof section carved into the stone by 2.5cm

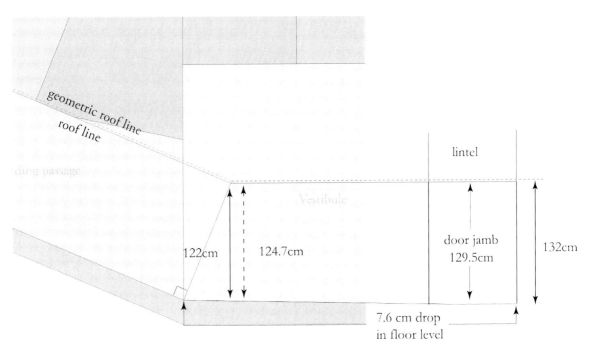

geometric roof line

roof line

ding passage

lintel

Vestibule

122cm

124.7cm

door jamb
129.5cm

132cm

7.6 cm drop
in floor level

The entrance passage surveying

The astonishing accuracy of the entrance passage surveying is detectable from the geometric composition of the system. The illustration shows the entrance passage with the middle section removed

can safely throw away all of our assumptions regarding the mathematical ability of the architects.

So we now know one more piece of information about the architects and their principles of construction. Although we chose to analyse the chambers starting from the inside, had we started at the entrance passage we could have immediately detected a series of mathematics that lead us into the inner chambers. This is point which is well worth us bearing in mind because it is more than likely going to be the method of breaking in to the architecture of many of the ancient monuments of Egypt if our experiences to date are to be repeated elsewhere.

A very primitive triangle

A VIEW FROM THE HEAVENS

Having found such an exquisite pattern to the design of the interior of the pyramid then we should now have a look at the exterior of the building to see if it also yields any clues which might assist us in realising the purpose of all of the architectural design.

If we turn first to the work of the Egyptologists we find that the details that are published in the work of Labrousse concerning the side lengths of the pyramid are quite vague. He states that they vary between 57m 60 cm and 57m 70cm although does not specify exact details of any of them. One can appreciate by looking at the external design of the pyramid why this might be the case. The illustration below shows a view of the north east corner of the pyramid of Unas on which it can be seen that the east side of the monument contains the remains of a temple. This temple was built onto the east face of the pyramid, and so one can understand that it is not possible to easily measure the length of the face of this side of the monument. Added

to the problem is the fact that the stonework is greatly dilapidated down this side of the building making the determination of a face line almost impossible to accomplish. Fortunately, as the illustration above shows, the other sides of the pyramid show well defined remains and include the foundation plinth upon which the stonework was laid. These remaining face stones of the pyramid contrast well with the debris that makes up

A view from the heavens   101

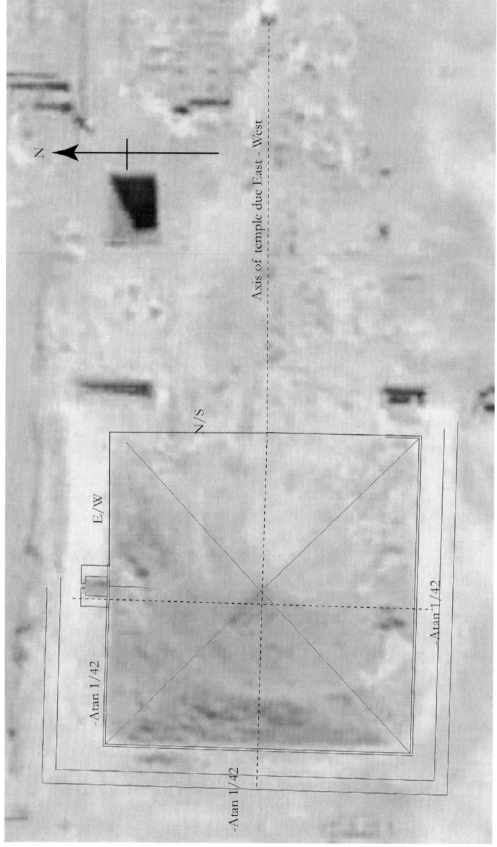

A satellite photograph of the Unas pyramid and temple complex with a provisional overlay of the pyramid structure

Axis of temple due East – West

N

N/S

E/W

-Atan 1/42

-Atan 1/42

-Atan 1/42

-Atan 1/42

the rest of the remains, and if one turns to satellite photography to assist in the analysis of the monument, even at the resolution of photography available for free to the general public, all of the face stones which remain in place can be detected in the images.

The illustration opposite shows a medium resolution satellite image of the pyramid of Unas and the area of the temple to the east of it. There are a couple of important points to note when looking at photography from space. The first is that the image may or may not be taken from directly above the object at which you are looking, and more often than not the satellite was at an angle to the area of the image being studied when the photograph was taken. This is known as being 'off nadir' and means that you cannot rely on the relative positioning of elements on the photograph which are at different heights, since parallax errors will be apparent. The second point of note is that the raw images from the satellite have to be geo-referenced before they are published to remove the distortions which are created by the off-nadir positioning of the satellite and the curvature of the earth. This process of geo-referencing is complicated and expensive and adds considerable cost to the purchase of satellite imagery. It is during the geo-referencing process that the true north of the photograph is determined, and one can be absolutely certain that the true north on such photographs is perfect.

With this in mind it is immediately evident on looking at the satellite image that the the pyramid of Unas is rotated in a clockwise direction when viewed from space. If the satellite image is placed into a CAD system and the builder's rotation angle of -Atan 1/42 is used to overlay lines on the photograph a very clear similarity between the rotation of the pyramid and the angled lines can be seen. In fact no discrepancy at all can be distinguished between the two, and one can reasonably deduce that the whole of the foundation of the pyramid is rotated from true north by

the angle that we have already seen so many times. The only exception is that the north east corner appears to be aligned with true north and the design of the exterior of the building does appear to mimic the interior design.

The resulting distortion in the east face of the pyramid remains neatly hidden behind the brickwork of the temple's walls, but the distortion on the north face does not. Fortunately Labrousse paid good attention to the analysis of this area of the pyramid, since the entrance area also appears to have been the home to a smaller temple structure. Amongst the detail that is included in the survey work is the exact layout of the paving stones which surround the entrance passage. These stones appear to have been irregularly laid onto the bedrock, almost like a crazy paving system, however on close inspection it is evident that they have been very carefully placed indeed. In the illustration on the next page you can see that the first two stones on either side of the entrance passage are aligned to be perpendicular to the face of the pyramid which is angled at -atan 1/42 and not to the axis of the passage which we

The south face

Extensive repairs have been done to the south face of the pyramid which now shows the first six layers of masonry

already know is aligned to north. The rest of the stones which make up the surrounds of the hole are roughly aligned to the angle of the passage, and the dark interior of the passage and rough workmanship around this area make the distortions difficult to detect. However, there is another feature which the architects have used to distract the eye from the difference in the axis. The large face stones of the pyramid which can be seen behind the entrance passage were carefully measured by Labrousse and he noted that the eastern face (on the left) of the stone on the first layer was cut vertically, yet the western face was cut at an angle.

I have illustrated this point on the photograph with blue lines which show where the verticals should lie on the stonework. By bringing in the stone joints at the top on the right side, the architects have used a highly sophisticated method of forced perspective, making sure that the vanishing point of the passage and that of the stonework coincide. So the eye is tricked by the combination of the paving stones and face stones and does not recognise the mis-alignment of the entrance passage and the pyramid itself.

Having seen from the satellite photography that the pyramid is clearly rotated and that the sides are not aligned to the true north axis of the entrance passage, we are left with an architectural design problem. Around which point has the pyramid been rotated, and have the architects left us a way of determining the answer to this question?

Since we now know considerably more about both the architecture and the architects of this building, let us return for

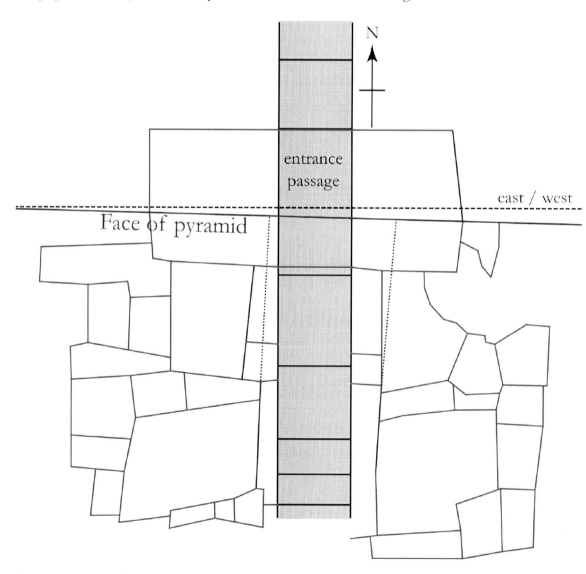

The entrance passage

(right) The alignment of the stonework on the entrance passage is designed to deceive the human eye

a third time into the underground chambers of the pyramid of Unas. On our first visit we just went looking at the chamber's walls and floors and made a note of the quite unusual features within the structure. The second time we went in we were armed with our cubit rod and our assumptions about the mathematical knowledge of the builders. This time we are going in with no preconceptions at all, just the knowledge that we have built up in the pages of this book, ignorant of all who have gone before us, for it is only in this manner that we will truly succeed on our quest.

What we need to bear in mind is that the architects are exceedingly clever, they are using illusions on us all of the time and that they are very good mathematicians. And one final point to note which is a logical conclusion from all we have seen so far : **they must also know that we are in there looking at their work.**

THE MODEL PYRAMID

If we consider all of the details that we have come across in the pyramid, and in particular the sections of damage that we have seen to the chamber walls which all served a purpose in hiding various aspects of the design, then we still have one unexplained feature in the main chamber. If you look at the doorway that leads from the chamber into the antechamber we see that it is very badly damaged indeed on its left side. We know from our analysis of the walls that there is no reason for this damage to be present, since the north east corner of the chamber is vertical and presents no optical conflict with the left side of the door, if the door is indeed vertical. If you have a good look at the illustration below, which is a duplicate of a section of one of Piankoff's photographs, you will notice

that the damaged section of the doorway is missing both width and depth, meaning that the top left corner of the passage when projected onto the plane of the east chamber wall would actually be situated slightly further to the left than one would assume from looking at the photograph. The exact location of this corner point can be determined by considering the artwork on the right side of the door which is 66% of the width of the hieroglyph rack above it. When this measurement is duplicated on the left of the door you can accurately pinpoint the location of the corner where the north wall of the passage, the passage roof and the east wall of the chamber all meet up. If you then try to drop a vertical line down from this corner it becomes quite evident that the left side of this doorway is not vertical and that the door is narrower at the bottom than at the top.

In the illustration the destroyed roof section has been repaired, just as it has been in reality in the pyramid of Unas, and one can now see the artwork and hieroglyphs that were missing from above the doorway. If you have a careful look at the artwork pattern you can see that it is not randomly designed, as was the case

The main chamber doorway

The left side of the main chamber doorway appears not to be vertical as deduced from photographic analysis

with the ends of all of the main walls, but that each of the pieces of artwork is regularly spaced. In total in can be calculated that there are 42 small squares of artwork which make up the full width of the top of doorway from the south wall of the passage to the north wall of the passage, and that the base of the doorway is slightly less than 41.5 units of artwork wide.

In does not take long to recognise that the design of this doorway and the design of the west wall of the chamber are very similar indeed. They both have their dimensions marked along the top which in both cases is 42 drawn sections, and contain an angled wall section on one side causing the base to be less wide than the top on the doorway and the top wider than the base on the wall. Having recognised this fact it is an obvious next step to check to see if there is any relationship between the two pieces of construction, and upon doing so one is presented with the remarkable fact that the width of the doorway of 137cm is exactly 7/16ths the width of the west chamber wall. **It is the fact that this is a rational fraction that makes it so remarkable.**

The west chamber wall is 6 cubits wide, or 314.0cm, and by reducing the wall down by 7/16ths the calculated door width is 137.4cm at the top, this value differing from the value measured by Labrousse by only 4mm, which is within the error margins of his report. The implication in the design is that it is possible to insert a 7/16ths scale model of the pyramid's chambers into the doorway, since both the dimensions and the shape of the passage and chamber match each other. In order to do this we need to build a new 3D model of the pyramid in which the air space inside the chambers is modelled as a solid object. Such a model is shown below and has all of the hieroglyphs and artwork rendered onto its walls for reference purposes. The underside of the model which is not visible on this illustration has been rendered with a black and white stripe pattern which represents the 42 palm measurement that we know stretches across the chamber floor and makes up the room's 6 cubit width. Visible on this view of the model is the hole in the floor of the chamber for the canopic chest, which can been seen protruding out

The model pyramid

An airspace model of the chambers showing the artwork and hieroglyphs reversed from their actual state on the walls

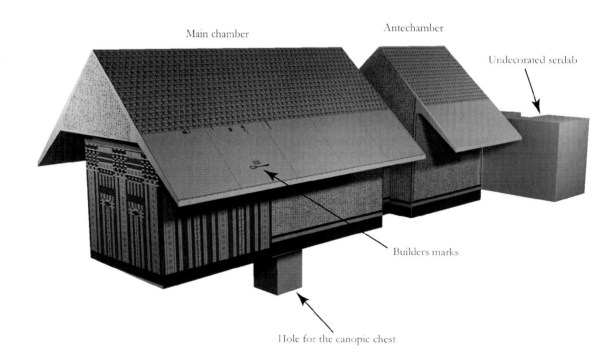

Main chamber

Antechamber

Undecorated serdab

Builders marks

Hole for the canopic chest

of the bottom of the model. This hole in the floor of the main chamber was measured by Labrousse as being 90cm square which he deduced from the remains of the canopic chest which were still in the chamber at the time of his work. Also visible for the first time on the model are the builders paint marks on the roof and the lack of decoration in the serdab is also quite pronounced when the chambers are viewed in this manner. The hieroglyphs which are rendered onto the side of the model are of course back to front with respect to their counterparts on the real chamber walls.

If we now reduce the size by 7/16ths and insert this model into the passage between the chamber and antechamber we have no choice but to rotate the model of the chamber along the east-west axis by 180° so that the angled south chamber wall on the model matches up with the angled north wall of the passageway. If this rotation is not performed then the north wall of the chamber and the north wall of the passage will clash with each other making any insertion impossible to perform.

The illustration below shows the results of carrying out the insertion which leaves the coffin end of the main chamber on the model sticking out into the chamber. This positioning is due to the south wall of the chamber not being vertical and therefore dictating the exact position in which

the model and the passage walls dovetail together. There can be little doubt that this creation is intended because the artwork across the door top and the floor measurements fit so perfectly and the rational scaling factor clearly points to intent on the part of the architects. Having said that, it appears to serve no purpose whatsoever and is a particularly ugly and cumbersome construction. The rest of the model is of course in the antechamber section of the pyramid and does not conform in any way whatsoever to the architectural features of the antechamber. The model of the serdab is left placed partially in a wall and partially in the antechamber, and the conclusion that has to be drawn from this exercise is that whilst the concept looks logical, in practice it clearly is not. What possible use, meaning or purpose could the architects have with a model such as this left in such awkward position ? Or is it that we have just extended the analysis of the architecture of this building one stage too far and ended up with an entirely ficticous creation of our own making ?

It is the juxtaposition of the perfect fit of the model and the ridiculous result that one obtains when doing so that leads one to think in depth about what could be going on with this concept. When thinking the problem through one

Inserting the model

The main chamber of the model can be inserted into the doorway only after it has been rotated by 180° around its east-west axis

thing that is apparent is that we could of course perform exactly the same insertion again on the model, in the same manner that a Russian doll is designed. We could take a 7/16ths scale model of the 7/16ths scale model (resulting in a 49/256ths scale model) and insert it in the doorway of the model and it is upon investigating this idea that things start to become clearer. If you have a good think about the design of the whole of the underground chambers, and in particular the areas that were highlighted in the clues section at the beginning you may well be able to see where the architects are leading us.

One of the clues we came across was that the doorway to the serdab from the antechamber was not completed and looks like it is missing a doorframe or some other type of construction which needs to be inserted into it. Now it may well be that the 7/16ths model that we have just placed into the antechamber-chamber passage looks completely out of place, but you can probably already start to sense that a 49/256ths model placed inside the antechamber-serdab passage would look considerably better suited to its location. To determine if the smaller model will fit into this doorway all we need to do is find the length of the serdab from the surveying information and scale it down appropriately. When we do this we find that the serdab is exactly 13

cubits long or 680.5cm and this value scales down to 130.25cm when reduced by a factor of 49/256. You may recall that in the original survey information from Maspero in 1881 he measured the width of the doorway into the serdab as being 131cm, and so it is abundantly clear that the serdab will indeed fit perfectly into this doorway when scaled in this manner.

The first question that arises when doing so is whether the new model should be rotated around its east west axis, or in other words which way up should it be. The answer to this will become clear in a short while, but for now we are going to insert it in the same manner that the original model was inserted into the other passage with its roof facing downwards. This arrangement is shown in the illustration below in which the central axis of the antechamber is shown as a red tube running through the drawing. What can be immediately seen from this illustration is that the hole for the canopic chest is perfectly lined up with the central axis of the antechamber, and if we did not know better, we would also assume that it was lined up with the central axis of the pyramid. What is of further interest is that the canopic chest which originally measured 90cm square, divided into four quarters, now measures 17.2cm and that each of the quarters is approximately 1/7th cubit square allowing for the

The second model

The second model can be inserted in the same manner as the first, and the canopic chest marks out the presumed center of the pyramid

Protruding section of model

*The model of
the serdab has
been designed to
perfectly dovetail
with the start
of the doorway
between the ante-
chamber and the
serdab*

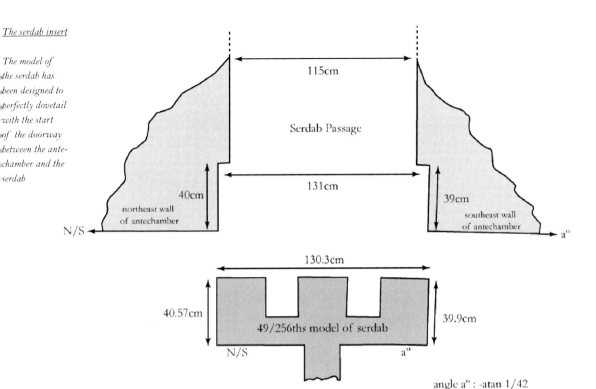

angle a° : -atan 1/42

width of the chest's side walls. It would be at this point that you would conclude that you had probably discovered the answer to the purpose behind this building's construction since you had just found a hidden model that perfectly marks out the central axis of the whole system. However, closer inspection tells us straight away that there is something wrong with this conclusion.

If you cast your mind back to the chapter concerning the serdab you will recall that the northern section of the room is aligned to true north and the southern section is angled at the builder's standard rotation angle, which resulted in the south wall being slightly shorter than the north wall. On the model that we have just inserted into the serdab passage this arrangement causes the far side of the serdab (as viewed on the illustration) to protrude ever so slightly from the doorway. Because the architects have been so utterly accurate in everything that they have constructed so far we know instinctively that this model placement is wrong, and that in marking out the central axis of the pyramid in this way they are telling us that our central axis is also incorrect. To find out how beautiful the correct insertion of the model is we need to have a close look at the design of

the door frame section of the serdab corridor.

The illustration above shows all of the pertinent features of the door frame section of the passage along with the 49/256ths scale model of the serdab. From it we can see that the doorway and the serdab have been designed to fit together in the manner shown, despite the fact that it is now evident that the surveying data error margins are no longer adequate for the detail which we are now looking at in the architecture. The model of the chambers needs to be inserted into the door frame the 'correct way up' with the roof at the top and the floor at the bottom, and this final correct insertion is shown in the illustration overleaf.

A point of note is that the base of the model is located 2cm off the floor at the serdab end where it is fitted into the door frame. This vertical positioning is because of two fully connected reasons. The floor of the antechamber in which the model is sitting slopes down by 2cm from the entrance passage to the serdab passage entrance and the model is a model of the airspace inside the chambers and so requires a gap below it to represent the floor of the chamber. Since we know

The model pyramid

The correctly inserted model

(left) When correctly inserted into the serdab doorway the model fits beautifully on the floor of the antechamber

The floor space

Below the model of the chambers the architects have deliberately left a space which represents the floor thickness of the chambers

that the chamber floor is about 10cm thick, then the gap below the model representing the floor should be about 2cm. When the model is correctly inserted in this way then the top of the serdab model perfectly aligns with the 51cm high paint work band than is evident at the bottom of all of the walls of the chambers as shown in the next illustration. This attention to detail in including this space under the model is particularly interesting and suggests that the floor is a highly significant part of the design.

The height of the model of the serdab is particularly easy to calculate since the serdab itself is exactly 256cm high as measured by Labrousse and so when scaling it down by 49/256ths the model's serdab height comes out at 49cm.

We are now left with just one unexplained feature of this masterful creation and that is the problem of the height of the serdab doorway. You will recall from the earlier chapter where the construction of the antechamber was analysed, that the architects have gone to considerable lengths to design the architecture of the east wall

of the antechamber around the door height of the serdab passage. We noted at the time that it would have been considerably easier for the builders if the door heights had all been the same in the chambers, and that by implication the height of the serdab door must be significant. In the illustration on the next page the purpose of the doorway's height is revealed.

At a scale of 49 : 256 the top of the doorway is located at ground level in relation to the model of the pyramid's chambers and perfectly sets it into a reference frame. The height of the serdab doorway given by Labrousse is 119cm +/- 0.5 cm, and so the scaled up height will be 622cm +/- 2.6cm. Since we previously calculated that the foundation level of the pyramid is 12 cubits below ground level or 628cm we can see that, allowing for a minor discrepancy in the surveying measurement (for example we do not know at which point on the passage Labrousse measured the height), the doorway is carved out to ground level on the same scale as our model.

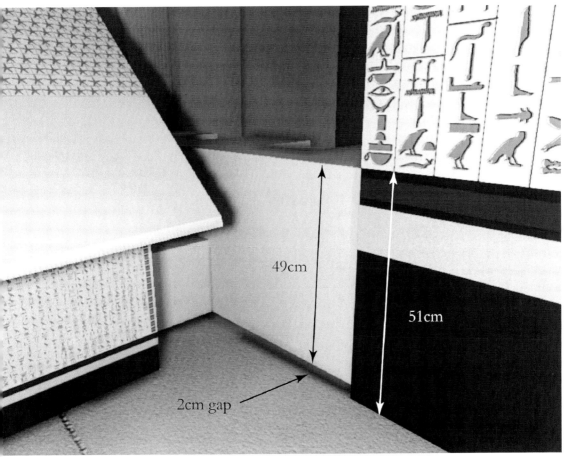

49cm

51cm

2cm gap

120cm

The whole of the system has been designed to perfection and there is one more feature which should give us further corroboration of the architectural principles. Because the artwork above the main chamber's door was regular and contained 42 sections which allowed us to make the first model insert, then we should find a similar system above the serdab door. For the systems to be the same we need to divide up the length of the serdab into palm measurements (1/7th cubit) and this should then give us the number of artwork sections above the serdab door. The serdab length was measured at 13 cubits, and therefore 91 palms, and so there should be an artwork pattern of 91 units above the serdab door. In the

illustration below, which is made from the original close up photography of Piankoff and then overlaid with CAD drawing lines, it can be seen that this is exactly the set up we find above the door, but strangely only on the right side. The artwork divisions, which are clearly visible in the photograph, are spaced perfectly so as to allow 91 divisions to be present across the width of the doorway, but the design has been changed at the half way point and the left side of the door shows a different pattern which would contain 119 divisions across the full doorway width. We will address the pattern on the left side of the door shortly, but not before we stop to fully appreciate the confirmation that the architects have just

The artwork above the serdab door

The illustration is a photograph of the actual chamber wall taken from the work of Piankoff

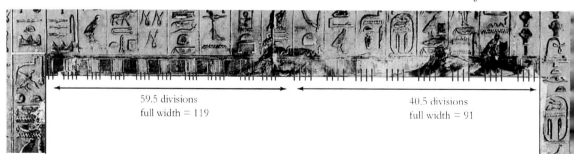

59.5 divisions
full width = 119

40.5 divisions
full width = 91

Ground level
marked across the
wall

The heights of the
serdab doorway is
designed so that
it marks out the
level of the ground
above the model of
the chambers when
looked at in the
scale of the model

The temple com-
plex and satellite
pyramid

given us.

Our 49/256ths model of the pyramid chambers is correct, and we are not looking at a fanciful creation in these images. We are looking at the very images that the architects laid out for us all those years ago and they beg to be completed with one extra item. With such a stunning model in front of us the natural desire is to want to also create a model of the pyramid itself, scaled at 49/256ths and it is when we do this that we realise that the architectural design that we have come across is immense. The illustration below shows the whole of the temple complex of the pyramid of Unas, and situated in the foreground of the photograph can be seen the satellite pyramid of Unas. Its base dimensions, as reported by Labrousse in his work "Le temple haut du complexe funéraire du roi Ounas" are 11m square, or 21.05 cubits. The satellite pyramid of Unas is a perfect 49/256ths scale model of the pyramid itself, reduced by a ratio which can only be determined by

an exhaustive inquiry into the internal architecture of the chambers.

What the architects have just managed to do is to transfer a precision measuring scale for the temple complex of Unas from the inside of the pyramid to the outside. The builder's units of the satellite pyramid are not cubits. They are 49/256th parts of a cubit, and by hiding the system of measurement in this manner they will have managed to completely confuse anyone looking for details within the temple construction. With this in mind we can return to the serdab doorway and now understand the second measuring scale that appears on the artwork.

Because we know that the artwork lines always represent one palm length measures in full sized objects then the implication of the measurements of the artwork on the left of the door is that we should also insert a scaled model of a 17 cubit wide object into the upper half of this door frame (119/7=17 cubits). We

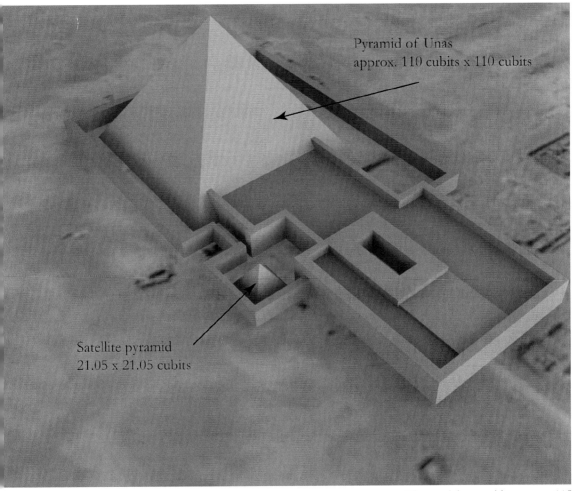

Pyramid of Unas
approx. 110 cubits x 110 cubits

Satellite pyramid
21.05 x 21.05 cubits

can also calculate the scaling required for the object since we know the door width and the number of artwork divisions within that width, and find that the scaling factor from the left side of the door is exactly 6/41, once again a perfect rational fraction. It is impossible not to notice the rather amusing sense of humour that the architects have just displyed, chosing a scaling factor of 6/41 for the top of the doorway insert when the principle measurement unit of the chambers is 7/42 of a cubit, reducing both the numerator and denominator of the principle fraction by one. Since we know that whatever needs to be inserted into the door must fit in the gap above the model of the serdab, we can calculate the other dimension of the object and find that we are looking for something that is 9 cubits in height or width before reduction. The illustration below shows the serdab doorway along with all of the information from the artwork pattern which is found above it.

Since the chambers of the pyramid are relatively small it does not take long to determine that whatever needs inserting in the top section of this doorframe cannot be found within them, and one can deduce at this stage that the most likely location for the object will be in the temple outside. This makes sense since by including one of the temple's features in the serdab door's construction, the architects will have managed to take yet another measuring scale from the inside to the outside of the pyramid with perfect precision. Somewhere in the temple construction there will be a section which measures 17 cubits by 9 cubits and it is this feature that we will now look for in the temple complex.

The serdab door

The space that reamins in the serdab doorway once the model of the internal chambers has been inserted

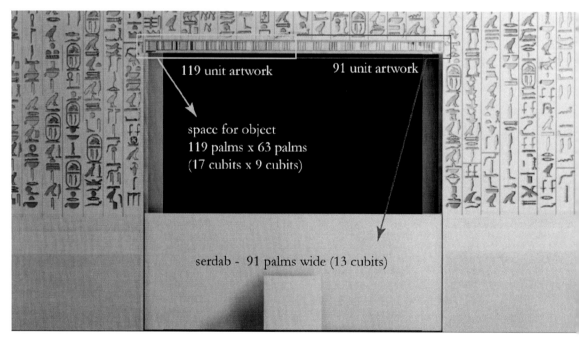

119 unit artwork   91 unit artwork

space for object
119 palms x 63 palms
(17 cubits x 9 cubits)

serdab - 91 palms wide (13 cubits)

A TWIST IN THE TAIL

The temple complex of the pyramid of Unas is fully explored in a second book by Audran Labrousse in which the highly detailed plans of the temple layout are published. The amount of work which must have been involved in reproducing the original layout must have been considerable, since all that remains of the temple today are fragmented sections of wall and stonework. The main technical drawings which are published in this work are drawn at a scales of 100:1 and 200:1 depending on the area covered by the drawing and from these plans and the accompanying text a detailed wall model of the temple complex was constructed. The purpose in building such a model on the CAD system was not only to produce a photographable model for the illustrations of this book, such as that shown below, but also so that each of the sections of the temple could be fully understood during the modelling process. In carrying out this task it did not take much effort to identify the area of the temple to which the architects are drawing our attention because the clues presented are strikingly obvious.

The temple contains a complex system of corridors which, starting from the causeway which leads from the Nile valley, eventually lead to the principle alter within the building. The proportions of the altar stone are immense with Labrousse showing that the reconstructed stone was at least 6 meters tall, and although it is clear that the side sections of the stone have been successfully reconstructed its exact height and design cannot be known with certainty. What is particularly interesting about the altar section of the temple is that the stone's width is shown as 9 cubits, and its estimated height by Labrousse is 12 cubits. Additionally, and the point which caught my attention first, is that this section of the temple contains two raised platforms. The first is the altar floor stone, and the second is a side platform and

The temple complex of Unas

The temple complex of Unas is shown with the walls reduced down to a height of about 1.50m for the purpose of clarity

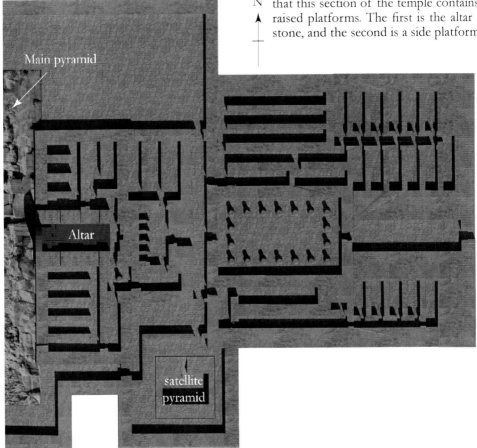

N

the combination of the two stone's geometry is quite obviously designed to parody the serdab doorway inserts that we saw in the last chapter. The illustrations below show two views of the altar area of the temple along with the dimensions of the two platforms.

There is no way that it is possible from the information available to deduce the height of the alter stone and there is little point in pursuing any investigation of this matter. However, when you enter an Ancient Egyptian temple looking for a highly significant object which is 9 cubits by 17 cubits, and find that the principle altar stone could well be exactly those dimensions, it is worth taking an educated guess that you have indeed come across what you are looking for. If we make that assumption at this stage then we can now see the symbolic purpose of the insertions in the serdab doorway. In the lower half of the doorway the architects have inserted the east side of the chamber system, and in the top of the doorway they have inserted the west side of the temple complex and by doing so have connected the two independent sections of the pyramid's architecture. If we review what we know up to this stage from all of the previous work it is possible, after a great deal of thinking, to understand what the architects have done.

We know that the main entrance passage of the pyramid is aligned to a true north, and we also know from the satellite image that the pyramid has been rotated by the architects standard angle in a clockwise direction when viewed from above. What we do not know is by which point the system has been rotated,

and therefore we are currently unable to attach the rotated part of the pyramid to the un-rotated part of the temple. In order to complete the architectural design, and thereby complete the logic puzzle that the architects have set out for us, we need a method of design that connects the two sections of the system. The part of the complex that we need to rotate includes the underground chambers and the west, south and north faces of the pyramid along with the external walls of the complex along the same sides. This implies that in a pre-rotated design plan that the entrance passage must not be aligned to true north since, after the rotation, we know that it is.

So to start the final section of our work we need a logical manner in which we can place the inner chambers into the preliminary un-rotated design of the pyramid. It is by carefully looking at the clues from the earlier chapter that we can see that we have so far not solved the riddle of the drill holes that were found behind the coffin, and that they would make a spectacularly sensible location in which to place the central axis of the pyramid. Since the original drill holes are located much too far to the west of the center of the pyramid to serve this purpose then we can investigate the drill holes in the model pyramid and

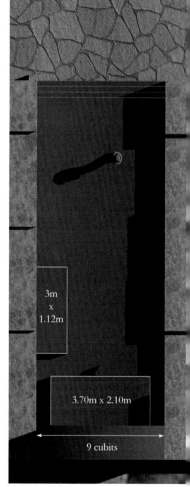

3m
x
1.12m

3.70m x 2.10m

9 cubits

The pyramid's
central axis

The central axis
is fixed to the
ground below the
pyramid so that
when any rotations
are performed on
the architecture this
axis line remains
stationary

in particular the northern of the two holes, since we know that in the full sized pyramid this hole has been placed in the floor in a logical manner being 2 cubits from the west wall and 1 cubit from the north wall of the main chamber.

If the whole of the chamber system of the pyramid of Unas is now placed so that the northern drill hole in the model is directly below the apex of the pyramid then we find that the entrance passage emerges from the north face of the pyramid exactly in the center and is also precisely the correct length. This is a quite remarkable construction since we are working not only from a drill hole which is only a few millimeters in diameter, but also the entrance passage system is rotated anticlockwise from north and the north face is at this juncture still aligned to an east/west line. The illustration below shows the floor of the model of the pyramid with the central axis inserted into the drill hole. What can also be seen on this illustration is that the stones which make up the antechamber floor have not been randomly placed as first appears, but they are purposely designed so that the model that the architects have created coincides

with the edges of the flooring stones. What is also important to note about this illustration is that the vertical red center axis line of the pyramid which passes through the apex above is *fixed to the earth* and not to the chamber floor. This means that when we perform a rotation on the whole of the pyramid system in the coming pages, that the red marker line is not going to move in relation to the earth below it.

The illustration on the next page shows the CAD drawing alignments for this initial setup. The whole of the temple complex and the pyramid is aligned to north south but the chamber system is rotated anticlockwise, as can be clearly seen since the entrance passage is not aligned to true north. When we place the chamber system inside the pyramid in this way, and then perform some checks on the system we come across something which has the architect's fingerprints all over it. The distance from the altar stone to the back wall of the serdab is exactly 42 cubits, and we can see that we have certainly correctly identified the altar stone as being the missing portion in the upper section of the serdab doorway. We started

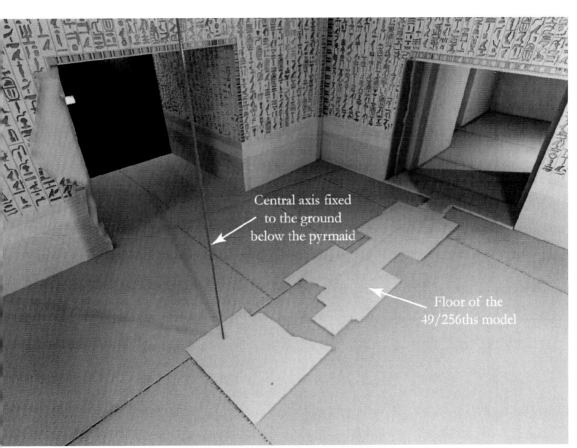

Central axis fixed
to the ground
below the pyrmaid

Floor of the
49/256ths model

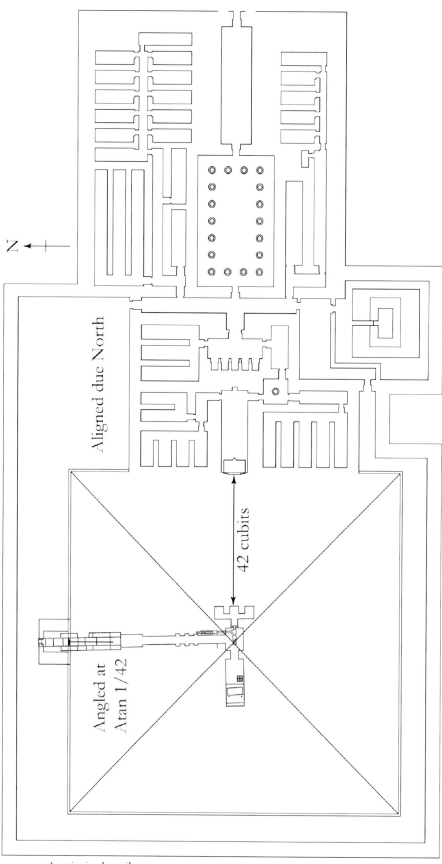

*The ground plan
before rotation*

*(left) So that the
final alignment of
the entrance pas-
age is correct after
the rotations have
been performed, it
needs to by rotated
anticlockwise in the
initial setup shown
here*

The rotation point

*The geometry of
the location of the
rotation point is
based on a simple
set of geometric
shapes, with the
triangle being a
duplicate of the
entrance passage's
slope angle*

the whole of our investigation into the pyramid of Unas by discovering the 42 racks of hieroglyphs which are located above the 'coffin' in the main chamber, and it is poetic indeed that we appear to be finishing with a 42 cubit long measure. The practical purpose of this measurement is that it confirms to us that the positioning of the chambers that we have just carried out is correct and that we should continue along the path we are investigating.

What we now require is the rotation point of the system so that we can re-align the entrance passage to north and create angles on the pyramid's external faces. The exact position and system of creation of the rotation point is not immediately apparent due to the fact that it also serves as the starting point for the temple's principle geometry and has therefore been well hidden in the design. However, after suitable logical analysis the system that has been used by the designers does

fall into place. The geometry of the rotation point uses one element from the chamber architecture that we have already seen and one element from the temple's architectural design which we have not yet studied, and these design elements are shown in the illustration below. The rather elegant use of the three primary elements of geometry, the circle, triangle and square leads to a relatively simple to calculate rotation point which is based on the same Pythagorean triangle that we were shown in the entrance passage, the 5,12,13 side lengthed triangle.

When the rotation point is placed in this manner, the distance from the center of the pyramid to the rotation point is 32.41 cubits or 16.96 meters. Having established this rotation point we can now select the sections that we wish to rotate, namely the chambers, all of the pyramids faces except the east face, and the external walls of the

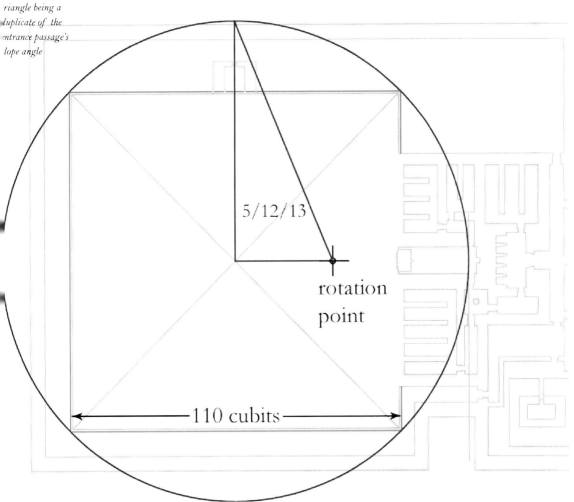

5/12/13

rotation
point

110 cubits

complex and colour them so that we can distinguish between the rotated and un-rotated sections when we are finished. If this construction is placed on top of the satellite photograph then the positions of all of the elements in the CAD drawing correspond to their respective points on the ground as far as can be seen and we can be reasonably certain that we have performed the rotation operation correctly.

There is however an extremely elegant check that can be done on this system that confirms with certainty that the procedure that we have carried out is correct. If we now go back to the antechamber and check what has happened to our original fixed central axis point we discover that, with the chambers having moved in the rotation process, the original axis line is now located in the second of our drill holes on the model. This utterly astonishing piece of architectural design is shown in the illustration below with the original red axis line falling into the southern hole, and the axis line of the rotated pyramid (shown in green) located in the northern hole. This elegant alignment system can be checked mathematically because we know the distance

from the drill holes to the rotation point, a fact that we determined from the rotation point's construction triangle. That distance is 16.96m, and therefore the distance between the drill holes in the model must be 1/42nd of this value, or 40.4cm. Because we also know the scale of the model in relation to the pyramid's chambers then we can calculate the distance between the drill holes at the back of the coffin as being 211.0cm which is exactly the distance that Labrousse measured them at in his survey work and confirms that what we have just done is correct. This remarkable architectural design permits us to perfectly recreate the combined plans of the pyramid and temple complex of Unas and that plan is shown in the illustration on the next page. The diagram shows a view of the whole complex with the un-rotated sections outlined in blue and the rotated sections outlined in red.

Before we can conclude our work and set out a list of deductions from what we have seen in the pyramid there is still one unanswered question to which we need to turn our attention. If the building is not a burial chamber, and all the evidence we have points to this fact, then why is there are coffin in the

The central axis holes

The two drill holes in the floor of the model align to the two axis lines of the pyramid before and after the rotation has been performed

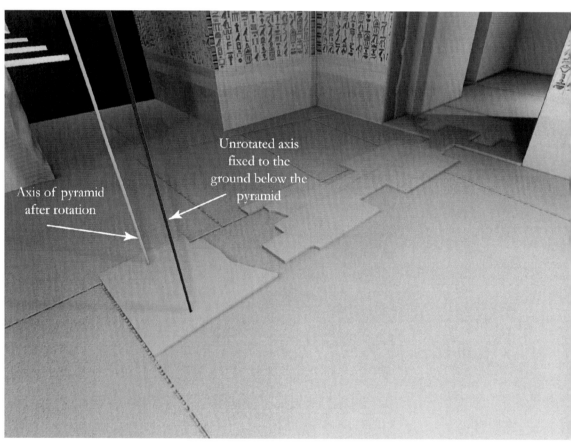

Axis of pyramid after rotation

Unrotated axis fixed to the ground below the pyramid

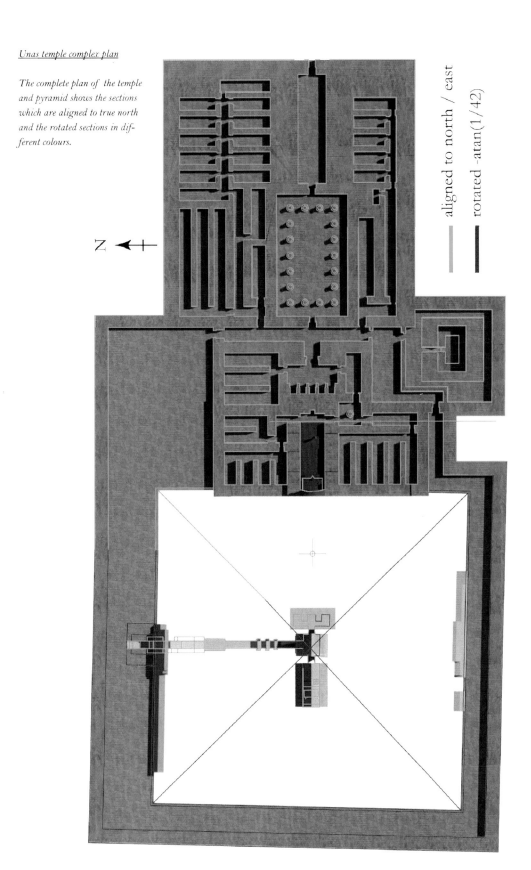

Unas temple complex plan

The complete plan of the temple and pyramid shows the sections which are aligned to true north and the rotated sections in different colours.

N

aligned to north / east

rotated -atan(1/42)

main chamber ? The only real clue that we have looked at regarding the coffin was the fact that the curved scar down the chamber's north wall could not have been made by the lid of the coffin it had the same profile as the coffin body. This question appears to have been resolved during the course of the work we have done, since it is now acceptable that the coffin lid is rectangular while the coffin itself contains a chamfered corner. This mimics the design of the rooms in the pyramid where each of the room corners is designed in a similar fashion.

The purpose of the coffin itself however is shown below and as can be seen its internal dimensions have been perfectly designed to hold a model of the chamber system. This model is aligned onto all six faces of the internal space of the coffin, with the serdab situated inside the stonework void on the south side of the coffin, a highly appropriate place to put it since it is not technically part of the chambers. The design of the coffin slices off the entrance passage at the exact point where the hieroglyphs start, and slices the serdab exactly along its western face. The measurements of the coffin contained in the

available sources of reference information are not sufficiently detailed to determine whether the small nuances in the building, such as the angled walls in the serdab, are also built into the coffin's walls. In the work of Labrousse he does include all of the basic dimensions of the coffin which show variances of a centimeter or two in various places. However, it would be unwise at this time to get into the exact construction details and scale of this model until a more detailed survey of the coffin's interior space is carried out. The final illustration on the page opposite shows the plan of the chambers when inserted into the coffin space, and it shows that the correspondence between the two is very close indeed with variances of only a millimeter showing on the technical drawings.

Conclusions

The 'Pyramid of Unas' is the modern name by which we refer to this monument, but the Egyptologists have of course translated the hieroglyphs which comprise the original description of the pyramid and temple, and they have it reading as "perfect are

The internal coffin space

The 'coffin' is designed to accept a model of the pyramid's chambers

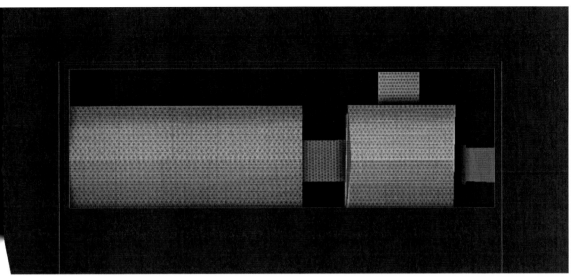

The coffin plan

*Viewed from
directly above the
model of the pyr-
amid's chambers
perfectly fits into
the internal space
of the coffin*

the places of Unas". The name is utterly befitting to the design because, as we have seen,
the architecture and planning is indeed perfect. There is of course a touch of humour in
the title because the currently accepted plans
of the pyramid show an imperfect set of wall
lengths and design principles.

The Egyptologists drawn plans have
the chambers of the building containing different length walls on opposing sides of the
same chamber. They have passageways which
have different lengths down each side, yet have
failed to question why this is the case. They
have a roof apex which is not in the center
of the room and angles on the roof stones
which are different on the north and south
of the same room. The coffin has a section
chamfered off one of the corners so that it is
not rectangular, and the heights of the three
passages in the building are different. There is
incomplete paint work on the west wall of the
chamber and drill holes in the floor located
at different distance from the side walls. The
stonework of the antechambers north wall
does not fit together properly, and there are
non horizontal stone joints in the main chamber. The north wall of the main chamber has
a section which appears to rise upwards and
an adjusted star pattern above it. With such a
list of imperfections in the building so clear
to see did it not strike any of the Egyptologists as strange that the building was named
"perfect are the places of Unas" ?.

What can be discovered within this
monument is a set of architectural design
principles which make it abundantly obvious
that the building was not designed or built by
the same people that the Egyptologists think
that it was. The mathematical ability of the

architects alone is far beyond the known
scope of the people of that period in the
middle bronze age. The ability of the architects to construct a logical but hidden design
system though the building speaks not of
the bronze age, but of much more modern
times. Having the conceptual imagination to
plan an optical illusion of such size and then
carry out its construction to the astonishing
detail that is apparent in this pyramid is not
something that one easily associates with ancient people from 4,500 years ago.

If the 'coffin' in the main chamber
is designed to hold a perfect model of the
pyramid's chambers then it is of course not
a coffin but simply a box. And if there is no
coffin then it follows that we do not have
a burial chamber beneath the pyramid but
only a very sophisticated architectural puzzle. And if there is no burial chamber and
no coffin, then there have to very serious
doubts indeed as to whether there was even
a Pharaoh named Unas. Disturbing as this
may seem initially it should be remembered
that the only reason that we think that this
building is the burial chamber of the Pharaoh Unas in the first place is that we were
told so in the hieroglyphs on the chamber's walls. As we know that the architects
were quite happy to destroy the hieroglyphs
wherever they needed to enhance the architectural illusions then, by implication, they
are telling us that the hieroglyphs are not important and that we can disregard the stories
that they tell. This fact is corroborated by
the placing of the model of the chambers in
the box thereby further negating the original story told in the hieroglyphs, and we can
finally come to some conclusions regarding

this building and its architects.

It was designed by someone with a commanding knowledge of mathematics and architecture who also understood the principles of optical illusions and how to apply them to real objects. The architectural design has been deliberately hidden from casual observation and this concealment has been enhanced by inscribing the walls of the building with the words of a story designed to detract attention away from the architecture. The architects had a complete grasp of logical thought processes and possessed the ability to create a path of logic through their work which we can still follow today. They had the ability to survey to the most astonishing accuracy and to line up complex combinations of objects to true north as and when required. And finally they appear to have had very few limits on either their use of time or energy, since the building contains 40 tonne slabs of rock carved to the most exquisite precession imaginable.

The story that we have been told about Unas by the Egyptologists is of course correct, but it is nothing more than a re-telling of the story that was laid down by the architects at the time that this building was constructed. When the Egyptologists tell us that 'this building is the burial chamber of a Pharaoh named Unas', the amount of effort that has been involved in making this statement by the academics should be appreciated by us. It has taken the combined group of dedicated Egyptologists well over one hundred years to painstakingly put together the scripts from the hieroglyphs and thereby the chronological list of Pharaohs and their respective times and places in the supposed history of ancient Egypt. Each of the ancient buildings' attributed Pharaohs has successfully been identified through rigorous and disciplined academic and archaeological research and the story of the old kingdom of ancient Egypt has been duly documented. The Egyptologists are no doubt correct in every detail that they have written, however they have been writing about the wrong subject. The stories of the Old Kingdom of Ancient Egypt are just stories.

These buildings do not contain the coffins of the fictitious Pharaohs of the Old Kingdom, and neither have they been robbed by a band of deliquent tomb robbers sometime after they were built. The treasures that were placed in the chambers of these pyramids are still there today - one simply needs to understand how to look for them.

With that in mind, lets go treasure hunting in the Great Pyramid of Giza.

126   A twist in the tail

The Pyramids of Giza

Architecture beyond our wildest dreams

THE WORLD IS NOT ROUND

In comparison to the pyramid of Unas the Great Pyramid of Giza is massive. It's volume is 25 times larger than that of Unas's and the complexity of its internal architectural design makes that which we have just studied look like the preliminary sketches of a junior school science project. However, we have learnt some very valuable lessons in looking at the architectural design of the Unas pyramid and we know the logical concepts involved in its architecture. The first thing that we should look for in the Great Pyramid therefore is a mathematical design in the entrance passage and one which is concealed from us by the clever use of architectural features.

Without getting into any detail at all at this stage, what happens when you try to apply the lessons that were learnt in the Unas pyramid to the Great Pyramid is that you get nowhere at all. There is no simple triangular construction method used in the slope and length of the entrance, and no amount of manipulation of the geometry on a CAD system yields any results of significance. This should really come as no surprise to us because the Great Pyramid is probably the most studied ancient building on the planet and it would be highly unlikely to discover anything so easily accessible that had not previously been noticed. It is only after vast lengths of time studying the monument's architecture that one can start to make any progress at all, and it took nearly six years to completely pull the design of the pyramid apart.

When you do eventually get to the stage where you thoroughly understand how the architectural design has been conceived the problems that were encountered when trying to locate the geometry of the entrance passage become clear. It is not that the triangular construction of the entrance passage slope has been concealed in any particularly difficult way, or that the architects have used an especially complex combination of triangle side lengths and builders units, the cause of the problems is actually something much simpler to understand. The entrance to the Great Pyramid of Giza is not located where the Egyptologists think that it is and the 'entrance door' and 'entrance passage' are actually nothing of the sort. In later chapters all of the constituent components of the pyramid's architecture are explained, and illustrations of the 'entrance' area will make the picture just presented a lot clearer. For now we need to start our journey into the Great Pyramid in the most peculiar way - our quest to unravel its mysteries will start in France and England towards the end of the 17th century where there is an interesting story to be told.

The invention of the long case or "grandfather" clock, in which the movement of the clock mechanism is regulated by means of a large pendulum which swings from side to side within the casing may seem far removed from the subject at hand, but actually provides the most suitable starting place for our quest. The length of the pendulum in such a clock is not a quantity which can be varied by the clock designer as the amount of time required for the pendulum to swing from side to side is dependent exclusively of the pendulum's length. Or so the inventor of the clock thought as he happily started to produce these wonderful new time pieces in the capital city of his European nation. The clocks worked wonderfully, and in addition to looking elegant and quickly becoming a fashionable addition to the homes of the noblemen of the era, also kept the time correctly. These clocks kept time so well that the government decided that they would be of great use in the offices of the many overseas territories that they 'owned' at the time, and dully loaded the clocks onto the best boats of the day and set sail for far off shores.

Much to the dismay of the clock's British engineers and inventor, it was not long before the postal system was bringing home news of how awful these new clocks were at keeping time - apparently they were losing significant amounts of seconds in a day and what was worse, within the political context of the era, was that it was a Frenchman who had found the error.

Once the mechanical elements of the clocks had been diagnosed as functioning perfectly, the time keeping problem was sent back to the scientists of the epoch who immediately recognised where the problem lay and, in a manner in which only scientists can, they became quite excited. As they explained at the time, the accurate timekeeping of the clock depended on two factors and not just the one that they had previously thought. The length of the pendulum is the first of these factors and the force of gravity acting on that pendulum is the second.

This meant that if the clocks were functioning mechanically correctly, then the gravitational force at the locations where they were malfunctioning must be different from in London where they had been invented. Once they had got over the shock that anything could be different than in London, they quickly realised that if the gravitational force was different at these overseas locations, then there was a very good chance that the world was not round. To be more precise, since they had long since gone into three dimensions, what they actually realised was that the world was not a perfect sphere. In fact they immediately realised that not only did they now know that the world was not spherical, they actually had no idea at all what shape the planet was, since the variations in the clock's timekeep-ing varied from country to country. What the scientists required was either a tabulation of the errors that each of these clocks was producing, so that an estimate of the distortion to the world's assumed spherical shape could be deduced, or a piece of inspirational and highly imaginative thinking from a genius.

The later was produced by the leading scientific thinker of the day, who performed some revolutionary calculations which left many contemporaries bewildered by their complexity and methods, after which he confidently declared,

"The distance from the North pole to the South pole is less than the equatorial distance from one side of the planet to the other by a factor of one part in two hundred and thirty".

The fact that he was wrong was luckily not noticed at the time because nobody had any way at all of verifying the informa-

Newton's Earth

Isaac Newton was one of the many physicists who attempted to calculate the exact shape of the earth's cross section and, like all others before him, got it wrong by quite a wide margin. His calculated value is shown here with the scale greatly exaggerated

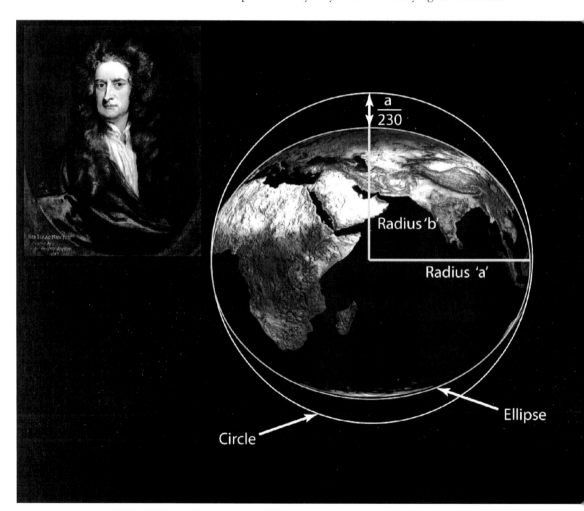

tion and mankind had not yet developed a desire to launch inter-continental ballistic missiles at each other, and the 6.5 km by which they would consequently miss their targets by would not become important for another few hundred years. It was also quite fortunate that the discrepancy in the calculation was not detectable as the scientist was Sir Isaac Newton, and his reputation as quite an exceptional Physicist may well have been questioned. This serves as an excellent example of one point which is salient to this book - if you collect large amounts of data from all over the planet, give the problem to the world's greatest Physicist of the time, arm him with a myriad of books and unique calculation methods, he will still get the shape of the planet wrong by a significant margin - it is a very difficult calculation to perform. What Newton did calculate was an approximation of the Earth's shape, along with a factually correct statement that the shape of the planet was that of a oblate spheroid (a polar flattened sphere).

We can come back to the shape of the Earth later in this chapter, but for now we should look at a second perplexing item from the seventeenth century regarding the planet on which we live. Not only was the shape of the planet unknown, but nobody either seemed to have the slightest idea what size the planet was. It was definitely quite big, as the scholars in Athens nineteen hundred years prior had been able to estimate the size of the planet by using an ingenious method using a stick located at various places around the countryside and the length of its shadow at various times in the day, and had come to the conclusion that the Earth was about 250,000 stadia around the equator. The French Royal court in the 17th century decided with wisdom that it was way past time that we stopped talking about the size of the Earth in terms of how many Greek stadia would fit around the equator and formally asked the French scientists of the day, in what must be one of the most grandiose requests of all time, if they could kindly measure the exact size of planet Earth.

The scientists who took up the challenge was Jaques Cassini who in 1700, along with his father, undertook the task of measuring the exact distance from the North to the South of France, starting in Dunkirk and ending in Collioure - an idyllic Mediterranean town situated to the south of Perpignan. The path between these two locations ensured that the measurements started and finished at sea level, encompassed the largest distance possible within the borders of France and lay on a North-South line. The results of the surveying work and accompanying mathematical calculations lead to two outcomes. The first was that France and England started to have a dispute about who knew the shape of the planet correctly, since the French had decided that the Earth's spheroid was flatter at the equator than at the poles in contradiction to Newton. The second was that the French invented the Metric system of measurement by basing it on a highly rational concept of dividing the distance from the equator to the North pole by an exact number, and calling the resulting distance 'one metre'. The most convenient number to divide the pole to equator distance by was 10 million, thus giving the length of a metre as being 39.37 British inches. The concept behind the French idea was eloquent as all measurements would be in natural units which related to the Earth and were therefore not based on arbitrary distances such as Roman stadia or British people's foot length.

Unfortunately, but not unsurprisingly, if you spend two years of your life walking from the North to the South of France carrying a tripod, notebook and pencil, you do not get a perfect measurement of the Earth's shape. Instead of the distance from the equator to the North pole being 10 million metres as was intended, it is actually 1965 metres longer, with the unfortunate result that the metre is an arbitrary unit of length measurement. In terms of surveying accuracy in 1700's, the accomplishment was extraordinary, but in terms of delivering the conceptual plan at the outset, it failed, and illustrates once again how difficult the measurement of the shape or size of the planet Earth can be.

So, at the start of the 18th century the French and the British were the only nations who were aware of the shape and size of the very planet that they lived on, and they were in disagreement with each other about it. Over the next 150 years the top names in mathematics all attempted to refine the calculations involved in determining the planet's shape, but it was not until the 1950's that any sort of consistent accuracy began to emerge in the quest for a definitive planetary shape and size.

During the Second World War many technological breakthroughs were made on both sides of the conflict, including the development of the aircraft detec-

Mountains

The reference
ellipsoid can
be thought of
as mesh which
encases the
planet. There
are areas where
the observer is
below the average
height of the
mesh and others,
such as the high
mountains, where
the mesh is below.

tion system now known as Radar. Once the war was over there was a vast surplus of large, powerful radar dishes available to the general public, and one or two of the more inquisitive members of society realised that the apparatus could be used in the detection of radio signals from outer space - and the science of radio telescope observation was invented. The early days of this subject are filled with fascinating stories of scientists on ladders scraping bird droppings out of antennas and other highly dedicated behaviour. The telescopes were refined and enlarged and not before long, radio telescopes began to go into operation all around the world.

One of the by-products of this scientific exploration of the universe was that by employing two radio telescopes which were situated at large distances from each other, and by pointing them at the same radio source in the sky, you could compare the results of the observations. And the comparison of the results of these observations can then be used to calculate the exact shape of the planet, assuming that you know exactly where the two radio-telescopes are geographically situated.

The latter point is another one of those annoying scientific problems, because if you have two telescopes on either side of the planet ,which would be the ideal situation to produce the best results, then you need to know the shape of the Earth to determine exactly where the telescopes are located. And since this is exactly what you are trying to measure, error margins once again arise in the results. However, the results are significantly better than those produced by any other means available, and the size and shape of the planet can at last be specified with some accuracy, with error margins reducing down to a few metres, rather than kilometres.

The breakthrough in the quest for the planet's shape eventually comes when you have the ability to launch objects into space, attached to which are measuring devices which can accurately determine the shape of the planet below. The first of the world's observation satellites were launched in the 1960's and this method of measurement solved the riddle of the Earth's dimensions with absolute certainty. Since the 1960's the interest in the mathematics of calculating the dimensions of our planet has completely stopped. We now know the exact shape and size of planet Earth.

That is except for one rather obvious point - that the Earth that we observe on a daily basis as we walk through the countryside has some very large lumps of rock protruding from it, in the form of mountains. It also has some very low lying lands which are lower than the average sea level around the world, and once again we have the problem from which this chapter takes it's title, that the earth is not round. What is required to accurately determine positional co-ordinates is some sort of idealised globe which gives the closest approximation to the shape of the Earth and one on which everyone on the planet is agreed upon. In some places the mountains will rise up above this ideal shape, and in some places the land will go below it, but as a reference system for locating places on the planet it will work perfectly.

This concept is what gave rise to the reference ellipsoid which is used for all modern navigation systems and which started out as a document known as GRS80 , the number at the end of the name being the year in which it was formally adopted by the world's scientific community. It was superseded in 1984 by a minor revision and given the name of WGS84 and this is the ellipsoidal reference datum by which aircraft navigate, global position systems (GPS) operate, and is essential to the functioning of much of technological apparatus which we take for granted each day.

So, from the early measurements of the Greek empire, to attempts in the late middle ages to determine the size of this wonderful planet we live on, it was not until 1984, only 26 years ago, that the human race finally settled on an accurate and unified result. There are a number of points to take from the story of the search for the Earth's dimensions which will become important to us as we make our way through this work. First is that you do not know that the Earth is anything other than round, or spherical, until you have some manner of observing the fact in detail - in our case the timekeeping errors of the 'Grandfather' clock. Secondly is that even when you have noticed that the shape is not spherical, it is then particularly difficult to determine the precise nature of the distortion of the planet's surface. Thirdly, that until electronic technology is available, the measurement of the Earth's size and shape are by no means accurate, and then the only way to determine the details with absolute precision is to send a spacecraft off the planet and observe from the outside, looking in.

Having comprehended the difficulty of determining the size and shape of the planet we live on it will come as quite a surprise to you, as it did to me, to learn that the Great Pyramid of Giza's architectural design is a geometrically *perfect* model of the Earth's oblate spheroid.

This statement is all that is required as the basis of a hypothesis to unlock the architectural treasures of the greatest building on this planet. It is also a statement which when proven, as it will be in the following pages of this book, has profound consequences on the comprehension of the origins of our very existence, since implicit within it are currently inexplicable historical anomalies.

Let us now make our way to the deserts of Northern Egypt and take our first look at the Great Pyramid of Giza.

THE INVISIBLE PYRAMID

If we are to apply diligent scientific analysis to the structure of the Great Pyramid in order to test the hypothesis that its architectural design is based on the Earth's elliptical shape, then a prerequisite of that analysis is the determination of accurate details of the dimensions of the structure itself. What we need as a starting point is a very accurate survey of the building.

This task was wonderfully accomplished in the late 1800's by an English surveyor, Sir William Flinders Petrie, who spent two years meticulously measuring the pyramids at Giza to the highest accuracy possible. His resulting work, 'The Pyramids and Temples of Gizeh' was published in 1883 and is a fascinating study of both the monuments on the Giza Plateau and the daily lifestyle of the Egyptians in Cairo at the time. The book is a large bound volume which would fill up a large portion of the table on which you would place it, and is nearly 10cm thick due to the elaborate hand bound pages and covers. Luckily, due to the work of specialists in the last few years, it has been fully digitised and made available on the internet.

To ensure that the vital dimension data contained in this work was indeed accurate, I compared the on-line and original manuscripts against each other and checked and compared all of the numerical data. There was only one discrepancy in the whole of Petrie's work which I came across, and this was not due to a type setting error in the on-line version, but an original calculation error on the part of Petrie during the transposition of his raw data. He unfortunately transposed some of his calculation mathematics and incorrectly stated the relative positions of the second and third pyramids on the Giza plateau - the details and corrections to this error have now been appended to the on-line version of the work, although you will often come across the consequences of this error appearing in quite significant published works, including those of academic institutions.

The second piece of survey work that is vital to the analysis of the Great Pyramid is that which was published by the German engineer who was commissioned by the Egyptian government in the 1990's to survey the small internal shaftways within the structure by means of remote robotic sensing. The robotics engineer in question, Mr. Rudolf Gantenbrink, published the results of the survey work on an on-line web site and it is due to this bold decision on his part that the structure can fully and successfully analysed. The results of the surveying carried out by Gantenbrink is contained within the CAD drawings which are available on his site, and it is this data which is tabulated in the surveying appendix to this book. For the reader who wishes to cross check this data, a CAD drawing display computer programme would be required which can be freely downloaded from a variety of locations on the internet.

The third and final source of information for the Great Pyramid's dimensions is the book of Dr. Mark Lehner "The Complete Pyramids" which is considered a standard introductory reference work for the study of the Giza pyramids along with the many other pyramids located around Egypt. Whilst not a piece of surveying work, the book does contain small details gleaned from the archaeological work of Lehner which fill in some of the small omissions in the earlier work of Petrie.

With this accurate surveying data to hand we are now in a position to be able to elaborate upon and test the hypothesis which is at the core of this analysis of the Great Pyramid.

The Great Pyramid of Giza

Scale drawing taken from the survey works of
William Petrie and Rudolf Gantenbrink.

Scale 1474 : 1
1mm = 1.474 m

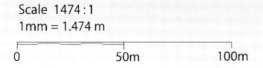

0   50m   100m

Upper South Shaft

Lower South Shaft

Upp
Cham

Few remaining Casing Stones

Granite bedrock

Subterrane

Principle features of the Great Pyramid

The named sections of the architectural features are shown in this illustration

Highly irregular core masonry of varying heights.
Upper North Shaft
Gallery
North Shaft
Ascending Passage
Blocking Stones
Descending Passage
'Well' Shaft

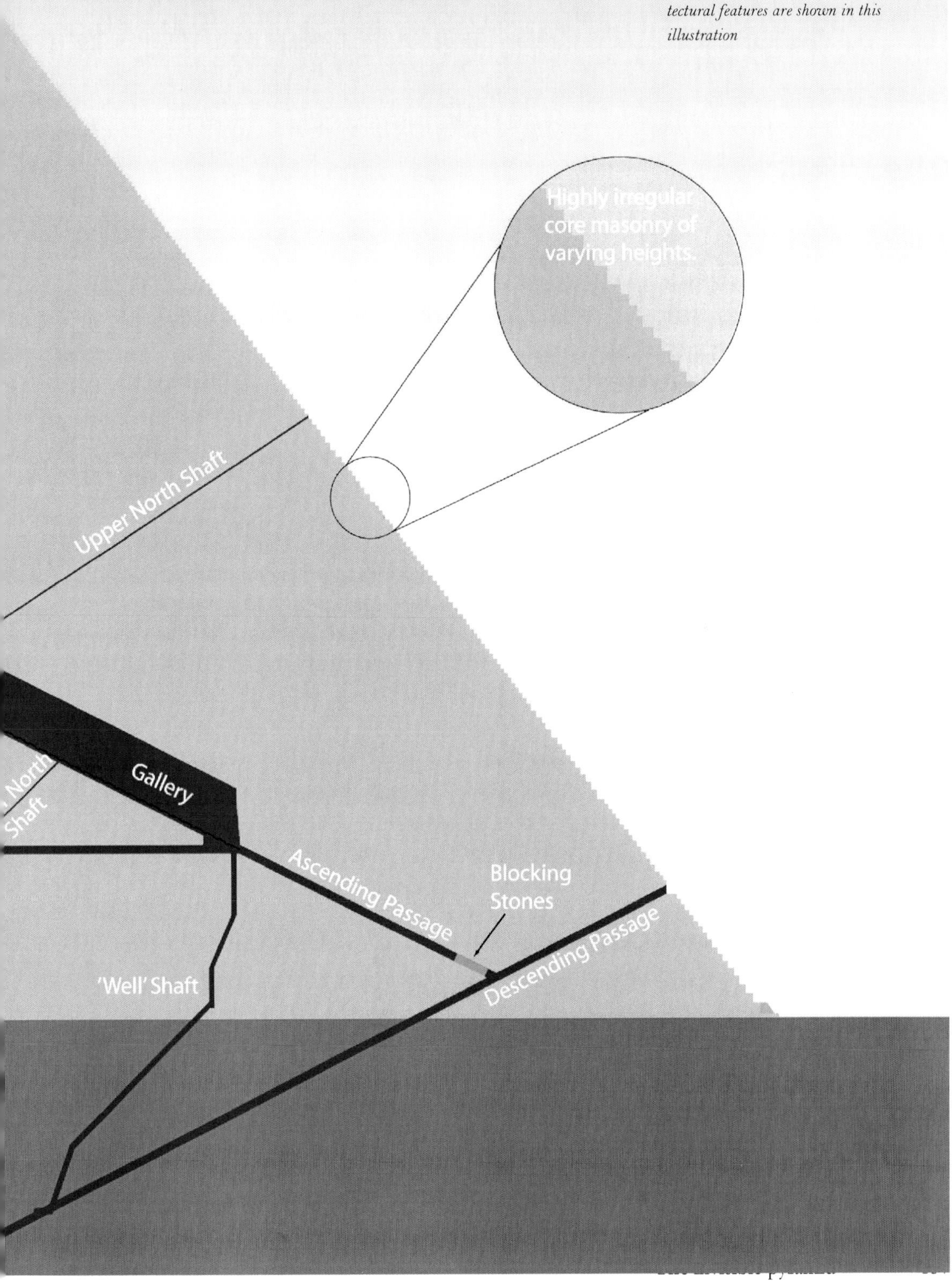

The Hypothesis

That the architecture of the Great Pyramid of Giza is based on a geometric model of the Earth's cross-sectional elliptical shape, and the base length of the structure is a representation of half the polar circumference of that ellipse.

What may not be immediately apparent from this statement, but which is essential to the understanding of the elaborate architectural design of the Great Pyramid is that if the hypothesis is correct then two possibilities arise from it. The first is that if the height and side angle of the pyramid are accurately known, then the base length can be deduced, but more importantly is that if the base length is known, then the height and side angle can be calculated.

Since the Great Pyramid is a structure which has undergone significant weathering and degradation since it was built approximately 4,500 years ago, it is in no state at all to give us accurate measurements of its external structure - something which the architects were no doubt fully aware would happen over time. The apex of the pyramid does not exist, and there are very few of the original casing stones which made up the external structure of the monument still intact which could give us a large enough distance over which to accurately measure the side gradient.

It was these facts that were in part the motivation behind Petrie's explorations in Egypt, to determine exactly what shape and size the original structure must have been from the remains that are present. Due to his meticulous attention to detail, he was able to calculate what the height and side angle of the pyramid originally were, giving error margins in his work which are calculated using standard statistical deviation mathematics, with results which can be used as an excellent estimation of the pyramid's origi-

The Great Pyramid stonework

The external stonework of the Great Pyramid is weathered and largely dilapidated.

nal external dimensions. This task however can also be performed on paper without ever visiting Giza, once the architectural design of the monument is understood.

If the hypothesis is correct and the base length of the pyramid represents half the elliptical circumference of the Earth, and if we know exactly the proportions of the Earth's elliptical shape as we do, then calculating the height and side angle of the pyramid is no more complex a matter than finding a suitable mathematical formula for the circumference of an ellipse. This can be then applied to the easily measured base length of the pyramid and the building can once again start to assume its former shape. This system of construction is shown in the illustration below.

The principle architectural design

The three steps required to create the external design of the pyramid are shown here

The formula for the circumference of an ellipse is not the simplest of mathematical equations, unlike it's sister shape, the circle, whose circumference formula is known to school student across the globe. In fact the formula for the ellipse is so complicated that it lead mathematicians to search for an approximation formula that could be used in every day calculations. The best of these formulae, and one which is used to this day, was calculated by the Indian mathematician Srinivasa Aiyangar Ramanujan, a self-taught genius who was born on 22nd December 1887 and who produced vast volumes of original work. His ellipse circumference approximation formula states that the circumference of an ellipse is given by

$$c = \pi(3(a + b) - \sqrt{(3a + b)(a + 3b)})$$

where a is the larger of the ellipse's two radii (known as the semi-major axis) and b is the smaller of the two (known as the semi-minor axis) and c is the ellipse's circumference. In an attempt to keep the majority of the mathematics of this book contained in the appendix, I shall not elaborate upon the mathematical workings required to understand the pyramids architecture in the main text of the book. If the reader wished to study the algebraic workings (which are fascinating) then they are laid out in the mathematics appendix and referred to in the text.

Using this formula on the known size of the Earth from the reference ellipsoid

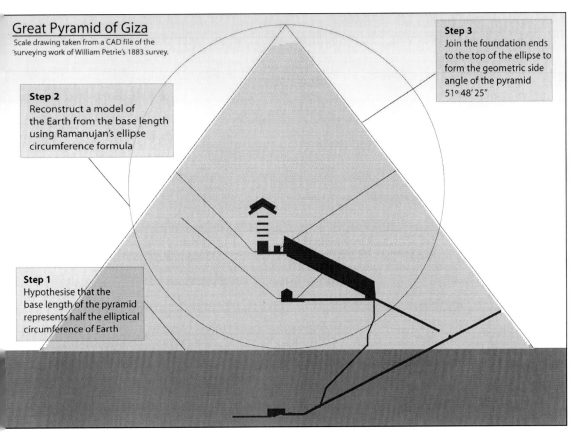

Great Pyramid of Giza
Scale drawing taken from a CAD file of the surveying work of William Petrie's 1883 survey.

Step 3
Join the foundation ends to the top of the ellipse to form the geometric side angle of the pyramid 51° 48′ 25″

Step 2
Reconstruct a model of the Earth from the base length using Ramanujan's ellipse circumference formula

Step 1
Hypothesise that the base length of the pyramid represents half the elliptical circumference of Earth

WGS84 referred to in the previous chapter, the circumference of the Earth's reference datum ellipsoid can be calculated accurate to one one thousandth of a millimetre. What is fascinating about Ramanujan's formula is not the astonishing accuracy that it produces but, as will be shown in a later chapter, that this is the same formula that was used by the pyramid's architects when the structure was designed.

However, for now we are trying to prove the hypothesis, and for this we need to rework Ramanujan's formula so that it gives us the polar diameter of the elliptical cross section of the Earth. Since the pole-pole diameter of the Earth is less than the equatorial diameter (as shown by Newton) and will represent the height of the pyramid if our hypothesis is correct, then we need to rework the formula so that the semi-minor axis b is given in terms of the circumference. What would also be useful would be to replace the term for the semi-major axis a in the formula and state it in terms of b, which can be easily achieved as we know the proportion of the Earth's radii. For this purpose we can introduce the letter f into the equation where $a=fb$ and also the letter L to represent the base length of the pyramid which, as the hypothesis states, is half the elliptical circumference. Ramanujan's formula can then be reworked to give the height of the pyramid.

$$H = \frac{4L}{\pi\left(3(f+1) - \sqrt{3f^2 + 10f - 3}\right)}$$

This is our first glimpse at the mathematical genius that is at the heart of the architecture of the monument. Notice that the height of the pyramid is defined in terms of a fraction, the numerator of which is $4L$, or four times the base length of the pyramid. And since the pyramid has four sides to it, all of which are a slightly different length, then we do not have to make an arbitrary decision as to which of the sides we use in the equation - we are being told to use them all. This immediately adds a statistical error balance into the equation for the height of the pyramid and starts us off in the accurate manner which will be required for the full analysis of the structure. It also strongly suggests that the perimeter of the pyramid's base is an essential part of the reconstruction of the building's architecture. The denominator of the equation has only one term in it, f, and since this

is the ratio of the Earth's elliptical radii, the denominator is a constant. In effect, the equation can be considered as stating that the height of the Great Pyramid of Giza is equal to its base perimeter divided by the shape of the earth.

The first test of the hypothesis is to plug in numbers into this equation, those numbers being the base perimeter of the pyramid and the ratio of the Earth's radii.

From the WGS84 reference datum on the Earth the radii of the planet's ellipse are given as

a= 6,378,137 m
b= 6,356,752.3141 m

which gives a ratio of the two radii f as

f= 1.00336409

This is effectively the same number that was originally calculated by Newton when it was first realised that the Earth was a oblate ellipsoid. The flattening of the polar radius stated in WGS84 is $1/298.257$ compared to the figure that Newton derived of $1/230$.

The second set of numbers that we require are the base lengths of the pyramid from Petrie's survey work, in which he documents the following

Northern Base Length	230.36276 m
Eastern Base Length	230.31958 m
Southern Base Length	230.36530 m
Western Base Length	230.34244 m

From which we can derive

Perimeter	921.39008 m

It should be noted at this point that the original survey of Petrie was conducted in inches, and that the exact measurements that he reported in his work have been transposed in this book into metric units. The five decimal places of accuracy which are shown above are not representative of the accuracy of the survey work, but are a consequence of that transposition.

Plugging in these numbers into the reworked Ramanujan formula gives the height of the pyramid from the hypothesis as being

Pyramid Height   **146.397 m**

From this height calculation the angle of the pyramid can be deduced by performing a simple trigonometry calculation with the average base length, yielding an angle for the pyramid's sides of

Pyramid Angle   51° 48' 25"

The simplest way of comparing these calculated figures to the structure is by visually overlaying them on top of a known drawing of the pyramid's cross section. In the illustration below the red calculated face angle of the pyramid is shown overlaid onto a CAD drawing of the pyramid drawn from Petrie's surveying measurements, and the remarkably close fit between the two sets of data can be seen immediately.

A second way of checking the numerical results of the calculation is to compare them to Petrie's surveying. He performed numerous angle calculations on the pyramid, many of these being based on assumptions regarding the way in which the various passageways within the

structure emerged on the outside stonework. Whilst these assumptions may well be true, it is wise to ignore them and rely on his measurements of the few remaining casing stones which still lie around the pyramid's base. In his work he reports that the angle of the stones is 51° 46' 45" which compares favourably with the numerical result calculated previously. The comparison of the height is largely academic (since it is dependent only upon the calculation of the side angle) but is non the less interesting as it gives us a linear measurement of the difference between the two sets of results - angular measure being much harder to visualise and therefore compare. Petrie calculated the pyramid's height as 146.71m which was deduced using assumptions in the side angle measurements, a figure which also compares well with that from the hypothesis and gives a difference between the calculated and 'surveyed' height of 31cm.

What can be concluded about this simple hypothesis is that it produces numerical measurement results which compare very well indeed with the existing structure. This,

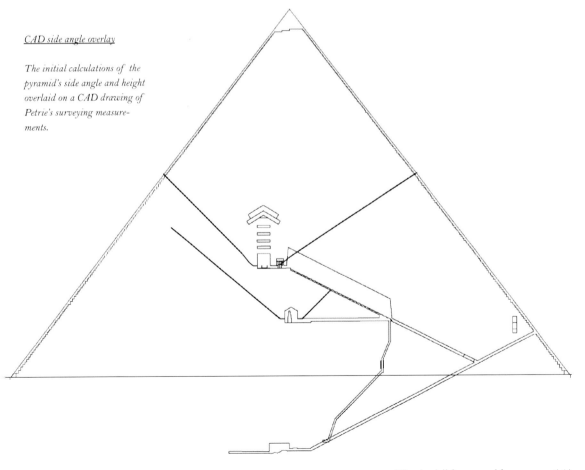

as classical Egyptologists would no doubt point out, could quite well be coincidence as the Great Pyramid of Giza must compare favourably with any number of geometric objects if sufficient manipulation of the mathematics is performed, and it would be impossible to argue with this position. What is required is further evidence that the mathematical similarities between the the building's architecture and the cross sectional shape of Earth's meridian are intentional. Luckily the architects have provided exactly this corroborating evidence, and in abundant quantities.

The base of the Great Pyramid is where the second clue to the design principles incorporated in the structure can be found. When the pyramid was constructed it was not simply placed in the Egyptian desert with nothing surrounding it, but was finished off with an elaborate pavement and foundation structure which encloses the whole of the base area. It is the remains of this pavement upon which the thousands of tourists who visit the monument walk each year, and to which Petrie and Lehner both pay close attention to in their works. In particular Lehner's detailed reconstruction of the building methods employed in this section of the site show quite clearly that the architects designed a precisely measured foundation plat-

form under the pyramid which he reports as extending 38cm outside the base line of the casing stones. The width of this foundation platform excess, which we can call the plinth, is important in the comprehension of the reason for it existence and it is fortunate that Lehner included the measurement of this feature of the pyramid in his work, as it is one of the few omissions from that of Petrie.

We know from Petrie that the average base length of the pyramid's constructed angular face where it meets the floor level of the building is 230.35m and the foundation platform excess surrounding it is 0.38m on both sides - giving the base length of the outer delimiting square boundary of the construction as 231.11 m. A simple calculation of the plinth width divided by the foundation platform length gives a quite fascinating result that the plinth is 1/304th of the platform length. This proportion is similar to one which we have seen before and is the measure of the flattening on the Earth's radii that Newton was so keen to determine and which he calculated as 1/230th , which was finally calculated with accuracy for the first time in 1980 as being 1/298.257th. Whilst the figure derived from the foundation platform is not exactly the same, the error margins in the reported works of Petrie and Leh-

Plan view of the pyramid

The plinth and the stonework form an elliptical base reference shape

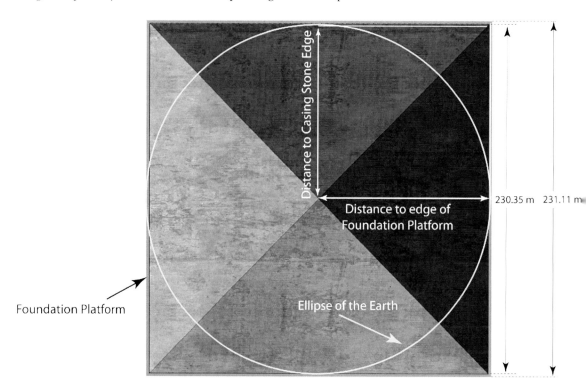

ner must be taken into consideration which are 1.27cm and 0.5cm respectively. So what we can factually determine about the value of the ratio of plinth to the foundation platform lengths is that it will statistically fall around the values of 1/308th as a maximum and 1/299th as a minimum.

When the pyramid is viewed from above and the two squares, that of the casing stone joint with the floor level and that of the plinth are considered, then the concept on display becomes apparent, as shown in the illustration opposite. By constructing an ellipse whose minor diameter touches any two opposite sloping casing stone edges of the pyramid, and a major diameter which touches the foundation platform edges, the resulting ellipse is an accurate drawing of the Earth's elliptical polar cross section, lending substantial credence to the original hypothesis. In fact it does more than add some credence to the original hypothesis, it suggests strongly that base length that was intended to be used when looking at the pyramid is that of the foundation platform and not that of the stone face blocks. If you consider the construction methods shown below, it is apparent that the foundation platform would have had to be accurately measured and aligned before the casing stones were laid upon it. The foundation platform edge must therefore have been the primary base reference point of this structure for the architects.

A reconsideration of our hypothesis also yields a problem with the first application of that hypothesis to the base length of the sloping pyramid casing stones. The world, as we sorted out in the previous chapter, is not a regular shape as the terrain of the planet includes mountains and valleys, and is as rough in form as the current state of the pyramid itself. So the thought of reconstructing a perfectly shaped ellipsoidal cross section of *the Earth it-*

self is an illogical concept. However, we can quite logically create a perfectly formed geometric reconstruction of the *Earth's ellipsoidal reference datum*. This masterful use of precise logic is exactly the same type of thinking that we came across in the pyramid of Unas and is why the architects left the foundation platform on the Great Pyramid extending 38cm out from the base line of the sloping pyramid face. By doing so a reference ellipsoid can be recreated from the foundation length of the pyramid, and it is this reference ellipse upon which *all* of the pyramid's internal geometry is based. The subtle variance between these two methods of reconstructing the ellipses makes little difference when initially recognising the geometric patterns within the pyramid's architecture, but makes a substantial difference in the latter stages of the work.

So we can now go back to the surveying data and re-apply the hypothesis to the foundation platform length of the pyramid in exactly the same manner as we originally applied it to the casing stone base length. The foundation platform perimeter measurement around the pyramid is an addition of 921.39 m (the surveyed length of the four sloping sides) plus 8 plinth widths of 38cm, giving the perimeter as 924.43m. This yields a height for the cross sectional ellipse of the Earth's reference datum, and therefore the height of the pyramids external reference geometry of 146.88m and of course the identical side angle as previously which is deduced mathematically from the height.

Applying the hypothesis in this manner to the foundation platform length could be considered as stretching the hypothesis slightly too far, but once again the architects have provided corroborating evidence which helps verify that this method of application is correct.

The foundation platform

The design of the foundation platform is the principle feature of the lower section of the pyramid to which the stonework is aligned

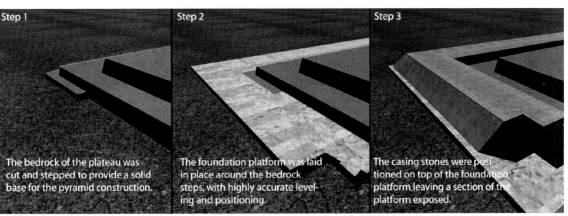

Step 1
The bedrock of the plateau was cut and stepped to provide a solid base for the pyramid construction.

Step 2
The foundation platform was laid in place around the bedrock steps, with highly accurate levelling and positioning.

Step 3
The casing stones were positioned on top of the foundation platform leaving a section of the platform exposed.

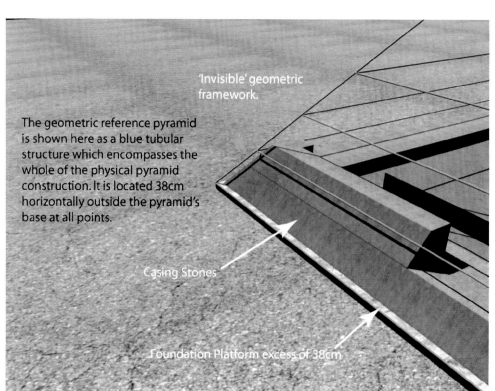

The purpose of the foundation platform is to provide a reference framework around the monument.

'Invisible' geometric framework.

The geometric reference pyramid is shown here as a blue tubular structure which encompasses the whole of the physical pyramid construction. It is located 38cm horizontally outside the pyramid's base at all points.

Casing Stones

Foundation Platform excess of 38cm

Revisiting The Cubit

We have already had a detailed look at the cubit measuring system used by the ancient Egyptians and have established that the monuments of the Old Kingdom were built using the cubit rod as a measuring standard.

The length of the cubit was diligently studied by Petrie in Chapter 20 of his surveying work in which he concluded that the best deduction of this measurement was 20.620 inches with an error margin of 5 thousandths of an inch, or 52.375cm with an error margin of one tenth of a millimetre. The accuracy of this measurement was achieved from surveying the main chamber of the pyramid in which he used callipers to determine exact distances involved with highly accurate results, and although this value can be shown to be slightly incorrect due to an assumption on the part of Petrie, this value for the cubit will suffice at this stage.

What has puzzled Egyptologists for many years is why the base length of the Great Pyramid is not an exact number of cubits in length, as would be expected since this was the starting point of the construction. Looking again at the four base lengths of the pyramid from Petrie's survey work, with the distances transposed into cubits, the reason for that puz-

zlement becomes apparent.

Northern Base Length	439.84 cubits
Eastern Base Length	439.75 cubits
Southern Base Length	439.84 cubits
Western Base Length	439.80 cubits
Perimeter	1759.22 cubits

None of the base lengths is a whole number of cubits and the perimeter of the base of the pyramid also does not give a regular figure. However, when the length of the foundation platform is considered things start to look considerably different.

North Platform Length	441.29 cubits
East Platform Length	441.20 cubits
South Platform Length	441.29 cubits
West Platform Length	441.25 cubits

Platform Perimeter   **1765.03 cubits**

The sides of the pyramid's foundation platform can be seen to come in adjacent pairs, where the addition of any two adjacent foundation platform sides will add up to a half-cubit measure, and the resulting perimeter of the structure is approximately a whole number of cubits. This fits in with the accepted system used by architects that we saw in the Unas pyramid, that they always tend to employ rational distances based on the measurement unit with which they are working. We should note, however, that we are using a value of the cubit which is derived from surveying measurements, and therefore adopting a perimeter length of 1765 cubits is nothing more than a good approximation with which we can work with for the time being.

If this calculation of the perimeter length is correct then the reason for the perimeter, rather than any individual side, being a whole number of cubits is, as we saw in the equation for reconstructing the pyramid's original shape, the numerator of the fraction is the perimeter of the structure. So not only have the architects pointed us in the right direction, they have also given us a way of measuring the foundation length of the pyramid from the comfort of our office desk. If we deduce that the perimeter of the foundation was intended to be a whole number of cubits, then we can easily determine the average length of each side of the foundation sides as being 1765/4 cubits or 231.105 metres and from it the height of the pyramid

as 146.878m.

Having determined what looks like the starting point for the Great Pyramid's architectural construction as being the foundation platform's perimeter of exactly 1765 cubits, we can now go back to our hypothesised method of construction and calculate with more accuracy the side angle of the pyramid. To do so we need to diligently analyse the construction logic that we have determined to this point to ensure that we do not make a mistake at the very beginning of our work. We know that

1) The foundation platform of the Great Pyramid probably has a perimeter length of 1765 cubits and so the average length of each side is 441.25 cubits

2) The core masonry of the pyramid is set back from the foundation platform base line by 1/298.257th of its length equally divided between both ends of the base , by a value of 0.74 cubits on each

3) The height of the pyramid can be calculated from the foundation platform perimeter length using the elliptical circumference formula of Ramanujan.

It may seem superfluous to re-state

The reference side angle

By using the foundation platform as a primary reference the angle used in the geometric construction can be found

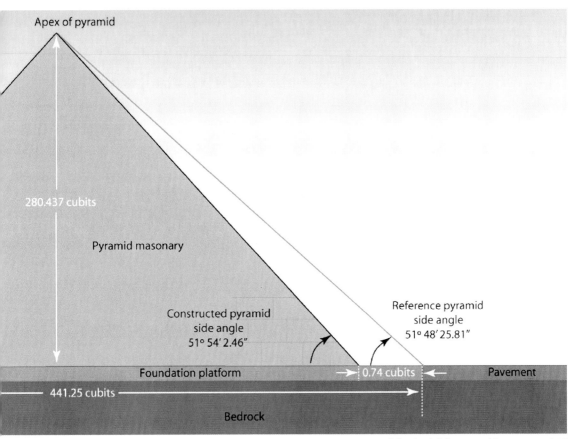

these facts but from them we can see one crucial point which may otherwise become lost in the work. That point is that there are two base lengths shown in the architecture, one for the foundation platform and one for the core masonry, but only one height. This means that the geometric reference pyramid and the core masonry must contain different side angles, as shown in the illustration on the opposite page with the horizontal scale grossly distorted.

At this stage in the analysis of the architectural design principles this tiny difference is largely irrelevant, but as we progress onwards it will become vital in unlocking the details of other pyramids in the Giza complex. It is also fascinating to note that if this is correct then the side angle of the pyramid's core masonry does not constitute part of the geometric design structure of the building, and other than it allows us to check our surveying data, it is essentially a highly crafted illusion. The only dimension detail of the pyramid that we really need to know with any certainty is the foundation platform length, and this principle design concept is one of the masterpieces of the building's architecture.

As the pyramid's external structure of the casing stones falls apart over time, and the sands of the Egyptian desert accumulate around the pyramid's base, debris will end up covering the pavement area of the pyramid, and will protect the primary part of the structure from damage. This is exactly the state that Petrie found the pyramid's to be in when he conducted his survey in the late 1800's, and he reports that piles of debris were stacked up to a height of several metres all around the pyramid's bases, causing him to have to bore down through them to determine base lengths.

What we have determined in this first look at the pyramid is that the hypothesis does seem plausible and there are significant architectural features within the building that conform to the proposal. It will not be until later that we will be able to see that there is actually a lot more accurate manner in which this base length was formed and that all that we have looked at so far is simply the architects rough workings which were specifically designed to attract our attention.

We are now in a position to be able to continue our search for the entrance to the structure, armed with a quite solid base to work from.

In Through The Out-Door

One of the criticisms often levelled at works which analyse the Great Pyramid's architecture is that they are loosely put together, rely on inaccurate information, and introduce random concepts throughout the work in order to substantiate incorrect results.

In order not to progress in a similar style we must be diligent in the extreme with the manner in which we look for the entrance to the structure. We have already set out a hypothesis, and to it we must add *nothing at all* if it is to stand up to thorough examination. For if they who designed and built this monument were so diligent in their work, then those who chose to analyse their work must

do so with the same immaculate attention to detail. Consequently the only item on the pyramid that we can use as a starting point in locating the entrance to the structure is the base of the pyramid, which we have determined in the previous chapter is probably the foundation platform edge. Even more restricting is that we only have the two ends of the foundations, the base centre, and the elliptical cross section of the Earth as currently defined reference points.

You will recall from the entrance structure of the Unas pyramid that there was a logical and linear design flow to follow, and so we find ourselves at the Great Pyramid stranded at the end of the foundation platform, looking for somewhere to which we can construct a geometric line. The are very few options indeed, and the one which is to help us on our way is the tangent line taken from the foundation platform end point up to the earth shaped ellipse. From this point on the ellipse we can now produce a second geometric line which returns back down to the foundation platform at its centre point. This simple geometric construc-

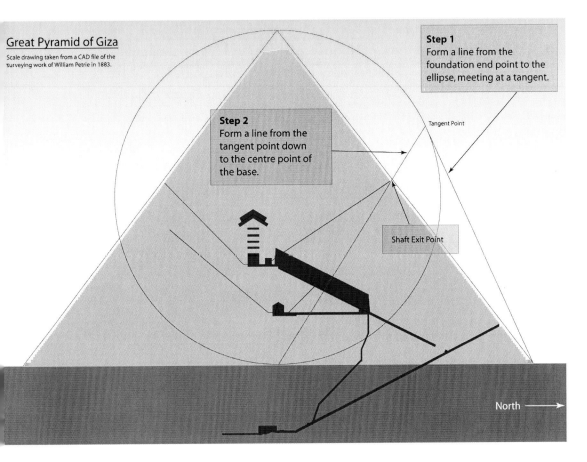

Great Pyramid of Giza
Scale drawing taken from a CAD file of the surveying work of William Petrie in 1883.

Step 1
Form a line from the foundation end point to the ellipse, meeting at a tangent.

Step 2
Form a line from the tangent point down to the centre point of the base.

Tangent Point

Shaft Exit Point

North ⟶

tion is shown in the illustration in which the remarkable geometric coincidence with the pyramid's upper north shaft exit is clearly visible. A similar coincidence at the south shaft exit point would be apparent if the same construction were to be repeated from the southern end of the foundation platform in the same manner. The geometric construction line which we have just created appears on the diagram to pass through the shaft's exit point on the pyramid face, an occurrence that is so unlikely to have happened by chance that we need to look at the precision of the coincidence in significantly more detail.

The first task in the analysis is to retrieve the accurate surveying information from the appropriate document so that the exact details of the shaft's construction can be quantified. For this we need the robotics survey of Gantenbrink in which the surveying data is presented in the form of a computerised CAD drawing. The data for each of the individual blocks of stone from which the shaft is constructed are listed in the surveying appendix, this tabulated data being taken directly from the original CAD drawings of Gantenbrink. The accuracy of this data is without question as when the Upuaut website was first launched on the internet the webserver directories where the CAD drawings are stored were left open to the public, allowing anyone who so wished to download the original CAD drawings and fully analyse the data within them. It is from these original drawings that the shaft block data is taken.

At the time of acquisition, the data was collect by means of a robotic device which was inserted into the shaft and inside

this robot were inclinometers which were used to detail the angle of the shaft all along its length. There are various blocks within the shaft which contain small anomalies, and I would advise that anyone wanting to read through the numerical data relating to this survey in the appendix do so in conjunction with viewing the excellent CAD drawings on Gantenbrink's website.

The first question which needs answering regarding the shaft is whether the roof line of the shaft or the floor line of the shaft should be taken as a reference datum. This is a reasonably simple question to answer once the manner in which the shaft was constructed has been understood, and the illustration below shows the architect's construction method as explained by Gantenbrink on his website. As can be seen the shaft only has three sides to it, the bottom of the shaft being supplied by the core masonry of the pyramid structure. It is more than reasonable to take the roof of the shaft as being the reference line of the architects, as this is the line which they have had to carve out of the rock.

We now need to determine the exact position of the shaft's roof at its exit point on the pyramid face by examining the position of the last block of stone in the North shaft. This stone was originally integrated into the casing stones which made up the external face of the constructed pyramid, but unfortunately the end of the block has been lost during the erosion of the outside of the pyramid's masonry. The details listed in the appendix for this stone are its starting location (which is known since it is still in place),

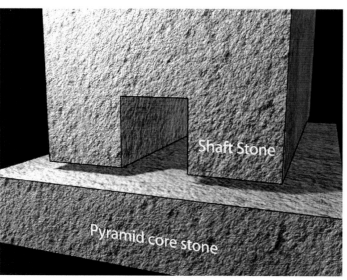

and its virtual ending place where it would intersect the reference pyramid which we constructed in the last chapter. The position of this intersect for the roof of the shaft is 51.82m North of the pyramid's central axis and 81.01m vertically from the level of the foundation platform (the floor of the shaft intersects with the reference pyramid at 51.96m North of the central axis and 80.83m above the foundation platform).

Once that the

Upper northern shaft stones

The upper northern shaft is formed by placing a carved section of stone upon a base bed

Upper northern
shaft cutting

A close up of the
shaft geometry
showing the ac-
curacy with which
the construction
lines fit the archi-
tecture

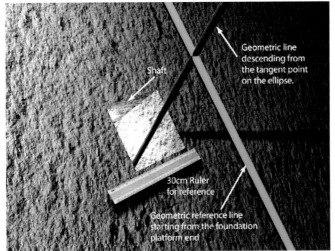

Geometric line
descending from
the tangent point
on the ellipse.

Shaft

30cm Ruler
for reference

Geometric reference line
starting from the foundation
platform end

coincidence in the two values
that the construction we have
just analysed is 81 metres
above the foundation platform and the difference is so
small that it would not even
be visible when viewed from
the ground. A close up of the
North shaft exit point and
the construction geometry is
shown in the accompanying
illustration.

With such a precise
definition of the shaft exit
point in our possession it is
now possible to return to the
original hypothesis and test
to a high degree of accuracy

shaft exit is specified with this accuracy, the
intersect point from the geometric hypothesis
can be compared on a CAD drawing. Doing
so yields a geometric intersect point located
51.83m North of the central axis and 81.00m
above the foundation platform floor. Therefore the proximity of the pyramid's construction from the geometry to the theoretically
constructed point is 1.7cm in a northerly
direction and 0.4cm vertically - both figures
falling close to the tolerance of 1.27cm of the
surveying data being used. It should be kept
in mind when contemplating this very close

the precise shape of the ellipse that we are
using, since any variation in the shape of
the ellipse will yield variations to the shaft's
exit point. This task can be performed most
informatively on the CAD drawing of the
pyramid, where the various ellipse radii
proportions can be varied and the resulting
exit locations plotted as a series of points.
The resulting theoretical geometric North
shaft exit points are shown below, a drawing
which is taken directly from the CAD original and which warrants explanation..

The North shaft is clearly shown,

The upper north
shaft geometry

This complex il-
lustration shows the
assortment of geo-
metric locations of
the geometry based
on the flattening of
the ellipse in use

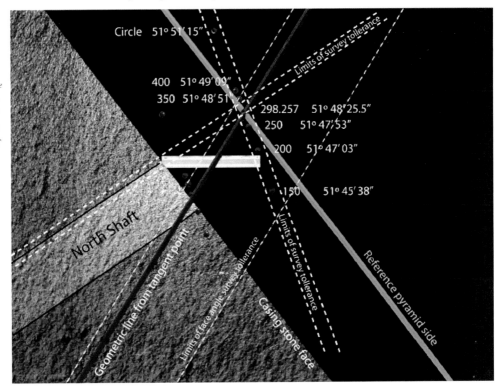

Circle   51° 51' 15"

400   51° 49' 09"
350   51° 48' 51"

298.257   51° 48' 25.5"
250   51° 47' 53"

200   51° 47' 03"

150   51° 45' 38"

Limits of survey tollerance

North Shaft

Geometric line from tangent point

Limits of face angle survey tollerance

Casing stone face

Limits of survey tollerance

Reference pyramid side

and the two dotted white lines which are parallel to the shaft's roof line are the limits of the vertical surveying errors reported by Petrie of +/- 1.5cm. The series of red dots contained within the second set of dotted white lines are the intersect points that would be created from using various shaped ellipses with a reciprocal polar flattening of the number accompanying them. By varying the ellipses' shape, the angle of the reference pyramid's face would alter, and the corresponding angles for each ellipse is shown next to each dot. A second series of red dots which can be seen much closer to the shaft are the corresponding points which would be created if the casing stone length of the pyramid was used as the initial reference datum in the calculations rather than the foundation platform. The blue line is the reference pyramid's face line, and the red line is the line from the tangent point on the ellipse which descends 81 m down to the base centre of the pyramid. There is also a 30cm ruler placed in the drawing to give an idea of scale. For the geometry to correctly concur with the survey

the intersect must fall, as it does, between the three sets of dotted lines and this target area which our geometric lines have hit is approximately nine square centimeters. We are still a long way from determining the exact details of the elliptical shape that the architects have used in the construction, but we know for sure that it will be very close indeed to the elliptical cross sectional shape of the Earth.

From this analysis we can state that if the overall hypothesis is correct, and if we are to stay within the tolerances of the surveying data of Petrie, then the polar flattening of the ellipse which was used by the architects falls within the range 1/295th to 1/330th. We appear to have extended the original hypothesis with a remarkable geometric fit to the pyramid and once again we need to find corroborating evidence which shows that this geometry is intentional on the part of the pyramid's architects and not just a highly improbable coincidence. This confirmation comes when the manner in which the angle of the North shaft was designed is considered.

Upper northern shaft angle

The construction of the upper northern shaft angle follows the same pattern of geometry

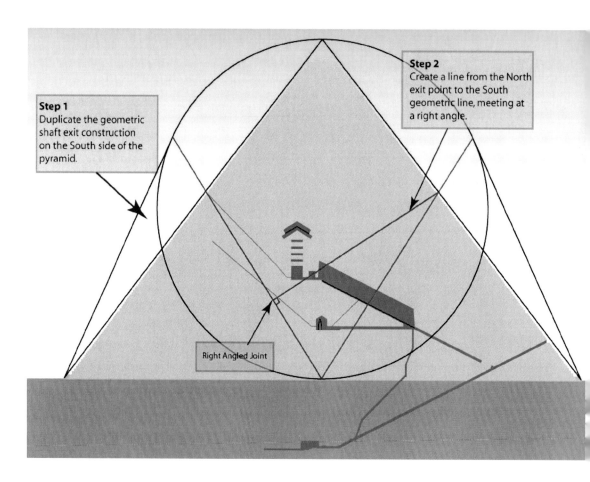

Step 1
Duplicate the geometric shaft exit construction on the South side of the pyramid.

Step 2
Create a line from the North exit point to the South geometric line, meeting at a right angle.

Right Angled Joint

North Shaft Angle

The geometric construction that we have just used to find the North shaft exit can also be used to determine the South shaft exit in a similar manner and with a very similar margin of error. To do so requires that a geometric construction line is also taken from the southern extremity of the foundation platform up to the tangent point on the Earth shaped ellipse on its South side and back down to the base centre. By connecting at a right angle the North shaft geometric exit point to the line which is used to locate the South shaft exit point , it is immediately apparent that we have determined the North shaft's angle of construction. This can be first verified visually and is shown in the illustration on the opposite page where the constructed shafts' roof line and that of the geometric line show no variance whatsoever in a diagram of this size.

This method of constructing the angle of this shaft could of course be performed without having first created the external ellipse by simply connecting the shaft exits down to the base centre. However if this were to be done, then the actual shaft exit points on the casing stone face would have to have been used, and the resulting shaft angle line would vary from the one shown.

The angle of the upper north shaft line when the construction is performed on a CAD drawing is 32° 37' 01" in comparison to that of the shaft floor reported by Gantenbrink in his survey drawings of 32° 36' 08"

showing a discrepancy of 53" of a degree, which relates to 2.5cm of linear discrepancy over a distance of 100m. Unfortunately Gantenbrink did not specify the type of inclinometers which were used in the robot to take the angular measurements and no error margins are reported in his work, so these two figures are difficult to compare. Currently in 2010 high quality inclinometers have a resolution of 10" of one degree and the lower cost portable ones 1' 48" of a degree, so it would be reasonable to deduce that at the time that the robot was built the resolution of the inclinometer must have been within these margins at the best. So our hypothesis is still fully intact and we have just entered into the pyramid's core and in so doing **found the mathematical entrance to the Great Pyramid of Giza**. Or to be more exact, we have just found the two entrances to the pyramid, one located on either face and which are currently described by Egyptologists as the shaft *exit* points. It will become clear as we continue our investigation through the structure that these are indeed entrances to the pyramid, and not exits as is currently thought, but in order to reduce the confusion down to a minimum I shall continue to use the classical descriptions of the pyramids architectural features throughout this book.

We have stuck rigidly to our hypothesis and methods of working to this point, and if we are to continue in such a manner then we have just come across and apparently enormous problem, although one that may not be immediately obvious. We have correctly identified the North shaft's angle by constructing a line which passes down the shaft, through the main chamber of the pyramid and out of its South side, meeting the south side's geometry in the middle of nowhere. There are no other points that we can justifiably use to terminate the shaft to the north of the main chamber and it appears that we have come to a logical dead end. Our last constructed point is the right angled joint which is situated amongst the core masonry of the pyramid, is completely inaccessible and an utterly illogical place to move on from. However, we have to remember that we appear to be dealing with an architectural masterpiece which has proceeded to this point in an immaculately logical manner. So if we are to trust the architects then we have only one piece of information which we can utilise, that being

Geometric grid system

To keep a consistent reference system a grid square can be overlaid on the geometry

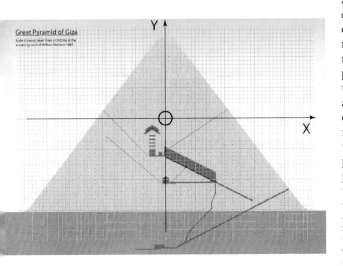

Great Pyramid of Giza
Scale drawing taken from a CAD file of the surveying work of William Petrie in 1883.

the North shaft angle. And it is at this point that the architectural design departs from being remarkable and enters the territory of the utterly extraordinary.

So far all of our calculations have been performed on a CAD programme, and all of the reported angles and lengths have been read from that programme. Computer programmes are not of course magical devices which compute the impossible, but are a collection of mathematical algorithms which are being rapidly performed in order to supply us with our tangent points and right angles. To understand how to proceed at this juncture we need to look into the mathematics that is being used within these CAD programmes and write down the geometric construction that we have made in the old fashioned way - using algebra. I would very much like to have presented this work without recourse to using algebraic mathematics, but it is simply not possible as you will see, since it is at the very heart of the design of this building.

The first step in determining the algebraic components of our construction to date is to set out a co-ordinate system which will be our reference grid throughout the rest of this work. Since the primary geometric shape in the architecture is the ellipse, then the origin of the co-ordinate system should be set in the centre of this ellipse on the pyramid's central axis and 73.44 metres above the foundation platform as shown in the illustration on the previous page. We should now go back to the start of our hypothesis and calculate algebraically the points and lines that we have created up to now, remembering that the whole geometric construction in based on the ellipse which has a semi-minor radius of b, and therefore the reference pyramid has a height of $2b$.

The starting point of the hypothesis is the North end of the foundation platform, and this point can be given the algebraic location $(x,-b)$, where x represents half of the foundation platform length. From the mathematics of the ellipse shown in the appendix we can calculate that the tangent point on the ellipse must have co-ordinates of

$$x_t = \frac{2a^2 x}{a^2 + x^2} \qquad yt = \frac{-b(a^2 - x^2)}{a^2 + x^2}$$

The line connecting the tangent point to the base centre of the pyramid on the North side has the equation

$$y = \frac{bx_t x}{a^2} - b$$

and therefore on the on the South side

$$y = \frac{-bx_t x}{a^2} - b$$

Since the upper North shaft is at right angles to this line, then it must have the gradient of

$$\text{North Shaft Gradient} = \frac{a^2}{bx_t}$$

You will recall from earlier that we introduced the algebraic quantity f into our calculation for the ellipse, where $f=a/b$ so that we could express all of the work in terms of the pyramid's height and the radii proportion of the Earth's ellipse. So the gradient of the upper North shaft when expressed using 'f' is

$$\textbf{North Shaft Gradient} = \frac{f^2 b}{x_t}$$

There are two quite remarkable points to note about this gradient. The first can be easily comprehended if you imagine that the ellipse is in fact a circle, making the value of f equal to 1. The gradient is then the ratio of the circle's radius to its quarter circumference or in other words it is an expression of 2/Pi. This can be easily checked on a calculator by finding the inverse tangent of 2/pi which is 32.482 degrees and clearly very close to the North shaft's surveyed angle. It also helps to explain why so many articles and studies of the Great Pyramid have included the value of Pi as being part of the structure, but have always contained small numerical variations from the actual value of Pi, the difference being the minute variation of the ellipse's shape from that of a circle.

The second point to note is that both the numerator and the denominator of the fraction are **rational measurable quantities** on the pyramid's architecture. The denominator is one half of the foundation platform length, and the numerator is half the pyramid's height multiplied by the radii proportion of the earth. Both of these distances can be drawn onto the cross sectional drawing of the pyramid starting at the shaft exit point, and the resulting line with its mid-point also marked is shown opposite. As can be seen in the diagram the length of the North shaft appears to be half of this line distance, a fact which is so extraordinary that a close up of

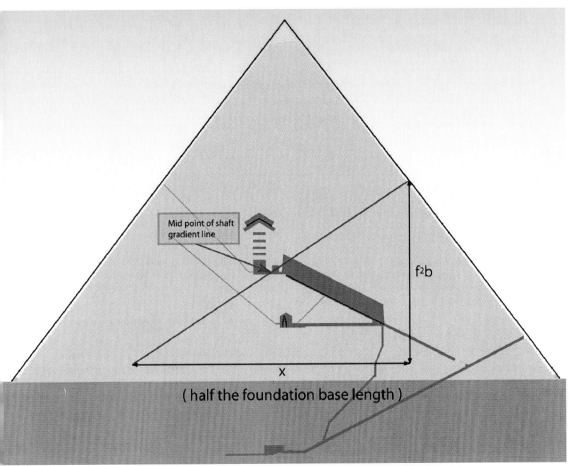

Mid point of shaft gradient line

f^2b

x

(half the foundation base length)

the geometric line's mid point area is required and is shown in the second illustration. For ease of viewing the geometric line is shown with its two halves in different colours, and the diagram clearly shows that the mid point of the line falls within the horizontal section of the shaft and close to the point where the inclined shaft begins. So it would appear that from our hypothesis not only have we found

the architectural design, but that the architects have employed the very same algebraic method for calculating the structural components of the building that we are using, suggesting that we are headed in the right direction.

To understand exactly what the architects are doing with this shaft construction we need to also form the South shaft in exactly the same manner. The South shaft of the pyramid is very simple to create, as we have already determined its exit point on the virtual pyramid face and the shaft has an angle of exactly 45 degrees. By the same reasoning employed on the North shaft its algebraic gradient

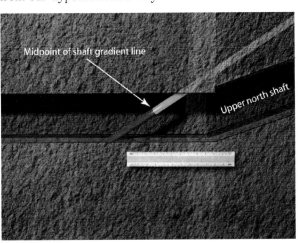

Midpoint of shaft gradient line

Upper north shaft

$$\text{South Shaft Gradient} = \frac{f^2b}{f^2b}$$

since it emerges at the same height as the North shaft, and the mid point of this gradient line is situated in the horizontal section of

In through the out door   153

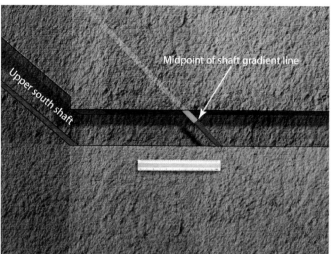

Midpoint of shaft gradient line

Upper south shaft

the North chamber wall is double the distance from the southern geometric point to the South chamber wall, the variance between the two measurements being 3.75mm and well within the surveying tolerances with which we are working. As a consequence, not only is it apparent that the geometric points are intentional, but much more significantly that **the chamber is positioned in relation to these points** and not the other way around, since the points themselves are deliberately not fabricated into the stonework and have been left floating in the middle of the shaft. Indeed this is the very reason *why* the shaft gradient midpoints are left floating - so that it is immediately apparent to the observer that the main chamber is positioned from them and not vica-verca. This seemingly innocuous statement has significant consequences.

If the chamber was placed in relation to the geometric shaft construction, as is apparently the case, then when the pyramid was constructed the chamber walls would have to have been placed to within 5.5mm of accuracy and to do so the builders *must* have been using sophisticated surveying techniques allowing them to measure the horizontal wall offsets with this amount of accuracy. It would also mean that the builders must have been working to a pre-determined architectural design which incorporated all of the mathematics that has so far been discussed. The implications in these statements to our current understanding of the pyramids does not require much further clarification as it is immediately apparent that this level of engineering could not have been carried out by

the South shaft as shown in the illustration above.

So we now have two locations given to us by the geometry and the apparently puzzling fact that neither of these points coincides with the stonework at the end of the horizontal shaft sections. What would be useful is some confirmation that these points are intentionally placed in these rather unusual positions in the horizontal shaft sections, and once again the architecture provides exactly that.

You will recall from our determination of the shaft exit points on the pyramid face that the roof level of the shaft was to be used as a reference line, since the bottom of the shaft does not exist. The very same principle has been used for these horizontal sections of the shafts, and using a design of masonry which is unique in the shaft's construction the architects have indicated that neither the roof or the base of the horizontal section of the shaft should be used as the reference line. The stonework construction for these shaft sections is shown in the illustration, with the roof section provided by the core masonry of the pyramid and the base section vertically split into two parts. This by itself is hardly sufficient corroborating evidence to suggest that the geometric point is intentional, but what is about to come certainly does.

The first job after creating these two shaft gradient mid points is to measure the distance between them, and also the distance to the North and South walls of the pyramid's main chamber. The results of these measurements are shown in the illustration opposite in which it is apparent that the distance from the northern geometric point to

Upper stone

West side stone

East side stone

*The main chamber of the pyra-
mid shown with the geometric
model of the earth contained
within it*

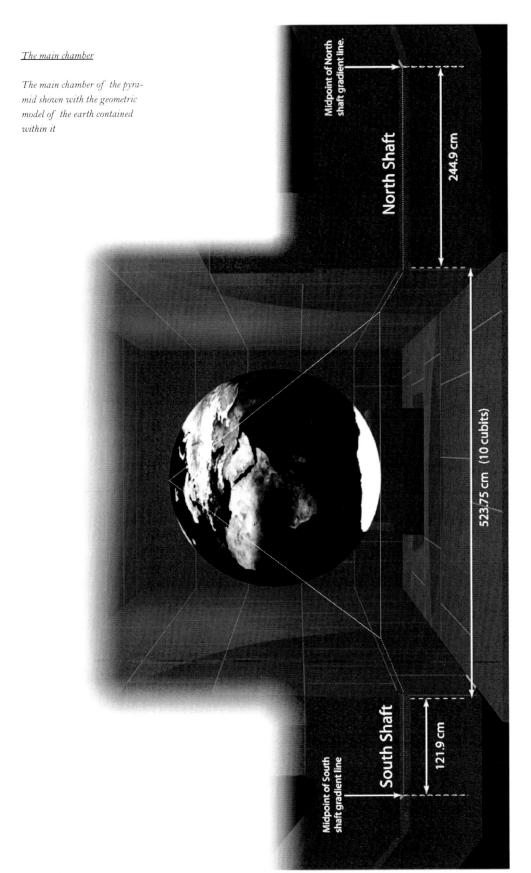

Midpoint of North
shaft gradient line.

North Shaft

244.9 cm

523.75 cm (10 cubits)

Midpoint of South
shaft gradient line

South Shaft

121.9 cm

the Ancient Egyptians.

A second consequence is that the bends in the shafts which are reported by Gentenbrink in the first 10% of both the South and North shafts are there for one reason alone - so that the geometric construction cannot be deduced from investigating from inside the chamber. The only way of ending up with the accurate analysis which we now have is by entering the shafts at the pyramid's face and working down the shaft, meaning that the lower bent sections are designed as a decoy device for anyone starting from the inside out. This would further imply that if the architects designed this building with the intention of its geometric principles being discovered, then they must have had to assume that those people discovering it would have been able to measure the shaft angles with a high degree of accuracy, which adds more fascinating consequence to what we are looking at.

So with such a significant discovery, we need to once again look for corroborating evidence. In the manner that we have used so far we need to carry on the logical sequence that is being presented in the architecture and look at the horizontal line stretching across the main chamber from the North to South shaft entrances, a line which is exactly 10 cubits long or 5.2375 metres. Since we are sticking rigidly to the opening hypothesis and cannot add anything whatsoever to it, then we need to look back at our work so far and find the only horizontal line that we have used in our work to date to understand how the architects put this section together. The horizontal line that we have already used is the base of the pyramid, and is the only logical item from the hypothesis that can be used when trying to progress from this point. The implication in the architecture is that the line joining the shaft entrances in the main chamber should be taken as representing the base line of the pyramid. The architects are asking us to build a small model of the pyramid itself onto this horizontal line for a reason which is currently not obvious in the same manner that we built a model inside the chambers of Unas.

The resulting construction is shown in the illustration on which the model of the pyramid with its base stretching across the chamber has been placed between the South and North walls, shown with a dotted white line, and the implicit model of the Earth constructed and on display in the chamber. The purpose of the whole of this construction is two-fold, allowing us to check that our sur-

veying is as accurate as the architects would want at this stage and then forcing us to place a model of the Earth inside the chamber.

When this construction is analysed in detail, there appears to be a small discrepancy on Petrie's surveying work for the main chamber, and if we have correctly interpreted the architectural design, then Petrie has the main chamber of the pyramid offset by 3.75mm to the North. In his work Petrie reports that the North-South error margin in this area of the pyramid is 20.3mm and so we can justifiably correct Petrie's errors and state that the whole of the Upper chamber surveying needs shifting 3.75mm to the South. The question then naturally arises as to why the architects would want us to make such a fine adjustment at this stage, and implies that the exact positioning of the chamber is highly significant in the overall design of the building.   What we are left with at the end of this geometric journey into the Great Pyramid of Giza is a model of the Earth suspended in the main chamber, and offset from the central axis of the building by what we know is a specific and highly accurately determined distance. The corroborating evidence as to why this small model of the Earth has been placed in the main chamber will not become apparent until we have finished our voyage around the internal structure of the pyramid and made our way back outside. For now we should finish this section of the analysis of the Great Pyramid and leave the model of the Earth suspended in mid air in the main chamber, hovering delicately just above the coffin (a poignant image in the age of climate change). We have come to the end of the mathematics which has taken us from the base end of the pyramid, in through the shaft exit point, and perfectly placed us inside the main chamber with an accuracy measured in millimeters.

As with all work it is worth going back over what we have just calculated and observed to check that the mathematics and logic is correct. If you do so, you will find that there is not one error in the logic, not one deviation from the original hypothesis and all of the structure fits perfectly into place with the geometry. However, if you really search deeply into the whole of this chapter then you find one very subtle point which we have overlooked. It is a tiny assumption in the algebraic mathematics which appears to have no consequence whatsoever to the work we have performed, but once the oversight has been detected then the key to the lower chamber in the pyramid, known by Egyptologists as the 'Queens Chamber', presents itself to us.

And that is where we are now going, down to the other chamber within the pyramid's structure to see just how diligently the architects have been working.

In through the out door

FINDING YOUR ROOTS

The lower southern shaft

The geometry of the lower southern shaft is based on that of the upper shafts

You will recall from the chapter "The Invisible Pyramid' that the height of the pyramid construction was determined entirely from the length of the foundation platform by making the hypothesis that the length of one side of the foundation represents half the elliptical circumference of the Earth. The mathematical formula that was used to perform the calculation was a derivation of the ellipse circumference formula of Ramanujan, and on closer inspection of his formula you will see that we have overlooked some of the mathematics during our work.

$$\pi\left(3(a+b) - \sqrt{(3a+b)(a+3b)}\right)$$

Ramanujan's formula is shown here and it quite clearly relies upon the use of a square root sign in the second portion of the formula. When calculating the circumference of an ellipse in this manner you are bound to end up with two different answers since there are always two results to taking a square root. One of the answers correctly gives the elliptical circumference and the other gives an answer which is incorrect and is discarded during the process of calculating the mathematics.

So when we used the formula 'in reverse' to deduce the dimensions of the radii of the ellipse which was formed from the base of the pyramid, we must also have thrown away an incorrect result for the height of the ellipse due to the square root sign. If we are pedantic in our algebraic calculations (and we need to be) then we should state that the minor diameter of the ellipse which is calculated from this formula when applied to the foundation platform base length is either 146.878 m or 29.376m. The larger value is the correct height of the reference

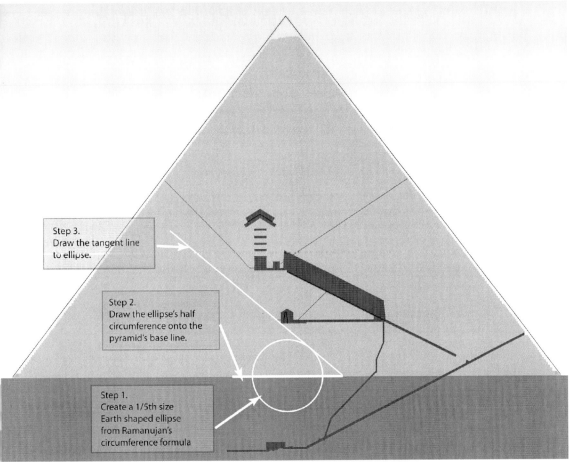

Step 3.
Draw the tangent line to ellipse.

Step 2.
Draw the ellipse's half circumference onto the pyramid's base line.

Step 1.
Create a 1/5th size Earth shaped ellipse from Ramanujan's circumference formula

pyramid and formed from the negative square root, and the smaller value formed from the positive square root we choose to discard because it is of no interest to us. However, we have learnt so far that the Great Pyramid of Giza contains some quite remarkable architecture and that the pyramid of Unas is full of deliberately constructed illusions, and it would be unwise in the extreme to discard any part of the mathematics just because we do not think it to be of any use to us. What we should do with this smaller ellipse, which is 4.99998 times smaller than the main ellipse of the Earth, is to place it onto our architectural structure and look to see if it corresponds to any of the architectural features of the building, rather than simply discard it.

When this smaller ellipse is placed with it's centre on the midpoint of the base line, which is quite acceptable with regard to the hypothesis as this point is part of our opening statement, then we can also draw onto the CAD drawing the ellipse's related circumference which will of course be 1/4.99998th of the foundation platform length. We can then start a geometric construction from the end

of this base line to the tangent point on the small ellipse, and by doing so we reveal what appears to be the gradient line of the lower southern shaft as shown below.

We are now back into familiar territory and need to look straight away to see if we have any corroborating evidence or whether this construction is simply a highly improbable coincidence or deliberate design work. However, we are now highly restricted in what we can use for supporting evidence, as whatever we use must be compatible with the logical approach that we used for the upper shafts. You will recall that the length of the upper northern shaft was formed by considering its gradient and then drawing the lengths of the algebraic numerator and denominator onto the geometric drawing. We therefore now have an acid test to determine whether the geometric structure of this building is arbitrary or carefully planned, by applying this same algebraic principle to this lower shaft.

The algebraic workings for the gradient of the lower southern shaft are available in the mathematics appendix and from them

The length of the lower southern shaft

By aligning the shaft by its midpoint and algebraic gradient components, the length can be calculated

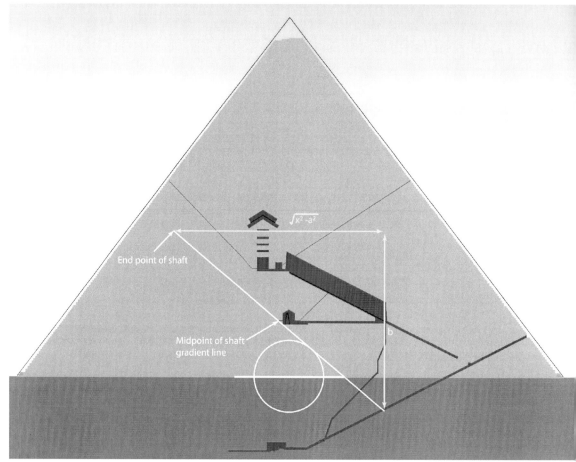

End point of shaft

Midpoint of shaft
gradient line

$\sqrt{x^2-a^2}$

b

we find that the gradient of the tangent line that we have just drawn is

$$\frac{b}{\sqrt{x_1^2 - a^2}}$$

where a,b refer to the radii of the original ellipse formed around the pyramid. We also know from the logic in the upper shafts that we have to place this line with its mid point at the point where the gradient line meets the horizontal shaft section. Now at this stage we do not have a horizontal line to work with, so we have no choice but to use the same system as we used upstairs and select the horizontal section of the shaft in the lower chamber. From Gantenbrink's work we can see that the shaft construction on these horizontal sections differs from that of the upper chamber, and the floor line of the shaft is being given as the reference datum by the architects as shown in the illustration below.

The resulting drawing of the geometry is shown in the previous illustration where it is quite clear that the length of the lower southern shaft is the same as half of the algebraic gradient line from which it is constructed. Without doubt we have just detected the system for the lower southern shaft construction and with it have confirmed that the hypothesis is correct.

On first appearances we appear to have very rapidly found out how the lower southern shaft was formed, but when we look closer we will see that we have a small error in the geometry. The angle of the shaft that we have just created is 39.5252 degrees and the angle of the shaft measured by Gantenbrink was 39.6078 degrees. This is quite a significant error and would represent a linear misalignment of 8.6cm over the length of the 60m shaft, a quantity which we know would not be acceptable to the architects. However, the length and placement of the shaft both look to be perfect, so the possibility arises that there is a small adjustment required in our construction that we may have missed.

The small adjustment in question is rather remarkable, since by rotating the Earth shaped ellipse through 23° in an anticlockwise direction the tangent line is elevated slightly and ends up with a gradient of 39.59°. Doing so reduces the linear error between the geometry and surveying work to 2cm, a figure which is much more acceptable than previously and most likely attributable to a further sophistication in the design that we have not yet detected. The angle of rotation for the Earth shaped ellipse has not been chosen arbitrarily - it is the axial tilt of the Earth, more technically referred to by astronomers as the Earth's obliquity to the ecliptic. The adjustment of the lower southern shaft angle in this manner is remarkable, and as usual we need to find corroborating evidence that this rotation is intentional on the part of the architects.

The lower northern shaft has not been considered yet, and of all of the shaftways within the pyramid is has proved the most difficult of all to measure for the Egyptologists. The first attempt was made by Gantenbrink in 1993 when he managed to send his robotic surveying mechanism up the first 18 metres of the shaft where he encountered a bend in the construction. He was unable to progress further, and it was not until September 2002 that the next attempt to measure this shaft was made. A team of engineers constructed a new robot and supported by the National Geographic television channel and the Egyptian department of Antiquities, the whole of the shaftway was eventually mapped out. The exact survey data has never been made public,

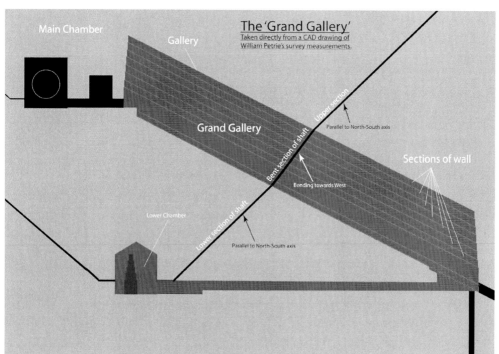

The 'Grand Gallery'
Taken directly from a CAD drawing of William Petrie's survey measurements.

Main Chamber

Gallery

Grand Gallery

Bent section of shaft

Upper section

Parallel to North-South axis

Sections of wall

Bending towards West

Lower section of shaft

Lower Chamber

Parallel to North-South axis

however there are sufficient details available in the public domain to be able to determine the nature of this shaft.

We know from Gantenbrink's CAD drawings that the shaft starts to turn at exactly 18.14 m from the chamber wall, the first 1.93 metres being on the horizontal section and the next 16.21m up the inclined shaft. We also know from Gantenbrink's CAD drawings that he was uncertain of the exact angle of the shaft, but has drawn it at 43.69°, implying that only the final precision is missing from the measurement. It is this partially measured lower northern shaft that has been shown on all of the previous drawings in this book, and the bend point appears to coincide perfectly with the floor section of the gallery when the pyramid structure is viewed from the East. The reason for the rest of the shafts data being withheld by the Egyptian authorities is not quite clear at present, but luckily the missing shaft information was disclosed by the director of the Egyptian Antiquities commission, Dr. Zahi Hawass, in a website article published in 2005. In that article he stated that :

"*We also sent the robot into the northern airshaft and found that after 20 m the shaft bent and continued for another 8 m. This bend may indicate that it was designed to miss the grand gallery and it also explains that it was carved during the construc-*

tion of the pyramid. The robot continued for another 60 m and then stopped in front of a door with two copper handles. It is the same distance as the door in the southern shaft with two copper handles."

Whilst hardly constituting a piece of archaeological surveying data, it does provide sufficient evidence when combined with the photographs taken by Gantenbrink inside the shaftway in 1993 to fully reconstruct this area of the pyramid shafts. What is particularly noteworthy once the shaft's construction is understood is that in the article the 8m section that Hawass describes is 8m in projection - which means that Hawass must be quoting the information from an architectural drawing and not from the raw data of the robot's linear traverse, which would have been closer to 9m as the shaftway bends away to the west during this section. It is this piece of information which makes one realise immediately why the Egyptian authorities have not released the full surveying data for this shaft - they are most likely stunned by what they are looking at. The illustration above shows a close up of the shaft section in question and the perfect correlation with the gallery of the pyramid which would be impossible to have been constructed accidentally.

Having determined the lower northern shaft section positioning in this way, we can now go back to the small Earth shaped

Great Pyramid of Giza

Scale drawing taken from a CAD file of the
surveying work of William Petrie in 1883

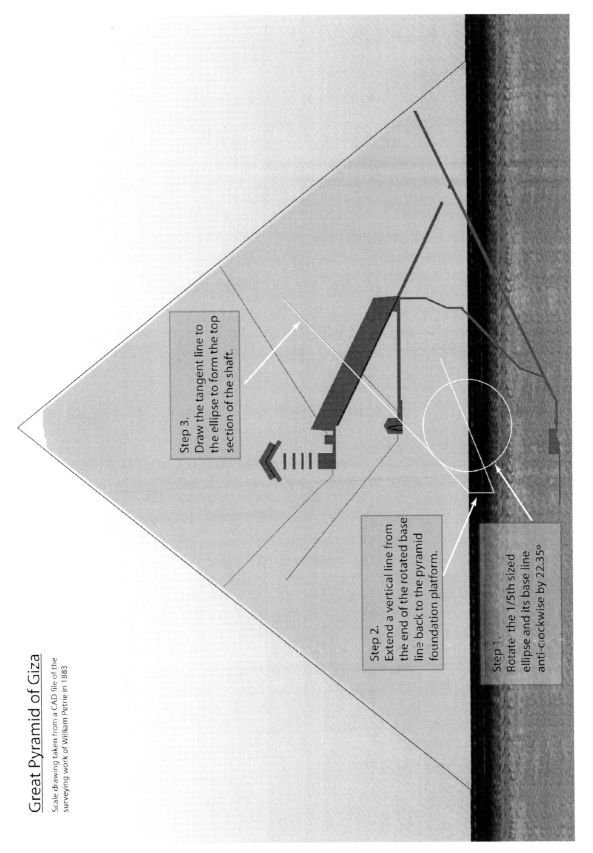

Step 3.
Draw the tangent line to
the ellipse to form the top
section of the shaft.

Step 2.
Extend a vertical line from
the end of the rotated base
line back to the pyramid
foundation platform.

Step 1.
Rotate the 1/5th sized
ellipse and its base line
anti-clockwise by 22.35°

ellipse which we rotated to form the lower southern shaft gradient and examine whether the logic of that rotation also fits in with the northern shaft construction. If we leave the Earth shaped ellipse in its rotated position, and also rotate the half circumference line, which we originally left lying on the base line of the pyramid when we examined the southern shaft, we come across a perfect geometric fit for the northern shaft's upper section. By taking a vertical line up from the end of the rotated half circumference line to the pyramid's base line, and then using this a the start of our ellipse tangent line, the upper section of the northern shaft is immediately carved out by the geometry as shown in the illustration on the previous page. It is probably this geometric fit above all of the others that tells us that we are quite definitely not dealing with ancient Egyptian architects and builders.

The dual use of the rotated ellipse which has to fit both of these elaborately created shaftways is precision engineering and must have involved surveying techniques of the highest quality during the construction of the monument. It is incomprehensible that these two shaftways could fit such an imaginative geometric design by chance, but in case we are in any doubt even at this stage, the architects have provided further corroborating evidence which will leave us in no doubt

whatsoever.

In the creation of these two pieces of geometry we have drawn two tangent lines which cross over just below the lower chamber in the pyramid, commonly referred to as the 'Queens chamber' by Egyptologists. Close inspection of the tangent line intersections shows that their horizontal intersect point is in a vertical line with the carved out section of the lower chamber's Eastern wall. In fact the carving, known as the 'Niche', serves one particular purpose - to mark out this intersect point and allow the correct diagnosis of the shaft geometry. The geometric design of this intersect point and the positioning of the 'niche' is shown below. (The niche also serves a secondary purpose which becomes apparent later in the work).

The second piece of evidence is dramatic, and allows us to look further into the architects technical abilities as well as confirming the validity of all of the geometry shown up to this point. The original geometric line which defined the upper shaft exit points crosses over the lower southern shaft at a point which can be clearly seen on illustration opposite This cross over point only occurs in the theoretical geometry, but has been clearly marked off inside the lower southern shaftway by a small horizontal shift in the shaftway's bricks and a red stripe down

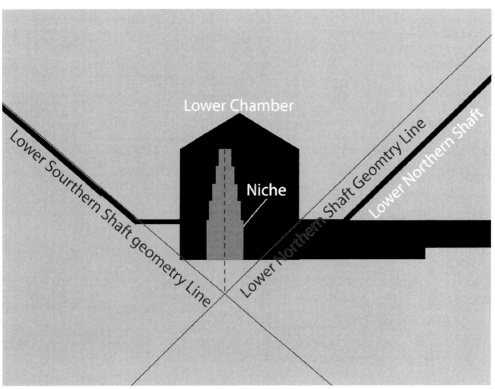

The niche in the lower chamber

The central axis of the niche coincides with the intersection of the geometry from the two lower shafts

The marked off crossover point

The location of the point in the lower southern shaft where the geometric lines cross over

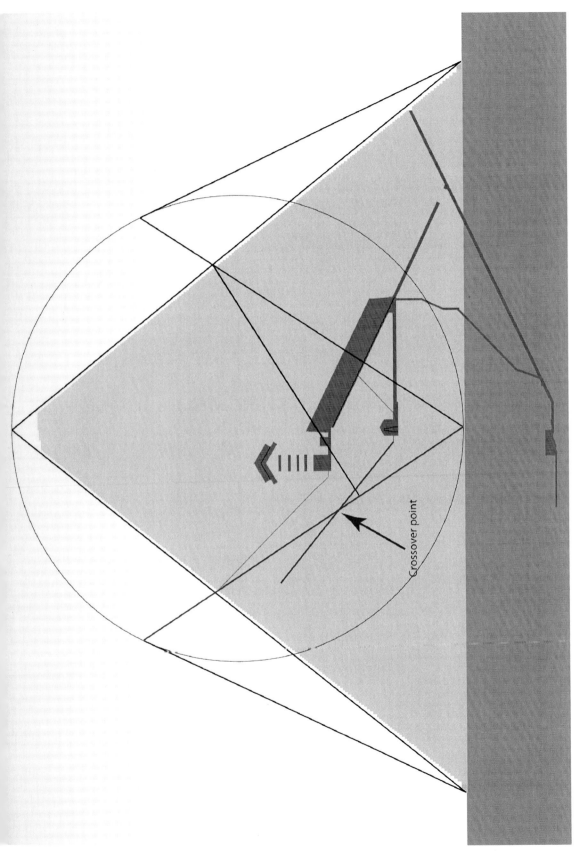

Crossover point

the shaftway wall as shown in the diagram This point in the shaft was remarked upon by Gantenbrink on his website and its position was carefully measured during the robot survey and corresponds to perfection with the geometric location of the intersect point. The implications from this small architectural feature are immense as implicit in the design is that the red paint line marking off the theoretical intersect point **was designed to be found**. This suggest that the architects expected someone at some point in the future to be able to view this paint mark, a task which is only possible for us through automated inspection, since the shaft is only 20cm wide and high. **It is one of the smaller features of the Great Pyramid, but one which has some of the most profound implications associated with it**.

It is at this point in the comprehension of the Great Pyramid of Giza that one has to accept that we are not dealing with what was previously supposed to be a construction by ancient people. The evidence already presented to this point precludes any possibility whatsoever that a society with the technical abilities of the Ancient Egyptians could possibly have designed, surveyed or constructed this building. Whilst I appreciate that this fact is quite difficult to absorb with the historical education that most of us have received, it is non the less factual, and I would recommend at this point that any reader who is still in any doubt should re-read the evidence presented so far, as it is compelling and beyond doubt. (The mathematical proof of the construction of the lower shafts is explained in the mathematics appendix, the contents of which are vital to the comprehension of the pyramid's true purpose.)

We now need to progress on to the next section of the pyramid which requires analysis, and to determine where we should go next we simply need to follow our standard procedure, and look at the last piece of information that was presented to us. The lower northern shaft has two bend points in it, which perfectly coincide with the massive gallery in the heart of the pyramid. It is therefore to this section of the building that we now go, and where we are about to come across the most masterful piece of building work that we will see in the pyramid.

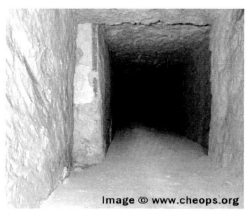

The dramatic builder's mark

The theoretical cross over point between the geometry and the shaft has been marked on the shaft wall with a red line.

ONE SMALL STEP

Located at the heart of the Great Pyramid of Giza is a massive inclined room, named in the 19th century as the 'Grand Gallery'. It is an elaborate construction consisting of a sloping floor either side of which are bench like sections made from stone, with walls which taper off towards the roof of the room so that the ceiling is only half as wide as the floor. The wall sections are not flat, but consist of seven sections of stonework, each section protruding slightly over the one below so that the roof takes on its narrower aspect. One of the sections of overlapping stonework on both of the side walls, the third from the bottom or fourth from the top, contains a carved groove running all the way along it and is remarked upon and measured by Petrie in his work. The roof itself is formed from many angled blocks of stonework each one embedded slightly into the side walls so that in profile from the East it looks like the teeth of a saw. The whole of this construction is attached at its lower end to a sloping passageway, and at it's top to the horizontal passageway which leads to the pyramid's main chamber. The grand gallery construction is shown in diagram on the next page.

To understand how this room was constructed we need to first of all carefully read the surveying work of William Petrie with regard to its angle and that of the sloping passageway to which it connects. Petrie states that the passageway at the bottom of the gallery has an average angle of 26° 2' 30" and that the gallery itself has an angle of 26° 16' 40". This slight variation between the two sections is entirely deliberate on the part of the architects and facilitates the full analysis of this portion of the building once the discrepancy between them is understood. What we must first determine is the geometric construction which was used to form the passageway angle, using nothing more than the principles already determined from our starting hypothesis, and that can be accomplished in the following manner.

The original construction of the primary Earth shaped ellipse, which was determined from the foundation length of the pyramid's base, positioned that ellipse on the outside of the building structure. If that same shape of ellipse, the polar cross section of the Earth, is reduced in size so that it is made to fit precisely *inside* the geometric pyramid construction then a similar set of geometry to that used previously can be constructed which forms the angle and position of the lower section of passageway. As with the previous geometric constructions, the algebraic geometry of this section is vital in the analysis of the pyramid's architecture, and is shown in the mathematics appendix.

This geometric construction, shown in the illustration on the following page, gives an algebraic value for the gradient of the passageway angle which, when evaluated using the pyramid's assumed principal datum of a foundation platform perimeter of 1765 cubits, gives an angle for the passage of 26° 1' 34". This compares well with the reported value from Petrie's surveying of 26° 2' 30", although we are probably now at a stage in the work where the comparisons with Petrie's work serve more to show how accurate he was with his surveying, rather than confirm that what we are looking at is correct. What we need to determine next is how the gallery floor angle was constructed, and for this we have to return to the main chamber of the pyramid.

You will recall that in the main chamber we left a model of the Earth suspended in mid-air in the middle of the room, a model which was formed from taking the width of the chamber as representing the base of the pyramid and reconstructing the pyramid's sides, and hence the Earth shaped ellipse, in the centre of that chamber. At the time we could not take the geometry and logic as to why it has been placed there any further since we did not have the rest of the pyramid in place. We are now in a position to continue the logic of the master room of the pyramid and join it up with that of the gallery.

In the main chamber, having formed the mini-pyramid between the chamber walls, the logic presents us with just one point in the room from which we can progress, that being the apex of the mini-pyramid, the same point as the 'north pole' of the model of the Earth which we also placed there. Close inspection of the gallery's architecture and that of the main

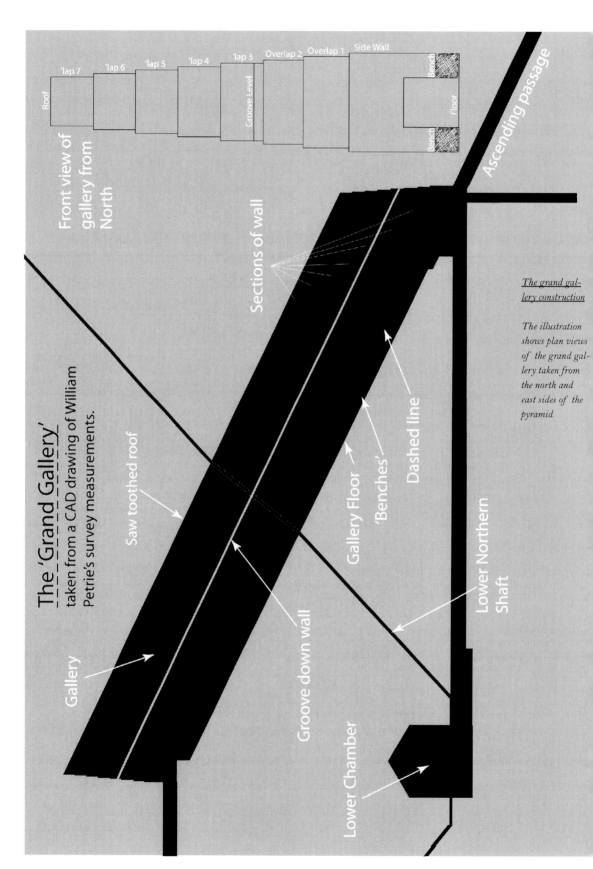

The 'Grand Gallery'

taken from a CAD drawing of William Petrie's survey measurements.

Front view of gallery from North

Roof
'lap 7
'lap 6
'lap 5
'lap 4
'lap 3
Groove Level
Overlap 2
Overlap 1
Side Wall
Bench
Floor
Bench

Sections of wall

Ascending passage

The grand gallery construction

The illustration shows plan views of the grand gallery taken from the north and east sides of the pyramid

Saw toothed roof

Gallery

Groove down wall

Gallery Floor 'Benches'

Dashed line

Lower Northern Shaft

Lower Chamber

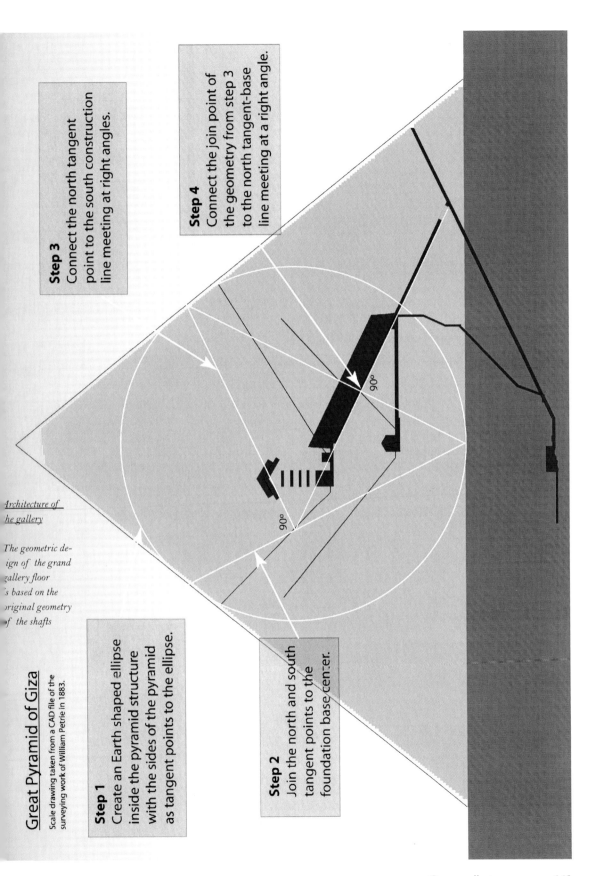

Great Pyramid of Giza

Scale drawing taken from a CAD file of the surveying work of William Petrie in 1883.

Step 1
Create an Earth shaped ellipse inside the pyramid structure with the sides of the pyramid as tangent points to the ellipse.

Step 2
Join the north and south tangent points to the foundation base center.

Step 3
Connect the north tangent point to the south construction line meeting at right angles.

Step 4
Connect the join point of the geometry from step 3 to the north tangent-base line meeting at a right angle.

*Architecture of
the gallery*

The geometric design of the grand gallery floor is based on the original geometry of the shafts

90°

90°

chamber reveals that the geometry continues horizontally from the top of the Earth model towards the North, bypasses the small 'antechamber' where the locking mechanism is located, and comes out at the exact point in the gallery where the lower edge of the groove is located on the side walls of the gallery, as shown below. This connection is found by comparing the exact position of the top of the mini-pyramid calculated from the algebraic geometry with the groove position reported in Petrie's surveying work.

It is at this point that the architects require us to use our own logical analysis and powers of deduction to progress, since we now need to determine the angle of the groove down the gallery wall and we do not know what that angle is. This is also the point where the architects incorporate probably the most obvious use of deception and concealment in the whole of the pyramid which will cause the untrained eye to miss the architecture if one was to simply rely upon assumptions from the surveying data.

You will recall that Petrie reported that the gallery floor angle is 26° 16' 40" but what he did not measure was the angle of the groove in the wall, the angle of each of the overlapping wall sections, or the angle of the roof. It has always been assumed that they were the all the same, and it is this very assumption which the architects are relying upon to hide the geometry of this section of the pyramid from even the most diligent of observers such as Petrie. It is also the reason why they made the room so tall and incorporated a saw tooth pattern into the roof, making the roof almost inaccessible and secondly, if anyone were to construct a set of ladders to reach the roof, the slope angle of the roof is not measurable by optical surveying methods. In addition, they included the benches into the gallery floor and finished off the tops of them highly irregularly so that it is not possible to measure from the groove or any of the overlapping wall sections back down to the floor using a plumb line, as can be clearly seen in the view of the gallery from the North shown in the previous diagram. This is precisely why Petrie was unable to measure these values and, as all before him had also done, **assumed that the groove and the wall sections were all of the same angle as the gallery floor.** This is not a mistake on the part of Petrie and other surveyors, but a piece of genius on the part of the architects.

To solve this section of the pyramid our logical analysis needs to stick rigidly to *only that information that we know*, that being the geometrically constructed angle of the lower

Connecting the main chamber to the gallery

The groove on the gallery wall connects through to the geometry in the main chamber

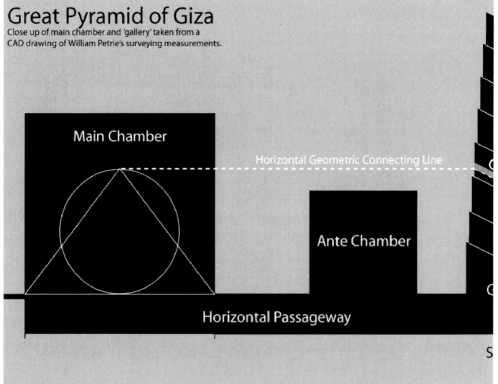

Great Pyramid of Giza
Close up of main chamber and 'gallery' taken from a
CAD drawing of William Petrie's surveying measurements.

Main Chamber

Horizontal Geometric Connecting Line

Ante Chamber

Horizontal Passageway

S

passageway, and the fact that the gallery floor is of a different angle. Applying logic to this situation dictates that the only possible angle for the groove down the wall of the gallery is that of the lower passageway angle, since at this stage it is the only angle which we have in our possession from the geometric analysis. It is a logical assumption that we must take, but one which proves to be entirely correct and allows us to continue our analysis of the rest of the room.

We are not quite ready yet to analyse the angles of the gallery as we need to understand one more piece of information before we do. What we will we require is a more detailed understanding of the cubit measure that was used inside the pyramid. We have addressed the cubit previously and explained that Petrie calculated its value as 52.38cm and that this value was based on an assumption. The assumption that he made was that the main chamber of the pyramid was the most important part of the building and therefore contained the most accurate value of the cubit. It is however the grand gallery that we are now studying that is the main section of this monument, and it is fascinating to take note of the fact that Petrie calculated the value of the cubit inside the gallery as being 20.605 inches or 52.337cm. The reason that this is fascinating is that we are about to determine the exact value of the cubit, and Petrie's surveyed value within the gallery varies by less than four thousandths of a millimetre from the correct value - a quite extraordinary achievement for

The top of the Great Pyramid

The surveying disk which is located on top of the Great Pyramid is shown in this photograph

a surveyor working by candlelight in the late 1800s.

Defining the Cubit

By now it should be abundantly clear that the Great Pyramid of Giza has origins which are quite extraordinary, and so the following determination of the value of the cubit, whilst clearly impossible for the ancient Egyptians to have performed, is more than plausible for the level of scientific knowledge already on display.

If we go back to the most fundamental property of the pyramid, we know that it is located in Egypt just to the west of Cairo. Its exact location is registered on the governmental geographic survey of Egypt as it has been used as a reference point for map making in Egypt for years due to the wonderful panoramic view from its apex stretching for miles in all directions. On the top of the pyramid, at a position that is as close as possible to the pyramid's central vertical axis is a small brass surveying disk and which is shown in the diagram. This disk was used by the Ancient Egypt Research Associates (A.E.R.A.) during their detailed survey of the Giza plateau and its exact geographic location is reported by them (http://www. aeraweb.org/gpmp_grid.asp) as being 29° 58' 44.3830" North and 31° 07' 57.0194" East when measured on the Helmert Spheroid of Reference. This reference ellipsoid is based on a 1906 measurement of the Earth's shape, and so is of little use to a modern GPS analysis of the plateau. The value that was adopted for this work was taken directly from the satellite photography and has a nominal value on the GRS84 ellipsoid of

29° 58' 44.96"   North
31° 08' 03.05"   East

If we convert the latitude of the pyramid into radian measure rather than the more traditional degree measure shown above, we find that the latitude of the Great Pyramid is 0.52323497 radians north of the equator. You may have noticed that this value is remarkably close to the metric value of the cubit measured by Petrie and

29° 58' 44.383" North
31° 07' 57.101" East
(Helmert Reference Ellipsoid)

immediately draws our attention to the fact that the cubit may well be defined from the radian value angular measure of the pyramid's latitude. Whilst the possibility that the architects of the Great Pyramid knew the buildings exact latitude may well appear ridiculous on first sight, one needs to remember that the hypothesis that we are following is still fully intact. And if the hypothesis is still intact then we still have a perfectly shaped Earth as the starting geometry, meaning that the latitude of the Great Pyramid would definitely be known by whoever built these monuments. Until such time as the hypothesis falls apart through scientific testing, then the knowledge of the latitude of the pyramid is implicit within it.

Since the unit of measure to which the radian latitude of the pyramid is so similar is the meter, we need to look back at the origins of the metric system which were explained in chapter one. The meter was *intended* to be one ten millionth of the distance from the north pole to the equator, but due to the manner in which the French scientists measured it they mis-calculated and left us with a distance from the north pole to the equator of 10,001,965.72 metres. If the architects of the Great Pyramid intended their measurement unit to be also based on one ten millionth of the distance from the north pole to the equator, then the calculation we need to perform to obtain the value of the cubit, if it really is derived from the latitude of the pyramid, is relatively straight forward. If we multiply the radian measure of the pyramid's latitude by the metric distance from pole to equator and divide the result back down by ten million, we end up with a definition of the cubit as being 0.5233350 metres or 52.33350 cm, and this, remarkable as it first appears, is exactly how the cubit has been defined by the architects.

It is the value that varies from Petrie's calculation by a mere 4 thousandths of a millimetre and one which, as with every other aspect of the pyramid's most important features, **is backed up with substantial corroborating evidence**. This corroborating evidence however is so remarkable that it will not be until later in this book, when we have fully analysed the rest of the Giza plateau, that the explanation can be understood. What is worth noting for now is that had the French correctly measured the size of the Earth and thereby correctly defined the meter, then the latitude of the pyramid in radians and the value of the cubit in meters would have been exactly the same.

What is of greater significance at this stage is to realise that we now have an incredibly precise definition of the cubit to work with and most importantly that the cubit measure is directly related to angular measure in radians. It is this second point that is vital to the comprehension of not only this pyramid but also the whole of the rest of the system stretching across the Giza plateau and beyond. The logic of why the architects worked in radian measure will be that degree measure is a man-made concept for dividing a circle into segments, and the radian measure is a natural system and one which would be understood by any mathematically developed

The top wall of the gallery

The logical construction of the gallery wall ends can be deduced from the architecture

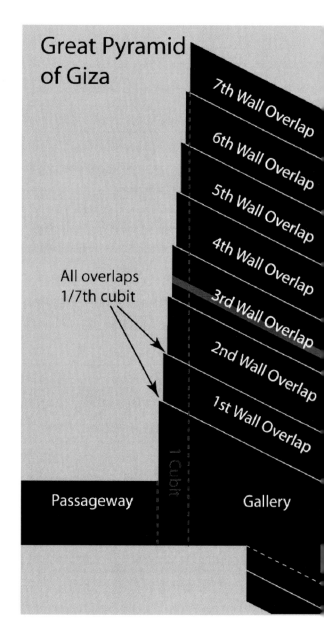

society and therefore a natural choice when trying to explain architectural concepts over large time spans - it does not rely upon units of measurement as it is an entirely natural ratio. Armed with both the value of the cubit and the concept behind its creation we can now continue our analysis of the 'grand gallery' and apply what we have just seen to the gallery's principle angles and architecture.

Our logical analysis has indicated that the angle of the groove down the gallery walls will be the same as the angle of the passageway below the gallery. That was calculated algebraically as being -26° 1' 34" degrees, and since we have determined that the architects are working in radians, this figure can now be converted to that angular measuring unit, giving the passageway angle as -0.4542413603 radians (rad.). We also know from our determination of the cubit measure's origins that radians relate to cubits directly, and a short investigation into the gallery length from the survey shows that the groove down the side walls has a length of 90.85 cubits - a value that is exactly 200 times its angular measure in radians. This correlation between angular measure and length measure is the key to unlocking the design of the gallery, since although we do not know the roof or floor angles algebraically we do know the lengths of each wall section of the gallery with absolute certainty due to the manner in which they were designed.

In Petrie's work he explains in great detail how the vertical ends of the gallery were constructed. Each of the sections of wall overlap the previous one by an approximately equal amount, so that the roof ends exactly one cubit short of where the floor ends at both the top and bottom of the gallery. The same system was also used for the wall sections which form the widths of the gallery, where each successive section of wall overlaps the previous one by 1/7th of a cubit to give a base width of two cubits and a roof width of one cubit. The arrangement of the gallery ends is shown in diagram opposite in which the lengths of the overlaps have been standardised from the values reported in Petrie's work in order to demonstrate the architectural principle involved.

From this construction principle we can now create a table of lengths and angles for each of the wall sections of the gallery in the following manner. We know the length and angle of the groove down the third overlap which can be inserted into the table first. Since we have to account for the wall overlaps both above and below this score line, we can then add on 2/7ths of a cubit to each wall length section as we descend towards the floor, and subtract 2/7ths of a cubit as we ascend towards the roof. Once the tabulation of the wall lengths is complete, the angles of each wall section can be calculated by dividing the wall lengths by -200, giving the angle of each wall section in radians. This radian measure can then of course be converted into degree measure to give a more familiar measurement for each section. The full tabulated results of these calculations are shown in the table below which shows all of the wall section angles and lengths with absolute accuracy.

This ingenious method of design allows us to determine theoretically the floor angle as being -26° 16' 18", compared to

The Grand Gallery details

*The angles and lengths of the Grand Gallery are set out in the table, with row 3 marked with * to denote the starting point of the calculations*

The Grand Gallery

Wall Level	Length (cubits)	Angle (rad)	Angle (d.m.s)	Width (cubits)
Roof	89.419700624	-0.447098503	-25° 37' 00.69"	1.0000
7	89.705414909	-0.448527075	-25° 41' 55.35"	1.0000
6	89.991129195	-0.449955646	-25° 46' 50.01"	1.1429
5	90.276843481	-0.451384217	-25° 51' 44.68"	1.2857
4	90.562557766	-0.452812789	-25° 56' 39.34"	1.4286
3*	90.848272052	-0.454241360	-26° 01' 34.01"	1.5714
2	91.133986338	-0.455669932	-26° 06' 28.67"	1.7143
1	91.419700624	-0.457098503	-26° 11' 23.33"	1.8571
Floor	91.705414909	-0.458527075	-26° 16' 18.00"	2.0000

Petrie's surveyed value of 26° 16' 40", showing once again how good Petrie's surveying measurements are and how remarkable the architectural construction system is. What is more important however is that we now know the floor angle algebraically, since it is simply a function of the ascending passage angle which we have already determined from the principle ellipse structure. Since each of the wall sections is 2/7ths of a cubit longer than the one above it in length, then the gallery floor must be 6/7ths of a cubit greater in length than the score line, and the floor angle consequently 3/700ths radian steeper.

The next question to be addressed in this highly complex engineering structure is how the gallery floor line is positioned, since at present we have only determined its precise angle but not its location. Once again the architect has reverted to using tangents to ellipses to create the floor positioning, and the illustration below shows how the gallery floor line is in fact a tangent line to the Earth shaped ellipse contained within the main chamber. Because we know the angle of the floor with precision then we must also know its vertical position from this construction with the same absolute accuracy, since the Earth shaped ellipse is also nothing more than a mathematical calculation. This construction explains why Petrie was so puzzled as to the fact that the floor line of the gallery does not meet up with the top end wall of the gallery - a discrepancy which clearly perplexed him as he makes frequent reference to the 'virtual' floor end in his work.

This geometry not only positions the gallery floor quite beautifully but also immediately confirms that the Earth shaped ellipse that we created in the main chamber is intentional within the architecture, and not a creation which we have accidentally inserted ourselves, since we now have our usual corroborating evidence. This in turn allows us to work out the exact algebraic equation for the gallery floor line by relating the gradient of the gallery floor to the tangent on the main chamber ellipse.

It is at this point that we need to refer back to the previous chapter regarding the lower north shaft to realise that we now have two geometric lines which intersect each other within the gallery. The lower northern shaft line construction which was created by rotating the ellipse centred on the pyramid's base line, and the gallery floor line which we have just determined. Because we have already seen in the previous chapter that the

Gallery floor line

(below) The ellipse in the main chamber connects through to the gallery floor line

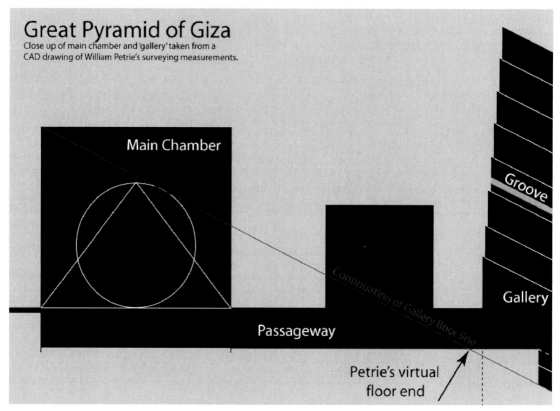

Great Pyramid of Giza
Close up of main chamber and 'gallery' taken from a
CAD drawing of William Petrie's surveying measurements.

Main Chamber

Groove

Gallery

Continuation of Gallery floor line

Passageway

Petrie's virtual
floor end

The gallery walls

(above) The marks
and cuttings in the
gallery wall follow
a logical sequence

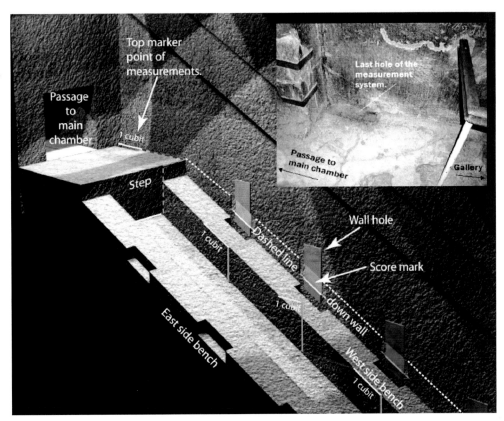

architects have marked off a geometric intersect point inside the lower southern shaft, then we can also expect to find some similar type of marking in the lower northern shaft. The intersect point of these two geometric lines can be mathematically deduced and the calculation, when enumerated using the principle foundation length of the pyramid, gives the intersect point as being 34.584 m vertically from the pyramid base and 15.182 m north from the pyramid's central vertical axis. We will have a look into the lower northern shaft in a moment, however the architects have employed just one more concept into the grand gallery which we must understand before we can deduce the reason behind so much complex architecture, and to find it we need to look more carefully at the walls of the gallery, and in particular the details of the 'benches' that run along either side of the gallery.

One of the features that has baffled Egyptologists in this section of the pyramid is the series of indentations, carvings and score marks which appear down the sides of the gallery walls just above these benches. These markings are shown in the illustration above, and it has been suggested over many years that perhaps the holes in the benches were designed so that cross beams could be

inserted into them for some reason. As we are about to see, that is very nearly the case, but the objects that needs inserting are far from what has been envisaged.

These holes are actually a measuring device which has been inserted into the gallery wall to be used in a very similar manner to a standard ruler. As shown in the diagram the measurements along the wall are positioned using whole cubit lengths, and line up with a final cut out section which can be found at the very top of the gallery where the horizontal passageway meets the gallery end wall, a photograph of which is shown inset into the illustration. The purpose of this measurement device is to allow the analysis of the gallery that has already been presented and in particular the top marker point gives the key reference for the positioning of the gallery's south wall, and hence the roof section in relation to the floor. Without it there would be no way of deducing the measurements and angles that have already been outlined, and it was these measuring marks the I used when reverse engineering the gallery - they served their purpose to perfection. In addition, across each of the wall holes is a linear score mark, and it is this mark which provides us with the final part of the puzzle. When these score marks are taken as a series running down the gallery wall, they present us quite simply with a dotted line - identical to that used by architects in their drawings where they are used to represent a measurement that is either hidden or approximate. They are used to imply uncertainty, and that is the same representation that they give in this case. The start of this dotted, or more strictly speaking, dashed line is the edge of the step at the top of the gallery - a point which is easily determinable algebraically. Since the dashed line is also parallel to the floor of the gallery we know its angle algebraically and therefore can determine the mathematical properties of its line equation. The purpose of this dashed line and how it relates to the northern shaft has been clearly indicated in the pyramid by the architects and to determine just where and how we need to have a look inside the shaft itself.

The lower northern shaft of the Great Pyramid is most unusual. It was originally constructed with its end bricked up and it was only by chance that the shaft was discovered. When the shaft's end in the lower chamber was opened by the Dixon brothers (who were essentially tourists to the area and not professional Egyptologists) they got the shock of their lives, because after a lot of rumbling and crashing, a small granite ball came shooting out of the shaft's hole and into the chamber. What happened next remains somewhat of a mystery as there is no documentation of the events (a perfect example of why Egyptologists alone should be left to examine these buildings) but what we do know is that the ball now resides in the British museum in London, and inside the lower northern shaft are a number of poles and other assortment of objects. Which of the poles were inserted up the shaft by the Dixon brothers and which were originally there remains an unknown, but a safe assumption would be that the granite ball was dislodged in some way as the brothers poked around inside the shaft.

If we look at the video evidence that was presented by Gantenbrink during his survey of this shaft we can determine that the length of a wooden pole that is located inside the shaft, and just around the first bend point, has a length of approximately 70-80cm and is most likely to be an original artifact from the builders of the monument because of its location. Further down this shaft is an object which appears to be a box or rectangular object of some sort and upon which the ball was originally resting. The determination of the size of the pole and other details from inside the shaft was deduced from analysing the diagram below which is taken from the video still on Gantenbrink's web site.

If we look at this section of the lower northern shaft in close up, and super-

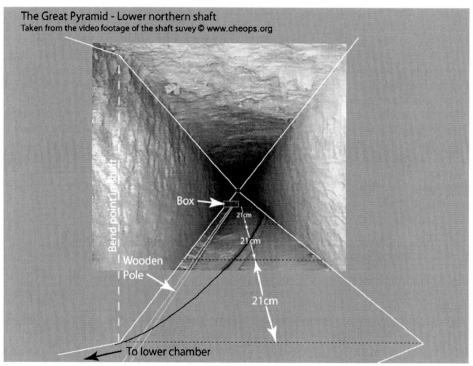

The Great Pyramid - Lower northern shaft
Taken from the video footage of the shaft suvey © www.cheops.org

Bend point in shaft

Box → 21cm

21cm

Wooden Pole

21cm

To lower chamber

impose the grand gallery details on the same drawing as viewed in projection from the East and shown in the illustration below, it is apparent that the small box like structure on the end of the wooden pole is located on the dashed line of the gallery wall, allowing for the errors in our estimation of the positioning of the item in the shaft and the length of the box structure which is unknown. The lack of precision in the measurements is irrelevant as what we are looking at here is a schematic illustration by the architects which will help us understand their design of this section of the structure. It would appear that the they have left the wooden pole across the bend in this shaft with the lower end of the wood protruding across the straight section of the shaft coming from the lower chamber, and with the small granite ball resting precariously on the box structure. It was when the Dixon brothers made contact with the wooden pole that they dislodged the object in the shaft, the ball then fell from the box structure and rolled down the shaft and shot out into the chamber.

Since we have a sound hypothesis that the Great pyramid is a geometric model of the Earth, then it does not take much imagination to deduce that the small granite ball that fell from the shaft is a likely to be a representation of the planet, and it has been positioned exactly inside the pyramid so that it is at the same height as the intersect point of the geometric line construction that was explained earlier in this chapter. The message that the architects are getting across is that it is at this geometric point in the pyramid where we can find the main representation of the Earth - the reason being that it is the first location they have chosen to physically represent it, using a small granite ball.

If we go back to the measurements that we took of the intersect point between the north shaft and the gallery floor, we can now extend our measurement horizontally through this point and along to the dashed line at the exact place where the granite ball

Plan view of the shaft

The approximate location of the ball in the shaft.

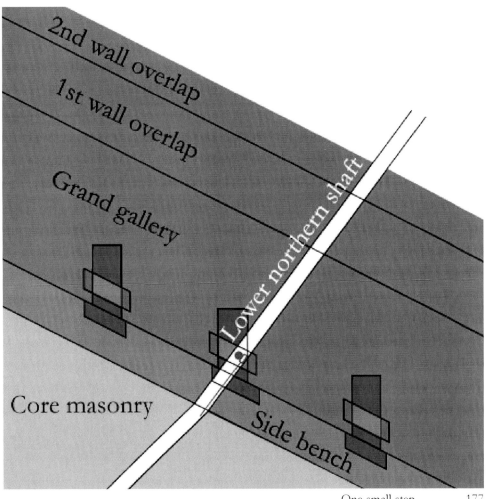

must have been located. By doing so we have just come to the final, remarkable purpose of the pyramid's construction. The illustration below shows the final geometric lines deduced from the complex calculations. The measurements involved in this geometry can be determined perfectly since there is *not one surveying measurement used to obtain the lengths* - they are pure mathematical distances and their values are determined by only two factors

1) The Earth's polar flattening
2) The length of the cubit

Since both of these quantities are known with a high degree of accuracy, the determination of the exact lengths of these lines is entirely in our own hands and is dependant upon out knowledge and ability to manipulate the mathematics and nothing more.

You may well be wondering why anyone would go to such lengths as to build a 53 storey high pyramid just to give us the lengths of a few lines, and it is this question that the architects are deliberately posing to us. The desire to answer that question will lead us to the meaning of the lines, and also explain the need for the incredible precision used in their construction. The algebraic calculations required to determine the architecture are com-

plex and involve not just the intersect point already determined but also the formation of the angled section of the shaft and from it the position of the dashed line down the gallery wall. If you study the mathematics it is quite clear that the whole of the system being described is a dynamic system with variables such as the axial tilt of the Earth all incorporated into it. From an in depth study of the mathematics is becomes clear that there are two distance being marked out by the architects and which are shown on the diagram below as d_1 and d_2 which are measured between the granite ball and the two central axiis of the pyramid. To understand what they represent we need to have a look at the original model of the Earth that is the basis of our hypothesis.

One of the points that was not discussed when we realised that cubit is defined from the pyramid's latitude was the fact that since the pyramid's foundation platform perimeter is known in cubits, then we must know the length of the platform sides to remarkable precision. That in turn means that we must know the size of the model of the Earth that we created at the start of our analysis, and can therefore determine the scale of the model with the same remarkable precision. Assuming that our value for the

The principle geometry line of the pyramid

The complex and highly accurate principle geometry of the pyramid

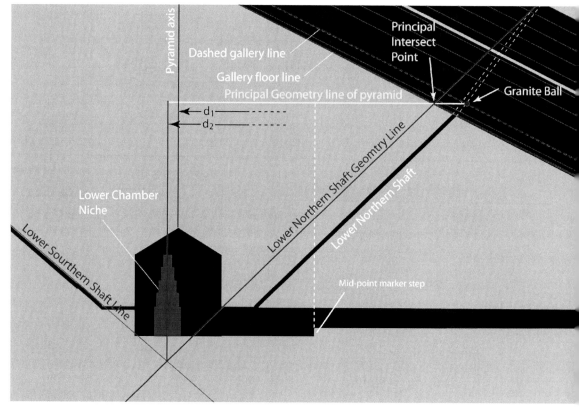

foundation length of the pyramid in cubits is correctly deduced then the value for the scale of the primary model of the earth is therefore 86626 : 1. Although *this is not a correct value* as we will see, for now it will suffice as the later adjustments are small as to not be important when explaining the methodology that the architects have used. We can use it to scale up the lengths that we have just discovered within the grand gallery area of the pyramid, and after a suitable adjustment of the decimal point these lengths come out as the following

$$d1 = 146,856,000,000 \text{ m}$$
$$d2 = 152,341,000,000 \text{ m}$$

Although only approximate distances at this stage it is already obvious that they are the measurements of the Earth's distance from the Sun during its annual elliptical orbit. The first of the values is known as Aphelion, the furthest distance that the planet gets from the Sun during the orbital year, and the second is Perihelion, the nearest distance that the planet gets to the Sun. The complexities and consequences of this subject will be covered in a later chapter, since they are at the very core of the pyramid's purpose, and also the subject matter is one which requires a complete understanding of the Giza Plateau.

The geometric line that gives these data is so fundamental to the pyramid's purpose that you would expect the architects to have backed it up with corroborating architecture, and that is of course exactly what they have done. In the passageway that leads to the lower chamber there is another one of the pyramid's features that has perplexed all who have looked at it. The small step which occurs just before the lower chamber marks off the exact centre point of the principal geometry line and is also shown in the illustration opposite. The use of this step as a marker point ensures that when solving the mathematics contained within the architecture that the principle geometry line is drawn to the central axis of the niche, and not just the central axis of the pyramid. This ensures that there the two line lengths are discovered, giving us the two distances between the Earth and Sun and is the final word from the architects within the Great Pyramid of Giza.

With such an astonishingly complex architectural layout in front of us there is a quite clear understanding that if we can correctly determine all of the features of this pyramid, then we will be able to accurately determine the values of Aphelion and Perihelion used by the architects. We already have a highly accurate value for the cubit by which to determine them, but what we cannot rely upon is our initial deduction of the length of the foundation platform of the pyramid. Our initial analysis and subsequent estimation of the length of the perimeter of the pyramid's foundation has served us well up to this point, providing us with the approximate scale of the model that is in use. Having just seen that the pyramid appears to contain some remarkably accurate details of the Earth's orbital characteristics, the question arises as to whether there is a more scientific manner in which the scale of our Earth model has been designed.

THE TIME SCALE

The Earths orbit

The variation
between the solar
and sidereal days
is shown in this
illustration

The value of the scale that the architects have used in the design of the Great Pyramid is currently calculated as 86626 : 1 and we need to have a long hard think about this numerical value to try to understand if it has any underlying logical meaning. We also need to avoid at all costs any foray into the realms of numerology and stick rigidly to scientific thinking if we are to progress satisfactorily and determine the origins of this scaling factor. Additionally we need to restrict our subject matter to that which we have already been presented with by the architects, namely the Earth and, as we have just seen in the 'Grand Gallery', the Earth's orbital characteristics. To start our search for the scaling factor let us first have a look at the basic details of the Earth's orbit around the sun.

From a very basic perspective we know that the Earth rotates around the sun once a year and that the heliocentric model of the solar system which was refined by Copernicus, Kepler and Galileo is today a well established standard model. In this model the orbit of the Earth is elliptical and as a consequence of interaction with other planets in the solar system the duration of one orbit around the sun is not a constant period of time. Some years the Earth takes perhaps 370 days to complete its rotation and in other years it may take only 360 days. This discrepancy is ignored by the vast majority of people who stick rigidly to the 365 day leap year model for their calendars and time keeping. The variation in the orbital characteristics are only of interest and importance to the scientific community, and the rest of us get on with our daily lives oblivious of the variations in the yearly cycles.

If we now have a look at the daily cycle of the Earth we come across similar variances in that they make no difference to most people on the planet but are highly significant to the scientific community. The basic unit of measurement that regulates our lives is the solar day. The sun rises at roughly the same time every day and sets in the evening in a similar manner. We know that the time of sunrise changes throughout the year, but on a day by day basis in makes little difference to us. The illustration below shows the way that the solar day is related to the annual cycle of the Earth around the sun, and in that illustration can be seen the fundamental problem that is inherent in the use of the solar day. As the Earth rotates

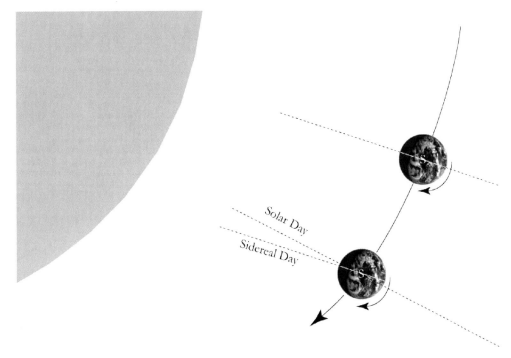

Solar Day

Sidereal Day

around the sun in its annual cycle, each day it has progressed about 1/365th of the way around its orbit. This means that in order for the same location on the planet to directly facing the sun at the same time on two subsequent days, and thereby have sunrise at the same time on both of these days, the Earth needs to be allowed to rotate upon its axis for a slightly longer time than one full rotation. This means that the 24 hour solar day that we use to measure time is actually slightly longer than the period required for the Earth to rotate once upon its axis. The later of these two time periods is known as the sidereal day and is defined as the time required for the planet to rotate once on its axis.

The sidereal day is an absolute fixed constant and does not vary by more than a millisecond or two every century and in comparison to the concept of the solar day is a utterly more sensible time reference to use in astronomical calculations. If we have a look at the values of the solar day and sidereal day when measured in seconds we find that the solar day is of course 24 hours long and therefore 86400 seconds, and the sidereal day is shorter and has a value of 86164 seconds. What is immediately striking about these figures is there very close proximity to the scaling factor that we have already come across in the Great Pyramid. Whilst neither of them is obviously the same value they are both of the same order of magnitude, and sufficiently close to make us take note.

Of course without a historical connection between our modern timekeeping and that of the Ancient Egyptians all that we are looking at in these values is nothing more than numerology of which we have no interest. But even the briefest of glimpses into the history of our time measuring units shows us that the 24 hour day, 60 minute hour and 60 second minute all date back to the time of the ancient Egyptians. We can therefore continue with the path that we are taking since it is more than likely that the architects of this building were using the same divisions of time that we are currently using, or more to the point were responsible for the initial definition of the time divisions which we still use today.

Because of the variations in the orbit of the Earth around the sun the solar day that we use must also vary considerably from year to year. It is not something that is noticable to us because its effects are so small on a daily basis, but never the less it is something which must be happening. So if we were to rational-

ise the way in which we measure time it would be a very sensible step to define the sidereal day as being the standard of time measurement because we know that this is the only fixed reference that we have.

It will come as little surprise to find out that this is exactly what the scientific world has already done and the sidereal day has been defined as being 24 sidereal hours long. This then gives rise to the sidereal hour, minute and second, all of which are quantities which are defined in absolute rational terms and which vary very little on a year by year basis. If we were to adopt this time system for our daily lives (which is not a practical idea) then we would of course have the situation where the sidereal day is 86400 sidereal seconds in length and the solar day would be slightly longer. The calculation to find the length of the solar day in sidereal seconds is not particularly difficult and yields the quite astonishing result that the solar day contains 86636.5 sidereal seconds. And it is at this point in the calculations and thought process that you realise that you have just discovered the primary scaling factor of the Great Pyramid of Giza. It is scaled to time. Sidereal time. Unmovable, constant, technical time. The architects are scientists, and of the highest order.

However, before we rush in and start to use this value as the primary scale we need to remember that the initial scale that we were using was only an approximate estimation based on our assumption regarding the foundation perimeter of the pyramid. Since it would be inconceivable that anyone with such a detailed scientific knowledge would rely on such a random starting point for such a group of technical calculations, we need to return once again to the plinth that surrounds the pyramid and look to see if there is further depth to the design that we can now detect.

In the earlier analysis it was determined that an Earth shaped ellipse could be inscribed upon the plinth of the pyramid, but since then we have developed the work considerably further and know for certain that the base length of the pyramid is a representation of half the Earth's elliptical circumference. This raises the possibility that the plinth's inner dimension (where the base of the pyramid meets the ground level) could be based on the circumference of something slightly smaller than the Earth, and that the outer edge of the plinth (where it meets the pavement) could be based on the circumference of something slightly larger than the

Earth. It is by following this line of logic that we eventually come across the definitive solution to the plinth's remarkably clever design.

The inner dimension is half the circumference of a circle with a radius equal to the scaled polar radius of the Earth, and the outer dimension is equal to the circumference of a circle with a radius equal to the scaled equatorial radius of the Earth. And since we know these points on the base with excellent accuracy then we can compare their scaled values to the real size values for the Earth, and we have *two* values from which we can deduce the pyramids scale, rather than just one approximate one that we used before. From comparing the numerical values from the surveying to the full sized values from the geodesic documentation the two possible values of the pyramids scale come out as

scale calculation 1 = 86704.9 +/- 4.8
scale calculation 2 = 86699.3 +/- 2.1

the first of these values being calculated from Petrie's base length figure and the second from Lehner's plinth width figure. With the numerical values being so close we can deduce that we probably have the scale correct, and so we now need to determine how the architects have come about this figure.

We have already seen that the length of the solar day when measured in sidereal seconds gives a very close approximation to this value, and it is when this figure is considered over the scope of a full year that the true primary scale of this monument comes to light. The length of a sidereal year (the time required for the Earth to rotate around the sun once) is 365.25 days, and it is because of the fractional part of this number that we have leap years every 4 years. However, if we consider that a standard year has only 365 days in it we can see that our calculated value for the length of the solar day measured in sidereal seconds cannot be correct. The average value over the full year must be 365.25/365 times this value. Taking the value of the sidereal year as being exactly 365.256363004 days, then the duration of one average day (1/365th year) in sidereal seconds, and hence the scale of the monument is

$$86697.4058$$

which is calculated as follows

$$\frac{365.256}{365} \times \frac{86400}{86164} \times 86400$$

We can now check this scaling value quite easily against the surveying measurements by calculating the inner and outer positions of the plinth from the GRS84 geodetic datum giving the base lengths of the pyramid as

Inner base length = 115.1725 m
Outer base length = 115.5600 m

with the resulting distances shown on the illustration below, along with the surveying measurements from the Egyptologists, (and a shoe for scale perception). The length of the base of the geometry, which is marked in red on the diagram, falls in the middle of

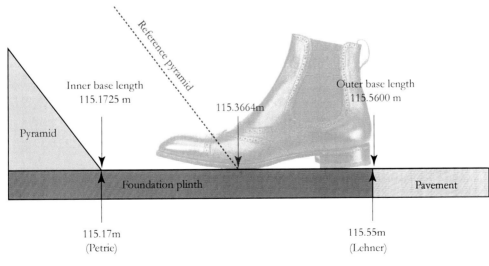

Reference pyramid

Inner base length
115.1725 m

115.3664m

Outer base length
115.5600 m

Pyramid

Foundation plinth

Pavement

115.17m
(Petrie)

115.55m
(Lehner)

the plinth and we can be quite certain that we have at last found the correct scaling factor for the model of the Earth.

What is strikingly obvious is that we are now outside the scope of the surveying if our deduction of the monument's scale is correct. There is little point in making a comparison with the surveying measurements other than to look at the accuracy of the survey itself. If our scale is correct, and it is, then we will have very little further use of the surveying measurements of the Great Pyramid of Giza because we know the exact dimensions of the monument.

Because we have already deduced that algebraic geometry on which the design is based and now also have a precise scaling factor to work from then our ability to recreate the original dimensions of the building is limited only by our own scientific knowledge. If we know the size and shape of the Earth and if we know the length of a sidereal day and year then we can use the geometric blueprint that they have given us and perfectly recreate the theoretical values inside the monument. If the lengths that we came across in the Grand Gallery are indeed representative of the Aphelion and Perihelion of the Earth's orbit then we will be able to determine their exact values with the information that we have been given. This is not something which I will be doing in this book, because we have now got to the stage where the work has moved out of the realms of the analysis of the pyramids and has moved on to a specialist subject field which will involve pages and pages of complex scientific argument. This science will need to be worked and reworked by the academic community so that a consensus is formed that is acceptable to all and it would be unwise to present the starting sequence of such a debate in a book such as this.

What we need to do is to concentrate on the overall picture that is before us and complete the analysis of the remaining sections of the Great Pyramid and its surrounding monuments. It would be only too easy to get sidetracked at this stage, but by thinking through what we have just seen it is possible to realise that we have just created a rather strange anomaly in our work.

If the pyramid is scaled using the sidereal day and year as its source then, as we have just discussed, we can accurately recreate the monument's architecture. But previously we have also deduced that the cubit measurement is based on the latitude of the pyramids location in Egypt and the problem that we

have created is as follows. If it is possible to determine all the architectural features of the building from the scaling factor alone, why would the architects have gone to such trouble to define the cubit so accurately?

We saw in the Grand Gallery that the cubit measure was related to the angles in the architecture, but since we can now recreate those angles with a very high level of precision, we can also derive an accurate value of the cubit from them. The possibility that arises is that there may well be some other feature of the cubit that we have not yet understood and that the latitude of the pyramid as its defining method is only an approximation. If this is the case then one can only imagine what the un-approximate definition of the cubit is going to be.

To find out the answer to this question we will need to progress through the remaining features of the pyramid that we have yet to study and then make our way outside onto the Giza plateau where we have all manner of riddles awaiting us. To do so we need to find our way out of the pyramid and in a manner that is connected to the geometric design that we have so far laid down.

WHICH WAY OUT ?

Having established at the outset of the work that the entrance to the Great Pyramid of Giza is situated at the upper shaft exits, it would be not at all surprising to discover that the exit is situated where we currently think that the entrance is placed. From the analysis of the 'grand gallery' in the pyramid we already know how the ascending passageway, which connects the gallery to the entrance passage, was formed and have calculated its geometric construction in the earlier chapter. What we now require is to determine how the entrance passage has been designed and work out its geometry so that the whole of the pyramid's internal passageway system fits together.

Its design is yet another piece of precision engineering and, as we are about to see, contains the now familiar mix of millimetre perfect construction, profound understanding of geometry, and curious but deliberate imperfections designed to make us think deeply. The mathematics upon which it is formed is based on a fundamental property of the earliest part of the construction that we have already put together, and in particular that section of the mathematics which relates the positioning of the upper shaft exit points, and their determination from the primary ellipse of the pyramid.

In the illustration below another internal ellipse has been added to our drawing and the defining properties of this ellipse are vital in the comprehension of its use in the entrance passageway construction. The defining properties are as follows; that the ellipse, shown in red on the diagram, touches the pyramid floor at it's base, has its highest point at the same height as the tangent points originally formed on the Earth ellipse, and it has the geometric pyramid sides as tangents. By defining the ellipse in this

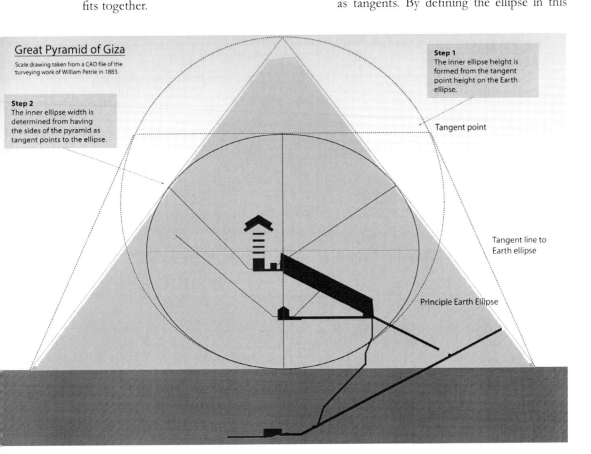

Great Pyramid of Giza
Scale drawing taken from a CAD file of the surveying work of William Petrie in 1883.

Step 1
The inner ellipse height is formed from the tangent point height on the Earth ellipse.

Step 2
The inner ellipse width is determined from having the sides of the pyramid as tangent points to the ellipse.

Tangent point

Tangent line to Earth ellipse

Principle Earth Ellipse

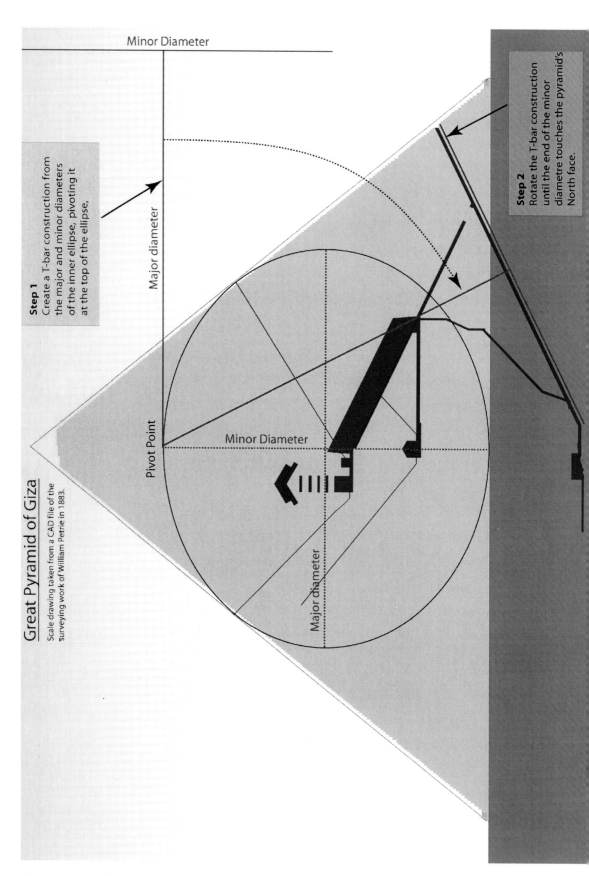

Great Pyramid of Giza

Scale drawing taken from a CAD file of the surveying work of William Petrie in 1883.

Step 1
Create a T-bar construction from the major and minor diameters of the inner ellipse, pivoting it at the top of the ellipse,

Step 2
Rotate the T-bar construction until the end of the minor diametre touches the pyramid's North face.

Minor Diameter

Major diameter

Pivot Point

Minor Diameter

Major diameter

The entrance passage geometry

By rotating the radii of the shaft ellipse the entrance passage slope and length are formed

way, the upper shaft exit points on the pyramid's sides coincide with precision with the tangent points formed on this new inner ellipse - a fact which is evident in the diagram.

This is not just a coincidence, but a mathematical property of this type of construction, and the lengthy proof of this geometric fact is shown in the mathematics appendix. The ellipse that we have just drawn, whilst mathematically perfect, is entirely theoretical since none of its primary characteristics appear to have been used in the construction. Having said this, smaller versions of this shape can be found throughout the pyramid's smaller architectural features and it is one of the major clues that the architects have hidden inside their work. For example, it is used as the defining shape in the construction of the coffin in the main chamber, can be found in the trial passageways (a set of small tunnels which are located just outside the perimeter of the pyramid) and it is also contained in the construction principles of the lower chamber. The details of each of these pieces of architecture are largely academic at this stage, since the purpose of the ellipse's inclusion into each of them serves just one purpose. When trying to work out how the pyramid was constructed it is the repetitious appearance of this elliptical shape in the small architectural details which leads you to finding its origin and principle use in the architecture.

It is used as the principle defining

The gallery end point

The lower end of the gallery is defined by the intersection of the T-bar construction with the gallery floor

geometry in the entrance passageway in a manner which is both clear and unambiguous and, as we will see in future chapters, the understanding of this entrance passageway geometry is vital in the overall system of which the Great Pyramid is a part. The architects have used the two different diameters from this ellipse and formed them into a 'T-bar' construction, which is then pivoted from the top point of the ellipse's vertical axis and rotated until it neatly rests inside the North face of the geometric pyramid - as shown opposite.

The underlying mathematics of this construction is shown in the mathematics appendix and the algebraic proof is particularly detailed and difficult to work out. The end result of that mathematics is that the gradient of the entrance passageway can be calculated in quite extraordinary detail and then compared to the surveying measurements from Petrie's work. The interesting point about this comparison is that the entrance passageway contains the most accurate of all of Petrie's surveying measurements because whilst surveying it he would have had reference points to work from which were external to the pyramid - such as a fixed horizon and direct access to his station marks. The comparison of the geometrically calculated angle and that of the survey therefore act as a particularly accurate test of the correctness of the mathematics.

Petrie reports the angle of the entrance passageway as being 26° 31° 23" +/- 5" , and from the geometric analysis the angle is calculated as 26° 31° 26', the variance between the two figures being 3" of one degree. To put the discrepancy between the two figures into perspective, it is the equivalent of viewing the width of your hand from a distance of 10km away. Once again Petrie has proven his surveying measurements to be of the utmost accuracy.

The usual corroborating evidence is contained within this construction method, and as can be seen in adjoining illustration, the major diameter line passes through the intersection point of the end of the gallery and the ascending passageway to which it is joined. To be more accurate in the description, the point in the architecture where the ascending passageway meets the gallery is defined by this major diameter line, and therefore shows us that we have correctly identified both these pieces of the construction.

There are however several rather

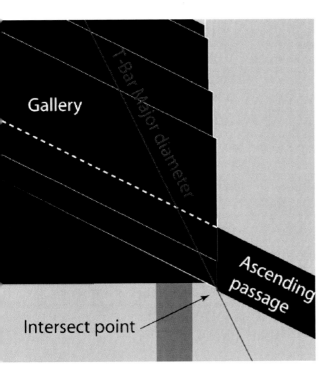

strange points contained within the mathematics and architecture of the entrance passage when it is formed in this way, all of which suggest that there is something not quite correct with what we have done. In order for the mathematics to correctly fit the architectural construction, the major diameter line has to be reduced by a 1/298.257th of its length to coincide with the constructed entrance passageway floor. This can be clearly seen in the diagrams where the red geometry line and the grey passageway lines have a gap between them. The reason for the reduction in length by this familiar fraction turns out to be a specific feature of the architecture, and one about which we need not worry too much. However you will notice if you look carefully that the architect has chosen to line the geometry up with the constructed face of the pyramid rather than the geometric reference pyramid face line telling us that something is deliberately incorrect in this construction.

It may seem a strange phrase to describe something as deliberately incorrect, but that is exactly what is presented before us here. We can perfectly deduce the angle of the entrance passage using algebraic geometry, yet to do so we have to deviate from the geometry that has formed all of the pyramid's internal features up to this point, and revert back to the stonework. It would seem that the architect is currently pointing us to the physical entrance/exit to the pyramid's structure, and that the mathematical one may well lie else where.

A second point to note, and a more significant one, is that at the lower end of the entrance passage the geometry does not coincide at all with either the floor or roof ends of the passage as shown in illustration above. This suggests strongly that the geometric construction only applies to the top of the entrance passage and is used exclusively to define the entrance/exit to the pyramid and not the lower end of the passage. The final point of note is that there is a very small discrepancy between Petrie's surveyed floor line position and that formed from the geometry, also shown in the diagram where the red geometry line and the passage floor line do not coincide. Whilst the angles of the geometry and the architecture match perfectly, the position of them does not and the error margin is a considerable 9cm.

Clearly something strange is happening in the architecture at this lower point in the passage although the top end is just fine,

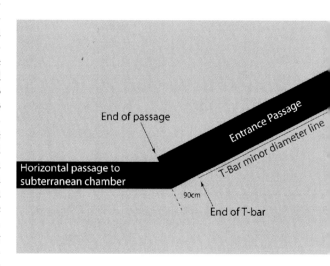

and if we take the premise that the mathematics is correct since it forms the top of the passage and its angle so accurately, then we need to delve into the mind of the architect to work out what is being shown to us at the lower end. We are being told that, although we have clearly found our way out of the physical pyramid construction by forming the entrance passage and thereby the entrance, we have not found our way out of the mathematical construction and we are being led in two directions at once. Further investigation into the T-bar, and its rotation around the top point is needed.

If, rather than lining up the top end of the T-bar with the pyramid's constructed North face we choose to line up the bottom end of the 'T-bar' with any suitable point on the pyramid, the architectural design for this lower section becomes apparent. By lining up the lower section of the T-bar with the floor level of the lower horizontal passage, the entrance door to the subterranean chamber becomes perfectly defined as shown in the illustration opposite. The discrepancy between the survey measurement for this doorway and that of the mathematics is only a few mm horizontally and vertically at the entrance to the subterranean chamber and so we now have a most interesting situation, that we have a piece of geometry that is telling us two things at the same time.

First we are being told that we have found the physical exit to the pyramid and can make our way outside, and secondly that we have found the mathematical exit to the pyramid, which is contained inside the subter-

Incorrect alignment in the entrance passage

The T-bar construction leaves an incorrect alignment in the lower section of the pyramid

ranean chamber - this deduction being more than reasonable since we are dealing with exit geometry in the formation of the subterranean chamber door. The first of these concepts gives us very few problems in its comprehension, but the second seems quite unusual as the subterranean chamber is known to have no exit other than the dead-end corridor which leads south.

At this stage in our analysis we can do no more than make a note of this section of the pyramid and come back to it in due course, once we have more information at our disposal. It will turn out that there is indeed an exit from the subterranean chamber, one which is marked out with absolute clarity, and one which contains the most breathtaking work in the whole of the pyramid. The exit from the subterranean chamber, as we will see later is architecturally stunning, lined either side with statues of the Sphinx and leads us to our first glimpse of the architects of this magnificent building.

It is typical of the deception and psychology of their work that they have chosen to conceal the mathematical exit from the pyramid in the subterranean chamber, with its walls and floor in such an unfinished state - causing anyone who chooses to casually analyse the building to leave this room alone. The subterranean chamber only appears to be a roughly cut out piece of the pyramid whereas in fact it is carved to perfection. The parallels between this section of the Great Pyramid and the serdab in the pyramid of Unas, where both are unfinished and designed to detract attention away from themselves, are clear.

We are well on our way to a full comprehension of this monument and should carry on exactly as instructed by the architects. We are about to leave the Great Pyramid via its physical exit, just as we have been told to do, leave the subterranean section for later, an look at the rest of the detail contained within the Giza plateau.

The door to the subterranean chamber

The doorway is defined by the geometry if the T-bar is correctly rotated around its pivot point

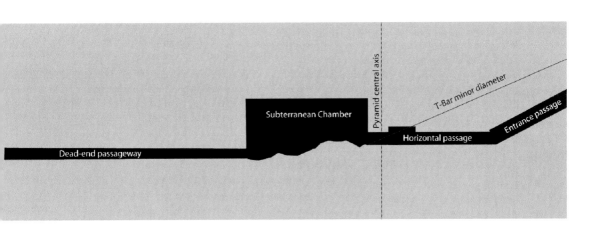

Dead-end passageway

Subterranean Chamber

Pyramid central axis

T-Bar minor diameter

Entrance passage

Horizontal passage

Which way out ?

THE SATELLITE PYRAMID AND THE SPHINX

Having spent so long inside the confined passageways of the Great Pyramid, the first view of the Giza plateau with the Great Pyramid replaced by the model of the Earth which it represents is spectacular, and is shown in overleaf. The pyramid is a geometric representation of the Earth, and can quite correctly be replaced in this manner with the ellipsoid representation of the planet, scaled at a ratio of 86697.4 : 1.

To start to comprehend what the other monuments on the plateau represent, we should go right back to where we started this book and reconsider how we measured the shape of our planet so accurately which allowed us to recognise the architectural features of the Great Pyramid in the first place. As stated in earlier chapters, it is impossible to measure the exact shape and size of the planet from taking measurements on its surface, and the only truly accurate measurements can be made from orbiting satellites in space. But where exactly are these satellites placed in relation to the Earth, and could it be that the second pyramid of Giza, rather than just being an adjacent pyramid to the first one is actually placed in a specific position relative to it. To answer this question, and it can be answered with certainty, we need to look into the physics of satellite orbits and understand the basics of their positions.

There are two physical forces, both of which are familiarly encountered on a daily basis, which dictate the location at which a satellite is placed in orbit around the Earth. The first of these forces is gravity, which will act upon the satellite and cause it to return to Earth in due course. However, as the satellite spins around the Earth it has a centripetal force acting upon it which makes it want to leave its orbit and fly out into space. For the satellite to remain in Earth orbit in space these two forces need to balance each other out, so that the gravitation pull of the Earth in one direction and the centripetal force in

the other have no detrimental effect on the satellites orbital radius. The mathematics of this harmonic balance concludes with a simple equation in which the distance from the Earth and the time it takes for one orbit around the planet are the only unknown quantities in the equation.

As a result of this equation there are three distinct areas of space into which a satellite can be placed. First is in low Earth orbit where, to maintain the balance between gravity and centripetal force, the satellite needs to spin around the planet quite rapidly. The orbital period of these low Earth orbit satellites is much less than 24 hours and they will consequently pass overhead, when viewed from the Earth, several times each day. They are used for a variety of purposes and are typical for most space shuttle missions, the International space station, and a large number of the world's communication satellites. The second area of space where satellites can be placed is high Earth orbit, and since these satellites have less gravity pulling upon them they need to orbit the planet slower so as to generate less centripetal force to balance out the weaker gravitational force. Consequently they orbit in more than 24 hours, and will pass overhead any given point on Earth every few days.

It is the third position which is by far the most interesting, and one which was first hypothesised by Arthur C Clarke in the early years of the last century. There must be an exact distance from the Earth where the orbital period of a satellite will exactly match that of the Earth's rotation on its axis. In simplified terms, it will rotate around the Earth in one day, and will consequently remain over the same longitude forever. This third type of satellite orbit is known as geosynchronous orbit, and is an especially useful orbit for communication and land mapping purposes.

Within the range of geosynchronous orbits there is one specific position, exactly over the equator at exactly the correct height above the Earth where the satellite will not only remain at the same longitude, but also at the same latitude for ever. This super specialised orbital position is known as geostationary satellite orbit, and is the one utilised by all of the world's television satellite systems. It has the unique property that any object placed into this orbit will remain stationary when viewed from the Earth, and hence permits wall mounted TV dishes to be firmly fixed to house walls without the

The Great Pyramid

The Sphinx

Pyramid 2

Pyramid 3

The satellite pyramid and the Sphinx

need of any motorised tracking equipment.

As well as the obvious practical uses of this orbit it also send out a strong message about the inhabitants of the planet to anyone who would care to be watching. It shows without question that the inhabitants of a planet, any planet, have technologically advanced to the stage where their physics and engineering is to a sufficient degree to be able to utilise this highly specific point in space. Once you place satellites in orbit at this distance from your planet, you have well and truly put yourself on the universal map.

The distance of geostationary satellite orbit from the Earth is relatively simple to calculate using basic physics constants. As with most equations the theoretical calculation is considerably easier to calculate than the true situation up in space, since we do not have to take into account factors such as atmospheric drag or the gravitational effects of the Sun and the moon. The result of this calculation is that idealised geostationary satellite orbit can be found at a distance of 42,164,169m from the Earth's centre. In practical applications this value has to be adjusted to take into account the perturbation from other heavenly bodies and a variety of other factors, but those calculations are outside the scope of this book and will contribute little at this stage to our analysis.

We already know that the Great Pyramid of Giza is a scaled model of the Earth, and that its scale can be deduced from knowing the value of the sidereal day and year. Sidereal day is of course the very time value that is required in the calculations for the orbiting satellite and by using this value and the scale of the model which was calculated at 86697.4 : 1 we can calculate where geostationary satellite orbit will be on this same scale. If we scale down the geostationary orbital radius of 42,164,169m then we find that the satellite orbit is 486.73 metres away from the centre of the model of the Earth that we have recently discovered.

If we now refer back to our master surveyor, Mr.. Petrie, we find that he measured the distances between all of the pyramids on the Giza plateau and reports in his work that the second pyramid of Giza's central vertical axis is located at a distance of 486.88 metres from the centre of the Great Pyramid. The second pyramid of Giza is positioned in geostationary satellite orbit around the model of the Earth, as shown in the next illustration with the small difference between the surveying measurement and the theoretical one be-

ing insignificant at this stage in the work.

Before looking for the corroborating evidence, it is worth stopping for a moment and contemplating what is on display here. We are looking at a 4,500 year old construction of geostationary satellite orbit - a representation of the conquest of science over space, and the biggest signpost that any civilisation could possibly put up to announce their technological level of advancement. We are being told in no uncertain terms that whoever built these monuments had the ability to play around with T.V. satellite orbits whilst the historically recorded human race was still living in mud huts and trying to work out how to make bows and arrows. The second pyramid has been built to make us sit up and take note, and that is precisely what we should do at this point.

There are two pieces of corroborating evidence that are available to confirm that the distance between these pyramids is a representation of geostationary orbit, the first of which links the second pyramid of Giza's architects to the those of the first pyramid with absolute certainty. You will recall from the chapter regarding the gallery in the Great Pyramid that cubit measurements of length were related directly to the angular measures of the gallery angles in radians by a factor of 200. It would therefore not be surprising to find that the second pyramid is 'rotated' around the first by an angle which is directly related to its distance from that pyramid. To start this calculation we need to convert the distance between the two pyramids into cubit measure, giving the distance between them as 930.05 cubits, when the scaled geostationary satellite orbit distance is used as being the correct distance between the two buildings rather than Petrie's surveying measurement (a difference of only a few centimeters).

We then need to refer to Petrie's work and take from it the angle he reported between the first and second pyramids which is 43° 22' 52" degrees west of the line running through the Great Pyramid and being parallel to the pyramid's North-South axis. This angle is shown on the illustration on the next page measured from the East-West line running through the Great Pyramid, and is consequently 90° larger, or 133° 22' 52". Since we know that the architects are working in radian measure, then we need to convert this angle into radians, giving the rotation of the second pyramid around the first as 2.32793955 radians. It is then a

Great Pyramid

930.05 cubits (486.73m)

133° 22' 52"

2.32793955 radians

Pyramid 2

The second pyramid
of Giza

The Giza plateau
with both the
first and second
pyramids replaced
by their respective
models

simple calculation to determine that the distance between the pyramids when measured in cubits is 400 times the angle between them within acceptable error margins, confirming with certainty that our deduction of geostationary satellite orbit is indeed correct. What is also confirmed immediately by this calculation is that the first and second pyramids of Giza were built according to a predetermined design *and by the same architects*.

There is a small discrepancy between the calculated position and angle of the second pyramid and that reported by Petrie. There are two possibilities as to why there should be a discrepancy between these values. The first is that in the 1800's the second pyramid of Giza had yet to be excavated, and therefore Petrie's deduction of the centre point of the pyramid carries an inherent error within it. Without a more detailed survey of the relationship of the two pyramids to each other on the plateau we are not in a position to determine whether Petrie's angle or his linear measurement contains an error, if indeed there is an error at all. What we can state is that if the linear measure were incorrect, then he missed the centre points of the two pyramid by 30cm respectively, and if the angular measure were incorrect then he had an error of 9' of a degree, or if both measurements contain errors, then he has an average linear placement error of 15cm on each monument and an angular error between them of 5' of a degree.

The other possibility is of course that Petrie's measurements are accurate, and that the architects have not calculated the theoretical value of geostationary orbit, but have taken into account all the minor gravitational adjustments of the advanced physics calculations, or perhaps that the second pyramid has had some minor adjustment made to it that we have yet to spot. This will turn out to be the case, but for now we can place this information at the back of our minds as it has little impact on this preliminary analysis of the monuments.

The second piece of corroborating evidence that confirms that the second pyramid of Giza is in an orbit around the first is utterly remarkable and to discover it we need to look at the way in which the architects have designed and built the causeway that leads down towards the Sphinx from pyramid two. To do this we need a detailed survey map of the Giza plateau, and we are in the fortunate position that enough archaeological survey information is available in the public domain

for us to be able to create one. The primary source of data is the survey of Petrie, from which we can recreate the three pyramids on the Giza plateau to an excellent degree of accuracy. To this we can then add the multitude of detailed archaeological surveys of the second pyramid's causeway and the Sphinx which are available from the Boston Museum of Fine Arts or any of the many Egyptology libraries in the world. Once these pieces of surveying work are combined they can be digitised and placed into a computer mapping programme, and an analysis of the causeway which leads from pyramid two can be undertaken.

In the illustration on the next page the preliminary design components of the second pyramid's causeway and the sphinx are illustrated, and *the estimates* of the manner in which this design has been architecturally planned is as follows. The second pyramid of Giza has its position dictated entirely by the distance and angle calculations outlined earlier in this chapter, making both it and the Great Pyramid immovable objects in the design. The North-South and East West lines which connect the two pyramids are then drawn on to the diagram with lengths of 354.69 m and 334.41m respectively as reported by Petrie. The East-West line is then divided into two equal lengths, and the temple at the East side of pyramid two is designed and built around this central marker point. The North-South line is then extended so that the extension length is 1/10th of the resulting overall length of this line.

We can now form the causeway which comes from the second pyramid temple by taking the temple centre point, joining it up with the end of the extended North-South line and continuing down towards the Sphinx area. The angle of this geometric line is 13° 24' 17.5" and is very close to that of the causeway when viewed either from satellite photography or more accurately when compared to the detailed 1936 survey of the causeway and Sphinx included in a work by S.Hassan. The detail of the pyramid two temple and its centre point taken from that survey are shown in the next illustration.

It is at this point that the purpose behind the construction becomes apparent, as by taking a line from the centre of pyramid two through our North-South end point, we have a geometric construction line which bisects the paws of the Sphinx. Additionally, if the East-West line is extended West by 354.69 m to a point which is at an

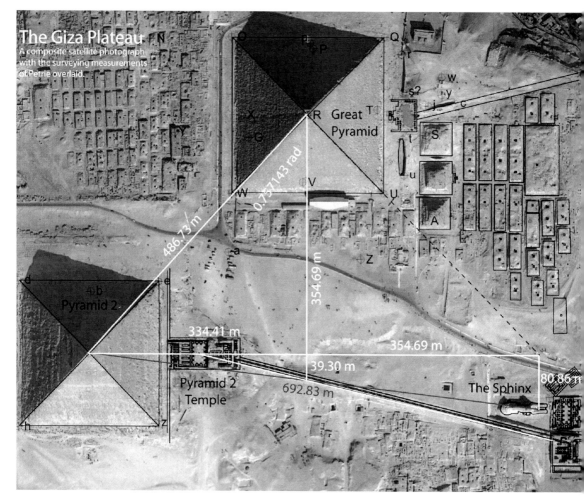

The Giza Plateau
A composite satellite photograph
with the surveying measurements
of Petrie overlaid

The primary distances of the Giza plateau are marked out on this illustration, with labels including N, O, Pl, P, Q, Great Pyramid, R, T, S, W, y, c, X, G, V, U, A, Z, 486.73 m, 0.737143 rad, 354.69 m, Pyramid 2, d, b, e, 334.41 m, Pyramid 2 Temple, 39.30 m, 354.69 m, 692.83 m, The Sphinx, 80.86 m, h, z

exact 45° bearing from the Great pyramid, then the stella which lies between the Sphinx's paws is marked off with decent accuracy. A photograph of the area between the Sphinx's paws that is marked out by this line is shown overleaf.

Even though we have temporarily departed from scientific data to map out these positions on the plateau, *and are therefore probably only looking at some preliminary calculations of the architects*, the question now arises as to what is significant about the line which comes from the center of the second pyramid to the Sphinx, and its length which is 692.83m or 1323.8 cubits. If we scale the line up by the scale of the Earth model we end up with a distance which has no meaning to it, and we are presented once again with a piece of design work which is going to require an additional piece of information before it is understood. What we are about to do is solve the riddle of the Sphinx, and in so doing add an extra piece of information to our knowledge base which

will allow us to comprehend the design of the third pyramid of Giza when we come to it. In order to solve the riddle, we need to go back to the Great Pyramid and review the details of how the upper and lower sections of that monument were designed.

Starting from a known base length we constructed our model of the Earth using an elliptical circumference formula which gave us two answers for the size of the Earth. The first of these ellipses we used to form the upper chamber and shafts, and the second we used for the lower chamber and shafts. Therefore there are two models being used and consequently two scales - the primary scale which we have already seen, and a secondary scale which will be 4.9998, or approximately 5 times larger, since it is based on the model of the Earth which was 1/5th smaller than the primary model. The architects can quite justifiably use either of these two scales on the Giza plateau, and it is by applying this secondary scale to both

The plateau distances

The primary distances of the Giza plateau are marked out on this illustration

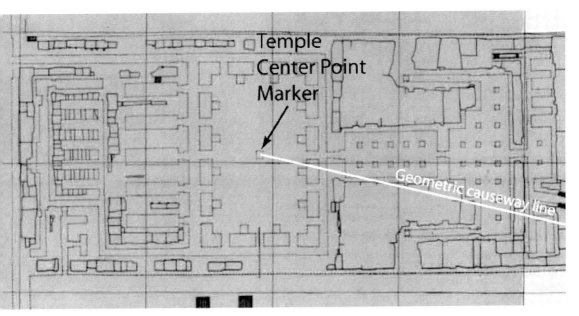

Temple Center Point Marker

Geometric causeway line

the Sphinx and later on the third pyramid of Giza that we can understand their positioning.

The marker point on the Sphinx, as we have already calculated, is 692.83 m metres from the centre of pyramid two, and when this is scaled up by the secondary scale the distance being given to us is 300,086,943 m. This value is astonishingly close to the value of one light second (the speed of light) which has the value of 299,792,548 m. Even though, due to our lack of accurate surveying information at this stage, we have some variance in our calculations which we cannot resolve, the architects appear to be showing us that the Sphinx is guarding the most fundamental of all physics constants. However, we have come across situations before where our surveying measurements contained errors, and a full analysis of the principles involved in the architecture resulted in automatic corrections appearing in the work. The same is the case with this distance.

Since we do not have the accuracy to work from in the surveying, we simply need to go back to the length of the cubit that we have calculated from the latitude of the Great Pyramid, and work out what the speed of light would be in cubits per second - always work in the architects units of measurement. This is not an irrational calculation because we know how the cubit is defined and we know that the primary scale of the Great Pyramid is based on the same unit as time that we currently use, or more likely actually defines it. The value of the cubit that we are using at this stage is

incredibly accurate but has an error margin dependant upon our ability to calculate the latitude of the Great Pyramid, in which we will have an error of no more than, for example, 20 centimetres. The resulting value of the cubit cannot therefore have an error of more than 4×10^{-8} m, and so whatever the value of the light second when measured in cubits, we know that it must have an error of no more than 10 cubits per second.

If we divide the light second of 299,792,458m by our currently known cubit value of .523350m, we find that the speed of light in cubits per second given by the architects is 572,850,006 +/- 10 c/s. From this it becomes quite apparent that the cubit measure, rather than being based on the Great Pyramids latitude, is actually based on the speed of light. The very positioning of the Great Pyramid has been chosen specifically to make this calculation work and has allowed us to start by measuring the cubit in the gallery of the Great Pyramid, refine the value via the pyramid's latitude, and now use the Sphinx to get our final and perfectly accurate definition of the cubit measure used in this magnificent construction.

The cubit is defined as 1 / 572,850,000 th of the distance that light travels in one second. The implications and conclusions that can be drawn from this piece of information are fascinating, and from it we can progress further in our understanding of the overall construction.

We now know that the architects are using the same unit of time as we are, or to be more precise, the unit of time that we are using is theirs. Secondly, since we now have a definition of the cubit down to almost infinite accuracy, then we can determine the exact latitude of the Great Pyramid of Giza by working our previous derivation of the cubit's length in reverse. From the speed of light deduction, we can define the length of the cubit as

1 cubit = 0.52333500567338745 metres

Since we know that the radian latitude of the Great Pyramid when multiplied by the distance from the equator to the North Pole will give us ten million times this value, we can calculate that the Great Pyramid's latitude must be 0.523232152 radians or

Great Pyramid Latitude
29° 58' 44.3786365869830

The first of these two pieces of information will allow us to go back to our CAD drawing of the Great Pyramid of Giza, and since the whole of the internal structure is based on algebraic mathematics and the cubit, recreate every passage and shaftway according to the original architects plans. It will allow us to eliminate any errors from the work and to correct any damage to the building that it has suffered over the last 4,500 years.

The second of these pieces of data allows us to compare our current measurement of the Great Pyramid's latitude to that of the architect's design. The final implication, and one that will most likely become the most important of all is that by defining the cubit from 'the speed of light', then the value of the speed of light in the architects units of measure is a round number ending with 4 zeros. The implication being that the frequency of 572.85 MHz may well be quite significant, especially since it is being shown emanating from a communications satellite.

With all of this information pouring out of the monuments of the Giza plateau, it is time to have a look at the second pyramid in more detail as we know that it appears to have been built to represent geostationary satellite orbit and its internal and external architecture may well hold further information.

The surveying point at the sphinx

The small construction between the paws of the Sphinx can be considered to be the primary surveying point on the Giza plateau

THE 2ND GREAT PYRAMID

On first appearances the second pyramid of Giza is completely different to the Great Pyramid in side angle, height and base length. In Petrie's surveying work he reports the base length of the second pyramid as being 215.26m, the side angle as 53° 10' and the height somewhere around 143.9m. In addition to these variations from the first pyramid, the structure is situated slightly higher up the hill on which the Giza monuments are built, having its base level around 10 metres elevated from that of the Great Pyramid.

The internal structure of the pyramid is shown in the illustration below which shows that the immense bulk of the pyramid contains no passageway system, and the only internal structure is that of the two entrance passages, and a horizontal corridor which leads to a chamber situated just to the North of the central axis. In addition to the central chamber, there is another chamber situated on the lower section of the lower entrance passage, built entirely into the bedrock of the plateau.

Each of the two entrance passages were original sealed off with a massive 2 tonne granite door, both of which were fitted from the inside of the pyramid at the time of construction - a point to which Petrie pays close attention. He was not so much concerned about how the builders would have got out of the pyramid, since they could have simply left via the central chamber before it's roof was laid, but more about the confined space in which the 2

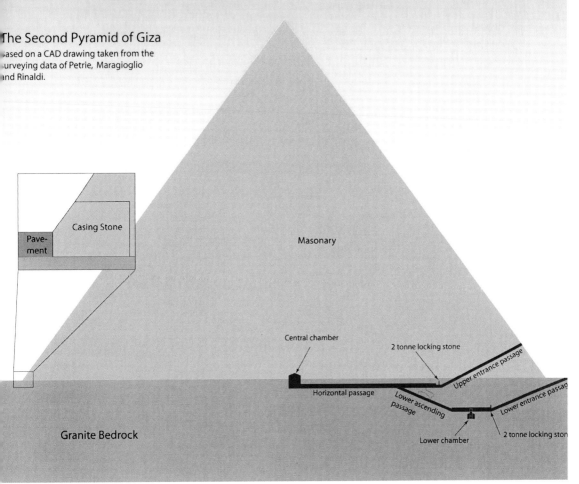

The Second Pyramid of Giza
based on a CAD drawing taken from the surveying data of Petrie, Maragioglio and Rinaldi.

Casing Stone

Pave-ment

Masonary

Central chamber

2 tonne locking stone

Horizontal passage

Upper entrance passage

Lower ascending passage

Lower entrance passage

Granite Bedrock

Lower chamber

2 tonne locking stone

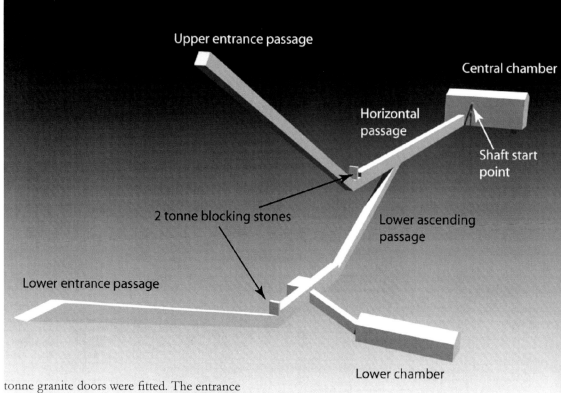

Upper entrance passage

Central chamber

Horizontal passage

Shaft start point

2 tonne blocking stones

Lower ascending passage

Lower entrance passage

Lower chamber

tonne granite doors were fitted. The entrance passages are just over one meter high and wide so that anyone traversing these passageways would have to do so in a bent over position with enough space for only a few people at the same time. Yet the granite door blocks weigh 2000kg, or about the weight of 25 people, dictating that about 40-60 people would be needed to lift the blocks into place. Whilst Petrie came up with no adequate solution to this problem, it is interesting to note that clas-

sical Egyptology must be fully aware of such implausible facts.

To get a better idea of the layout of the passages it is best to look at them in a 3D representation such as the one shown above where the passages and chambers are represented as solid objects, similar to the airspace model that we created in the Unas pyramid. This diagram is a view from the North of the pyramid and shows all of the major features of the passage system. Having then determined the characteristics of the pyramid from the surveying data, we can now move on to see if it is possible to interpret the surveying data and end up with the design principles of the monument. To do so we should use the same principles that were used in the first pyramid, and

The facing stones

(left) In contrast to the Great Pyramid, the facing stones of the second pyramid of Giza have the front face cut away

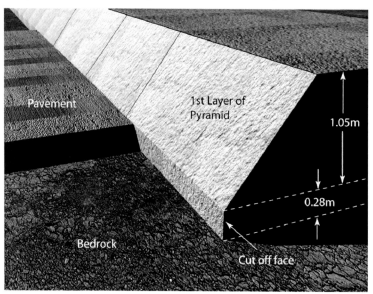

Pavement

1st Layer of Pyramid

1.05m

0.28m

Bedrock

Cut off face

he chamber and
ssageway system

he illustration
eft) shows a 3D
epresentation of
e chamber and
ssageway system
f the second
yramid

he shaft start
oints

elow) The upper
hamber of the pyr-
mid contains the
haft start points
nd several unusual
eatures

therefore start by looking at the core masonry and in particular the point where this meets the foundation platform of the structure as shown in the diagram opposite.

Here we come across a major design difference from the Great Pyramid, and one which is our first clue as to how this pyramid has been put together. The casing stones, rather than sitting on top of the foundation platform and pavement as we saw in the Great pyramid, have been cut off so that the vertical face of the stone butts up against the vertical face of the pavement. Petrie reports that the vertical face of these stones is 28cm high in the south west corner of the pyramid, and reasons that the feature was introduced to prevent the angular foot of the casing stone from becoming damaged. Since we know that every feature inside the first pyramid was significant in the building's architectural design, it would be reasonable to deduce that the cut off base stones of the second pyramid have been truncated for a specific architectural rea-

son. On its own this piece of evidence cannot help us, so we need to look for more features in the pyramid that can.

The second significant clue that the architects have left for us can be found in the central chamber of the pyramid, as shown in the illustration below. On both the North and South walls of the chamber, there is a small square hole in the wall situated high up on the chamber wall, which appears to be the start of the type of shaft that is constructed in the first pyramid's chambers. However, these holes only go back into the wall for a distance of 30cm at which point they stop, with the back face of the shaft hole left as rough rock. A red builders line runs from the east side of this shaft hole down to the floor level, passing on its way a square of about 21 cm^2 which has been drawn onto the wall but not cut out. Finally, from the surveying data of the pyramid we can determine that the shaft hole at the top of the wall lies exactly on the level of the

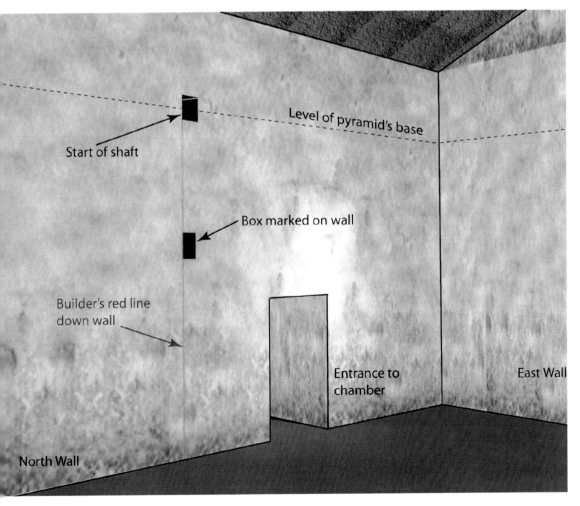

Start of shaft

Level of pyramid's base

Box marked on wall

Builder's red line down wall

Entrance to chamber

East Wall

North Wall

pyramid's base line and has approximately the same width and depth as the vertical cut off edge of the casing stones. It takes little imagination to realise that the area of the pyramid to which our attention is deliberately being drawn is the base level, and that we are being told two pieces of design information. First is that the face of the pyramid where it meets the pavement has been cut off, and secondly that the shaft hole that represent the base line is connected to a lower and similar structure. Finally, since we have seen red builder's lines before in the shafts of the Great Pyramid where they were used to mark out geometric design lines that had not been built into the monument, we are being told that there are geometric lines within this monument that also have not been physically constructed.

The conclusion that can be reached by following this logic is that the base of the pyramid that is at the pavement level is a *false base*, that it has been cut off vertically to indicate this fact, and that the shaft, red line and box system in the lower chamber is telling us to take a new base below that of the original.

The question then arises as to where exactly should we place a new base line in terms of height and width. We are given no other clues from the second pyramid and therefore have to revert to clear thinking to solve the architect's puzzle. There can be only one logical base to take for pyramid two, and its elevation and length determination are perfection itself.

We simply use the base length of the Great Pyramid as the hidden base length of the second and position it at exactly the same elevation on the plateau as that of the Great Pyramid. Not only does this lead to the solution to the architecture of the second pyramid, it also means that both the Great Pyramid and the second pyramid are architecturally identical in their bases, and since we know the base foundation platform length of the Great Pyramid to perfection, we will have generated a precise starting point for the geometry of the second pyramid.

As well as the architectural information contained within the pyramid, we also know from its positioning on the plateau

The face angle of the second pyramid

The geometric construction of the face angle of the pyramid is formed from the Great Pyramid's base length

Underlying construction principl

The system of positioning of the second pyramid is confirmed by the geometric layout of the building

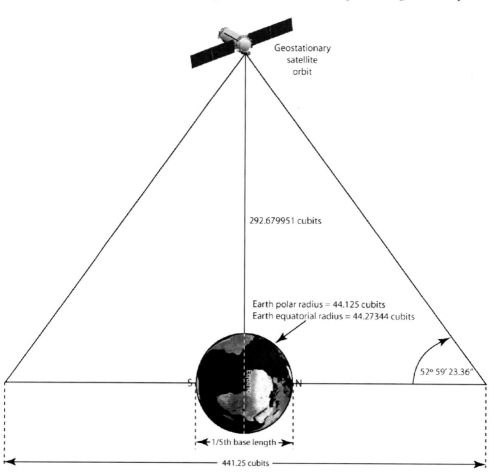

Geostationary
satellite
orbit

292.679951 cubits

Earth polar radius = 44.125 cubits
Earth equatorial radius = 44.27344 cubits

52° 59' 23.36"

1/5th base length

441.25 cubits

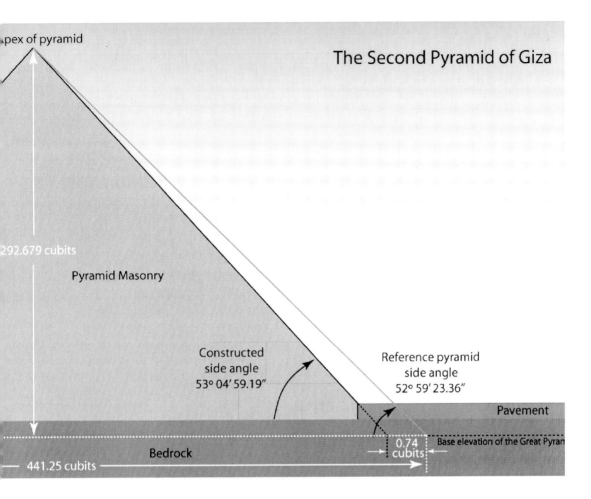

apex of pyramid

The Second Pyramid of Giza

292.679 cubits

Pyramid Masonry

Constructed
side angle
53° 04′ 59.19″

Reference pyramid
side angle
52° 59′ 23.36″

Pavement

0.74
cubits

Base elevation of the Great Pyram

Bedrock

441.25 cubits

that it represents geostationary satellite orbit. Combining all the information now at our disposal it is possible to accurately recreate the geometric design used by the architects in pyramid two in the following manner.

We can start our construction with a base length identical to that of the Great Pyramid's foundation platform. Since we know that we cannot create a model of the Earth in the same manner as we did for the first pyramid since the side angles of pyramid two are different from that of the first pyramid, then we need to find another logical way of creating an Earth model from this base length. Sticking rigidly to principles that have already been used in pyramid one, we can divide the base into fifths, a proportion which was used in pyramid one when determining the shape of the pyramid from the elliptical circumference formula. In order to mark out a representation of geostationary satellite orbit inside the pyramid's structure, we will need to have the polar axis of the Earth running parallel to the ground, and the equatorial line alligned vertically.

If we draw out this construction on a CAD system we can immediately see that the resulting angle between the base ends of the geometry and a position representing geostationary satellite orbit is very close indeed to that of the angle of pyramid two. In the diagram opposite all of the relevant dimensions are marked, and the drawing is constructed in the following sequence. First of all the base length is divided by five to determine the polar radius of the Earth model. The equatorial radius is then calculated from the WGS84 reference ellipsoid, and the scale of the model of the Earth can then be determined. Using this scale the distance of geostationary satellite orbit, 42,164,169m, is reduced down to give the height of the design of 292.68 cubits. At this stage the side angle varies from that of Petrie's survey by about 10′ of a degree, however we have not yet fully applied the lessons that we learnt in the Great pyramid to this geometry.

You will recall from the construction of the base of the Great pyramid that the architects built a plinth around the pyramid in order to help us pinpoint the edge of the constructed pyramid's side. They have done exactly the same with pyramid two, and the resulting geometric drawing is shown in the illustration on the previous page where the corresponding amount, 0.74 cubits, has been removed from the geometric base length before the side angle is calculated, resulting in an angle for the pyramid's casing of 53° 04' 59.19". This now brings us back into familiar territory, as we are starting to look at very small angular differences between theoretical and surveyed quantities, and there is no merit or purpose in trying to match up the two angles. Petrie has various measurements for the angles of the casing varying between 53° 02' and 53° 14' and settles on an estimate of 53° 10'. The linear variation between Petrie's averaged angle and that of the theoretical geometry when measure over the face of the pyramid amounts to a few centimeters and the state of preservation of the monument's exterior precludes any further accuracy in the comparison.

Now that we have a reasonable proposition for both the height and base lengths, we need to determine with what logic the pyramid's pavement elevation was positioned, since at present we have no indication of this. If we superimpose the geometric construction on top of an architecturally accurate CAD drawing of the second pyramid we can start to analyse the geometric features which were used to determine the positioning of the other features of the monument. We can start in the hunt for the geometry by drawing the half circumference of the ellipse below the model of the Earth, just as was done in the Great Pyramid although taking note that

the Earth model is rotated around by 90° in this instance. We can then apply the algebraic geometry that we determined for the first pyramid to position a tangent line onto the elliptical model of the Earth emanating from the end of the half circumference line, and from it we can see that the ground level elevation with reference to the geometric base line has been determined, as shown below. From these calculations it can be determined that the base level of the second pyramid in relation to the geometric base line elevation, and therefore also in relation to the base level of the Great pyramid by definition, is 18.798 cubits or 9.84 metres. The level of the pavement of the pyramid, which is higher by the amount of the vertical face of the core masonry where it was cut off to butt against the pavement will therefore be 28cm higher at an elevation above the Great pyramid's pavement level of 10.11m, a value identical to the elevation quoted by the Italian surveying of the Giza plateau carried out by Maragioglio and Rinaldi and the 1960's . This now puts us in a position to be able to accurately join up the CAD drawing of the pyramid and the geometric data, and from it we can extract two more of the major features of the design principles. The elevation of the entrance passage is defined by the top of the ellipse, and the floor level of the lower chamber is defined by the midpoint of the tangent line which emanates from the end of the half circumference geometry line. From here we can then determine the angles and positions of the passages, since they are formed from the same starting ellipse, using tangent lines once again to determine their angles, as shown in the illustration on the next page.

Geometry of the chamber system

The use of the ellipse and its tangent formed from a base length of half of its circumference is repeated in the second pyramid

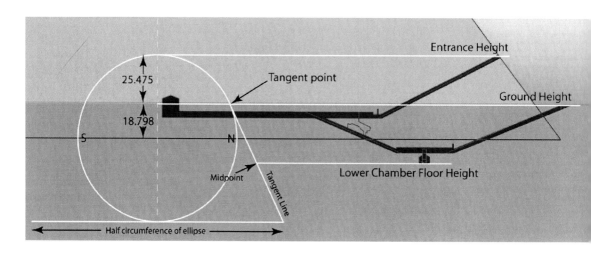

These angular passage geometry lines are constructed in the following sequence. First, from the end of the buried base level a point is taken up to the pavement level and from here a line is taken down to the end of the half circumference line to form the angle of the lower entrance passage. The midpoint of this line falls within the lower chamber, from which point a tangent line can be taken up to the ellipse to form the ascending passageway. The upper entrance passage is formed by taking a line from the entrance door of the pyramid, which was defined by the horizontal geometry, down to a tangent point on the ellipse.

In comparison to the Great pyramid, the geometry of the second is substantially easier to work out and all of the internal passages and angles can be deduced from one principle piece of geometry which fits all of the architectural components. However, knowing to what lengths the architects have gone to conceal their work, and knowing their remarkable perception of human nature, the ease with which this pyramid's geometry can be solved leaves you with a distinctly strange feeling.

Since we have no other data to work with, and are not about to get into the wonderful world of speculation, we can do no more with the second pyramid of Giza at this juncture. We should now progress on to have a look at the much smaller third pyramid on the Giza plateau.

The descending passage

A tangent to the ellipse is used for the formation of the descending passage

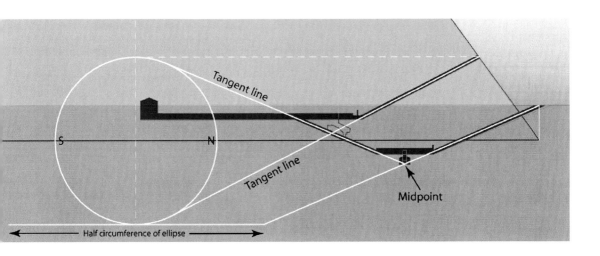

UNFINISHED BUSINESS

It has been a consistent aspect of the architects work so far that they set out the information required to solve the design in a logical order forcing us to understand one section of the work before we can understand the next. This is also the case with the third pyramid on the Giza plateau, a pyramid which is considerably smaller than the other two leading to the impression that it may not be part of the same design system.

Solving its primary design principle is relatively straight forward in comparison to solving that of the first two pyramids since we have quite a collection of information at our disposal. We know that the first pyramid is a model of the Earth, that the second is in geostationary satellite around the first, and that the architects are employing both a primary and secondary scale in their work. So all we need to do is to find the distance between the first and third pyramids and scale that distance up by both of the architectural scales and determine if this orbital distance around the Earth is of any significance.

It is at this point that we need to look at the surveying work of Petrie once more, and we come across a quite unusual discovery in his work. In the original printed copy of his 1883 survey he has made a mathematics error in his determination of the distance between the first and third pyramids. Although his surveying station marks on the plateau are correct, when he came to calculating the distances from the surveying points he inadvertently reversed the plus and minus signs in his calculations, an error which has recently been corrected in the on-line version of the book. The correct distance from the first to third pyramids according to Petrie's survey station marks is 936.1595 m.

We have already been able to determine the scale of the model of the Earth that the Great Pyramid represents with absolute accuracy as being 86697.4 : 1 and so the secondary scale used for the smaller Earth shaped ellipse from which the Great Pyramid's lower chamber system was formed must be 433486.7 : 1. If we apply the first of these scales to the distance between the Great Pyramid and pyramid three we find that the orbital distance is not significant, but upon applying the secondary scale the orbital distance of the third pyramid from the first becomes 405,812,657 m. To understand what this orbital distance relates to we need to have a slightly more in depth understanding of elliptical orbits around the Earth.

If we take the orbit of the moon around the Earth as an example we find that the distance between the moon and Earth varies during each rotation that the moon makes around our planet. The technical terms for the various elements of the orbit are shown below in which some recent actual distances have also been added to give the diagram a sense of scale..

The numerical data for each of the orbital elements varies each month due to the ever changing gravitational pulls within the solar system, and to find exact numerical figures such as those in the illustration one has to use an ephemeris table. An ephemeris table is a snapshot of where any celestial body can be found in the solar system at any given time, and to describe the body's position there needs to be a reference date and time to which the data can be related. This reference frame, or epoch as it is known, is the most essential part of the ephemeris

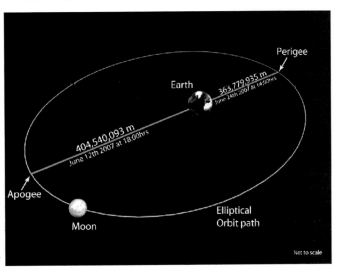

data, and currently the accepted reference epoch is known as J2000. In simplified terms this means that the positional data of the moon today, for example, is given with reference to where it was on January 1st 2000. It is a simple concept, but one which is essential to our ability to describe the planet and star positions with accuracy.

Comparing the numerical data in the illustration to our orbital distance for pyramid three it can be seen that the pyramid has been placed to represent the moon's orbit at its furthest distance from the Earth during is monthly cycle, a position known as apogee. The illustration below shows the moon orbit around the Earth on the Giza plateau model, with the perigee being derived from the average orbital eccentricity published in the header files of NASA's DE406 ephemeris tables.

At this stage the orbital ellipse has no matching points on the Giza plateau other than the third pyramid, which appears to specifically mark out the apogee of the orbit. What we need to do is to realise what the architects are showing us, and from there progress onwards in the design. The architects have not shown us the position of the moon in this diagram, they have shown us the orbital trajectory of the moon, and what is more they have used the secondary architectural scale rather than the primary one. Remarkable as it may seem, it would be entirely within keeping with their work so far if they have actually mapped out the Moon at the correct primary scale distance from the Great Pyramid, and that the orbital data derived from pyramid three is only the first step in the calculation. If this proposition is true then we will have to search beyond the Giza plateau for another monument, and one which will be situated at an exact distance from the Great Pyramid of Giza, a distance which we can calculate. If the third pyramid's distance from the first, when scaled up by the secondary scale, represents the Moon at a distance of 405,812,657 m from the Earth, then we need to reduce this real life distance by the primary scale of the Great Pyramid to determine where the architects should have placed the primary scale moon monument.

Performing the calculation gives a scaled distance of 4680.79 m, suggesting that

The third pyramid of Giza

The scaled orbit of the moon positions the third pyramid of Giza

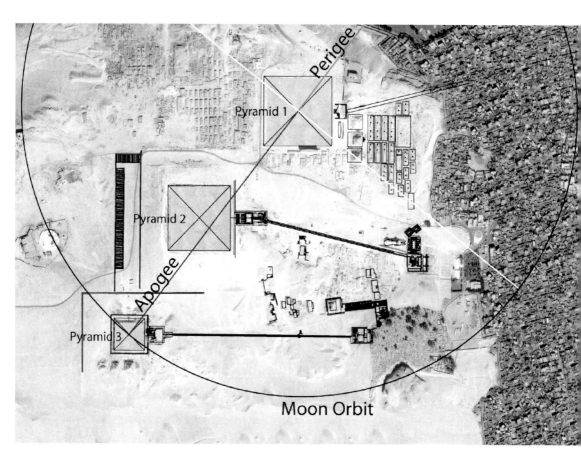

there should be a monument nearly 5 km from the Giza plateau which represents the moon, and it is at this stage that the overwhelming magnitude of the Giza Plateau construction first appears to us.

In order to determine the distance between two points on the Earth, one cannot simply draw a straight line between them and measure its distance. The reason for this being that, as we have discovered in our analysis to date, the Earth is an ellipsoid and so the shortest distance between any two points on the planet is actually a curved line. The mathematics of ellipsoidal geometry is a particularly difficult subject to comprehend and more importantly to utilise, and we are in the lucky position that there are numerous pieces of software available for computer systems which will make the calculations for us. These geodesic distance calculators are essential for calculating distances and bearings around the globe, although strictly not essential at this stage in our work since we are looking at a distance of only 5 km between two points where a linear path and elliptical one will show very little difference. However, since we are aware of the immaculate precision that has been shown by the architects in their design, it would be fully advisable to make any calculations with as much accuracy as we can.

A reasonable map of the locations of the Pyramids around Giza can be found in the reference work of Mark Lehner entitled "The Complete Pyramids" as well as from numerous on-line sources. From these we can see that if we go south from the Giza plateau, the next pyramid that we come across is the 'Unfinished Pyramid' at a town called Zawiyet al-Aryan. The reason for the pyramid's name is that, according to Egyptologists, it was a pyramid that was never completed, and the only sections of the building that were built were the entrance passage and subterranean chamber which was cut from the bedrock.

This pyramid can be located on satellite photography programmes that are commercially available today, such as 'Google Earth' which, while not purporting to be a specialist programme, do provide sufficiently accurate data for the position of the monument to be determined within a few decimetres or so. In this stage of our analysis such accuracy is acceptable, and we can determine the position of the 'unfinished' pyramid as being 29° 56' 24.54" N 31° 09' 5.56" E as shown in the illustration on the next page which is a screen shot taken from the 'Google Earth' computer programme on which the latitude and longitude of the point can be seen in the lower left corner

We then need to acquire a geodesic distance calculator, and this can be downloaded from the American National Geodetic survey or, alternatively the on-line calculator provided by the Australian Government mapping department can be used. Both of these computational methods give the same results and plot distances accurate to one millimetre across the whole face of the Earth.

If we plug in the latitude and longitude of the Great Pyramid and the 'unfinished' pyramid into either of them, we find that the distance between the two pyramids is 4638.85 m - compared to the distance at which we have predicted to find a monument at 4680.79 m. The 'unfinished' pyramid at Zawiyet el-Aryan is the fourth pyramid of the Giza plateau and is a model of our moon, although there is clearly a small discrepancy in the calculation of 41 meters which at this point cannot be explained. In addition to telling us the distance between the two monuments, the geodesic distance calculator also tells us the bearing between the monuments, which is 158° 49' 19.88" East of North when measured from the central axis of the Great Pyramid of Giza. We already know from the positioning of pyramid two that the architects have used angular rotations related to cubits for its positioning, so we need to now check if the same system has been used to position the pyramid at Zawiyet El-Aryan which represents the Moon.

We can convert its angle from the bearing shown in the previous paragraph, which is measured from North, to the angle when measured from East following on from the method that the architects have shown us in the positioning of pyramid two. We should also convert it into radians giving an angle of 1.2012 radians between the Great Pyramid and the unfinished pyramid. The distance between the two monuments is 4638.85 metres, and since we know the exact value of the cubit, we know that this distance between the monuments is 8864.01 cubits. Dividing the length by the angle gives a ratio of cubits per radian of 7379.45 - a figure which is meaningless and which would tend to lead to the deduction that there is no correspondence between the angle and the distance. We must remember however that as well as designing the construction of the monuments, the architects also had

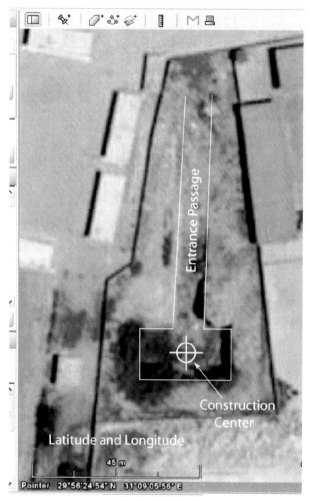

Entrance Passage

Construction Center

Latitude and Longitude

45 m

Pointer 29°56'24.54" N 31°09'05.56" E

The unfinished pyramid of Zawiyet

(left) The remains of the hole carved into the ground are visible on satellite photography

ferred to from here on as a 'natural meter' or 'nm'.

The distance between the Great Pyramid and the 'unfinished pyramid' at Zawiyet El-Aryan is 4637.93 nm and dividing this length by the angle between the monuments gives a ratio of 3861 nm per radian - once more a meaningless value. However, if we perform this set of calculations on the distance that we expected to find the monument at, which was 43 meters further, then this angular rotation comes out at exactly 4000nm per radian - a highly logical ratio and one which relates perfectly to the 400 cubits per radian rotation ratio used to position pyramid two on the Giza Plateau. Although we are clearly in the realms of estimation, and lacking some knowledge of what we are looking at, we can still plot a spiral emanating from the Great pyramid of Giza at 400nm per radian and from it find the unfinished pyramid at Zawiyet as shown opposite, although missing the center of the monument by the amount shown on the inset graphic.

The curved path of 400nm per radian starts from the center of the Great Pyramid, and when it is drawn in detail it can be seen that the immense causeway which leads from the Great Pyramid appears to have its architectural geometry defined from this curved path, as shown in diagram on the next page. At 400nm from the pyramid's center the first section of the causeway is marked with a perpendicular bisector, and the linear section of the second section of the causeway is marked out. At 800nm from the center point, the bend in the causeway is defined, and at 1600nm from the pyramid center the end of the causeway is defined. Finally, the building dimensions at the end of the causeway are defined by the tangent to the curved line as it bends around to make its way down to the 'unfinished pyramid'

Having discovered what appears to be the architect's method of positioning of the Zawiyet El-Aryan structure, which represents the moon, this then allows us to go back to the Giza plateau and accurately plot all of the data that we have just collected onto

The zawiyet spiral

(right) The location of the unfinished pyramid is seemingly dictated by the curved path from the Great Pyramid of Giza

the task of making sure that their design was concealed from casual observation, and so it is worth investigating this apparent anomaly in more depth.

You will recall from the definition of the cubit that it was calculated originally by taking the latitude of the Great Pyramid in radians, and multiplying that figure by the distance from the equator to the North pole. You may also recall that when the French invented the Metric system they defined the metre as one ten millionth of the distance between the equator and North Pole - and got the calculation wrong. It was the similarity between the French metre and the distance used to define the cubit that led us to the cubit's definition in the first place. So it is worth checking that there is no connection between the angular rotation of the pyramid in Zawiyet when measured in radians, and the distance used to define the cubit. This distance, which is one ten millionth of the equator to pole distance has a value of 1.000196572m and will be re-

East

Giza Plateau

Path of 400 natural metres per radian from due East

Entrance Passage

Center of Construction

'Unfinished Pyramid'

Zawiyet El-Aryan

the principle geometry of pyramid three and understand exactly what the architects have done with the smaller model of the moon that they located close to the Great Pyramid.

They have used the secondary scale from the Great Pyramid to illustrate the Moon's orbit, since an elliptical orbit at the primary scale would have been too big to be represented and identified, and they have used the primary scale to position the monument of the Moon in Zawiyet. The two pieces of geometry are then beautifully put together by marking off the moon monument's position in Zawiyet onto the moon's elliptical orbit representation on the Giza plateau as shown in the illustration opposite. This marked off position on the orbital ellipse is in a direct North-South line with the marker point in the paws of the Sphinx. The angle from this point back to pyramid three is very similar to that of the angle to the Sphinx from pyramid two, and is also duplicated to the north of pyramid three with a large building structure marking out the same angle. Finally the marked position on the orbit, the end of pyramid three's causeway, and the structure to the north of the causeway are all lined up with the centre of pyramid two's temple.

The point that we have found on the orbital ellipse is clearly intended to be found within the architecture, although there are a number of items that leave us with a sensation that we may not have the full story laid out infront of us. The distance down to the unfinished pyramid was shorter than we expected, and the geometry that we have ended up with on the Giza plateau has not been marked out definitively by the architects - it is all implicit rather than explicit construction. For certain there is something in what we are looking at, and it will not be until we know a little more about the whole remarkable construction system that we will be able to find out exactly what the architects have done with this part of the design.

To start out on the final part of this remarkable voyage of discovery we will need to go back to the Great Pyramid once more and discover its one remaining big secret - that of how to get ourselves out of the pyramid mathematically from the underground chambers where we last ended up in our investigation of that monument.

The complete lay out of the Giza plateau

(right) The moon orbit completes the geometric layout of the Giza plateau

The Great Pyramid's causeway

(below) The complex geometric construction of the Great pyramid's causeway is based on the spiral which connects to Zawiyet

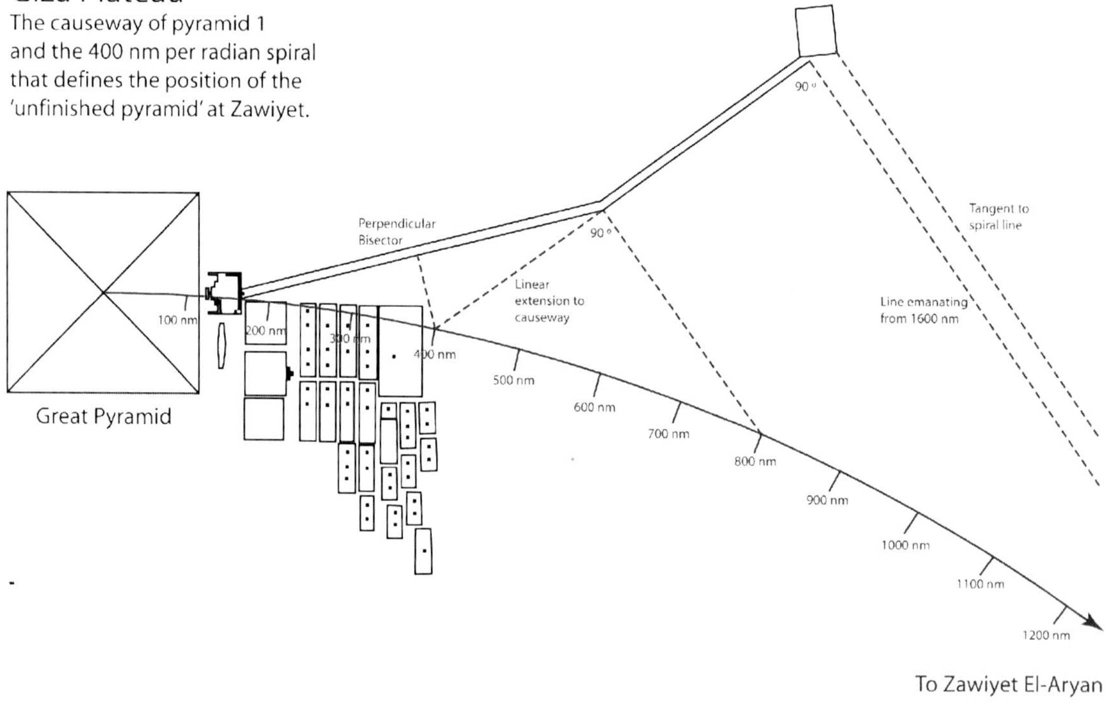

Giza Plateau

The causeway of pyramid 1 and the 400 nm per radian spiral that defines the position of the 'unfinished pyramid' at Zawiyet.

Great Pyramid

Perpendicular Bisector

Linear extension to causeway

Tangent to spiral line

Line emanating from 1600 nm

90°

90°

100 nm
200 nm
300 nm
400 nm
500 nm
600 nm
700 nm
800 nm
900 nm
1000 nm
1100 nm
1200 nm

To Zawiyet El-Aryan

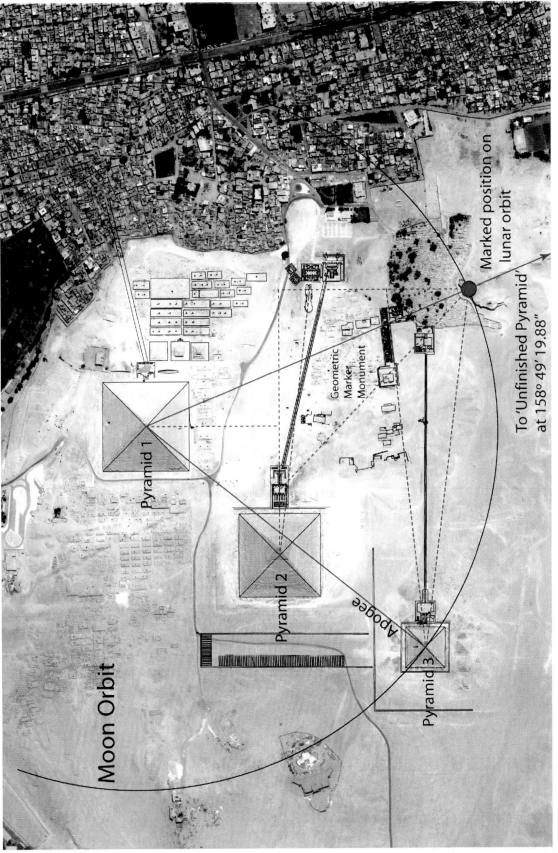

Moon Orbit

Pyramid 1

Pyramid 2

Apogee

Pyramid 3

Geometric
Marker
Monument

Marked position on
lunar orbit

To 'Unfinished Pyramid'
at 158° 49' 19.88"

ANOTHER TWIST IN THE TAIL

There is a section of the Great Pyramid which we have disregarded up to this point, and that is the subterranean chambers which were carved into the bedrock 30m below the pavement level of the pyramid. We briefly looked at them when we were analysing the construction of the entrance passage and determined that the rotated T-bar construction was designed to be aligned with the entrance to these underground chambers.

As Petrie describes in his surveying details, the workmanship appears to be very rough in this section of the pyramid, with unfinished floors and walls and irregular angles throughout. This lack of finishing could lead to the assumption that this lower section of the pyramid contains little important information, and it is exactly this assumption that the architects are relying upon to hide the details contained within this section of the building. The details of the passages and chambers of the subterranean area of the Great Pyramid are shown in the accompanying illustrations, with the passages and chambers shown as solid objects in the second of the two illustrations overleaf, and in which the following details can be seen.

The pyramid's sloping entrance passage joins to a horizontal passage which is 8.8m in length and runs through to the doorway of the main subterranean chamber. A small side room which is 1.8m in length from North to South has been carved out of this passageway, and between this small chamber and the main chamber, the central east-west axis plane of the pyramid can be found. The main subterranean chamber opens up towards the west, and is considerably rougher in finish than is shown in this diagram. The floor of this chamber varies vastly in height, with the distance between the roof and floor being only a few centimeters towards some sections of the west wall. It has been shown in this diagram in schematic form to give an idea of the general proportions of the room. Close to the East wall of the chamber can be found a square hole, the sides of which are set at an angle to the chamber walls and which drops 10m into the bedrock below the floor surface. From the South door of the main subterranean chamber, a passage has been carved

The subterranean chambers in 3D

(right) The unusual construction of the subterranean chambers with the immense square hole in the base of the floor

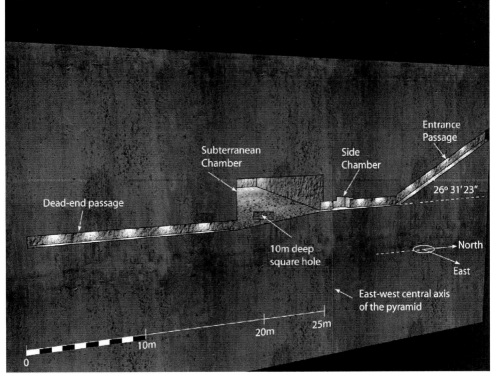

Subterranean Chamber

Side Chamber

Entrance Passage

Dead-end passage

26° 31' 23"

10m deep square hole

North

East

East-west central axis of the pyramid

20m   25m

10m

0

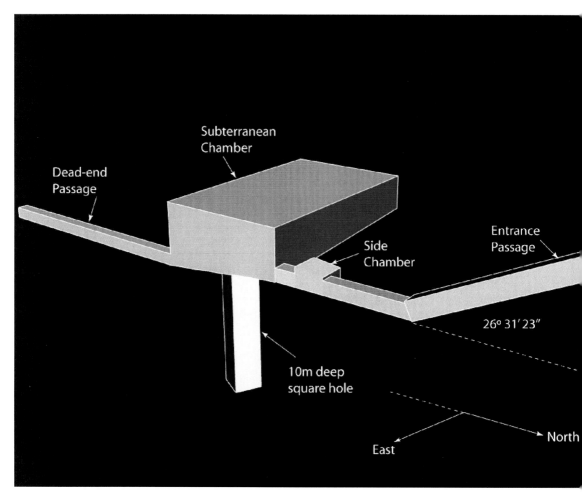

Dead-end Passage

Subterranean Chamber

Entrance Passage

Side Chamber

26° 31′ 23″

10m deep square hole

East

North

very roughly out of the rock, and after 16.5m it comes to an end. This section of the Great Pyramid has been thoroughly scanned using ground penetrating radar and, as is whown in the diagram, the passage does indeed stop where it appears to - there are no hidden passages or chambers beyond.

Yet you will recall from the section regarding the entrance passage to the pyramid that we deduced that the mathematical exit from the pyramid was not to be found at the top of the entrance passage, but at the lower end of it in these subterranean chambers. The architectural and logical design tells us that somewhere in this subterranean chamber there is and exit from the pyramid, and since we know that it is not a physically constructed exit, it must be a geometric one. To find this geometric exit takes a large amount of work, but it is work which fits in perfectly with the logic of what we have come across so far. We know that we have a model of the Earth as the primary piece of geometry from which

the building is designed, and up to this point we have worked all of the mathematics and geometry in 2 dimensions. However, having seen the depth of knowledge on display from the architects in would not be beyond credibility if the construction was actually based upon a 3 dimensional model of the Earth and not a flat 2 dimensional one. If this were to be the case then the cross sectional shape of the Earth from which all of the geometry has been formed could actually be an orthographic projection of a full 3 dimensional ellipsoid, with the resulting complexities in the mathematics that would entail. If this is the case then there is also the possibility that the ellipsoid of the Earth has also been rotated, and it is once that this possibility is investigated that the solution to the underground chambers starts to take shape.

If we take the bold and imaginative step of rotating the whole of the Great Pyramid of Giza using three angles, the first angle being that of the axial tilt of the Earth, and

The elements of the subterranean section

(below) Although roughly carved, the exact measurement details of the underground chambers is known

the others for now being chosen arbitrarily, and then spend significant amounts of time analysing the resulting structures, something quite breathtaking appears. The illustration below is a plan view from above the subterranean passage system after the pyramid has been rotated by three specific and highly logical angles. The first angle is the axial tilt of the Earth, the second angle is the angle of the Earth's ecliptic to the invariable plane of the solar system, and the third angle is a geometric reference angle of 225° (45°). The details of the diagram may well look confusing at this stage, but as the comprehension of this highly developed section of the pyramid's architecture becomes clear, then so will the contents of the illustration.

The dead end passageway has ended up at approximately 45° east of North, the descending entrance passageway is at about 36° degrees east of north, and the central axis of the pyramid, which is marked in red on the diagram, is at an angle of 50.5°. The whole of the system is skewed around so that the original west sides of the passageways are now visible from above, and the roof of the small side chamber protrudes over the original east wall of the passage in which it sits. In summary, the subterranean area of the pyramid has ended up looking like a piece of modern art, and it would appear that rather than having solved anything we have actually created a much more complicated structure and for absolutely no apparent purpose. To see just what we have done, we need to travel 500km down the River Nile to Luxor, the ancient capital of Egypt, and have a look at the main temple of Luxor which is shown in the illustration overleaf.

The temple is a magnificent structure, and one of very few of the Egyptian ancient monuments which can be found on

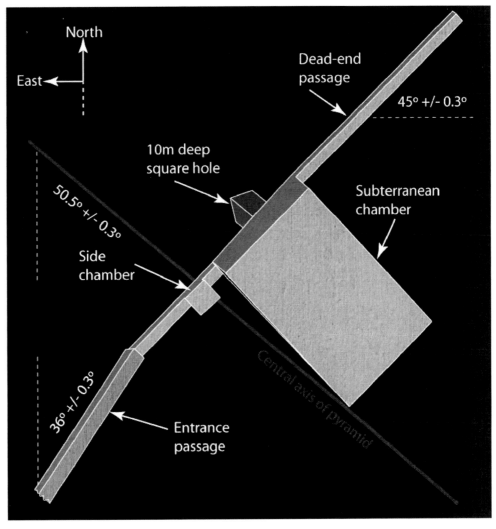

The rotated subterranean chambers

The three angle rotation of the subterranean chambers results in an obscure plan view

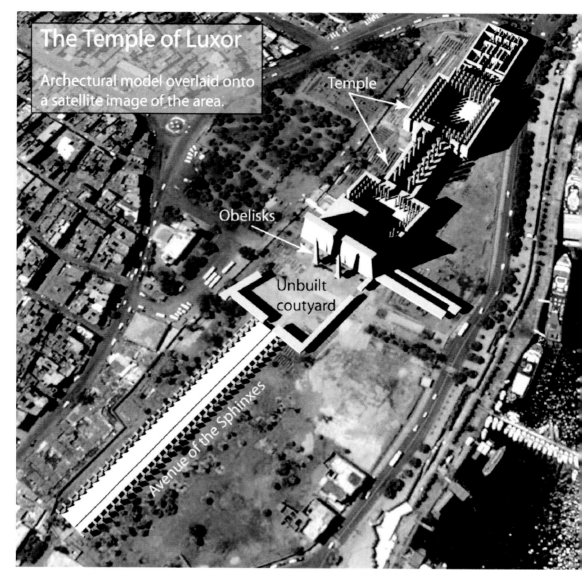

The Temple of Luxor

Archectural model overlaid onto a satellite image of the area.

Temple

Obelisks

Unbuilt coutyard

Avenue of the Sphinxes

the East side of the Nile rather than the West, where all of the pyramids can be found. The temple comprises of a majestic avenue lined either side by statues of the Sphinx; and unbuilt section which is enclosed by walls, but which has no internal structure; two colossal obelisks, one of which has been removed and can now be found in the Place du Concorde in Paris; a towering wall structure which marks out the start of the temple proper; and a series of temples and courtyards. It was surveyed in detail over an eight year period by Egyptologists and its dimension and angles are known with absolute certainty.

Exactly what the connection is between this temple and the Great Pyramid becomes clear when the ground plan of the Temple of Luxor and the rotated Great Pyramid plan view are superimposed upon each other, as shown in the diagram opposite. The bizarre looking rotated structure of the subterranean chambers is a perfect model of the temple of Luxor's ground plan precise in all dimensions and angles, with the central axis of the pyramid after rotation clearly marked out in the Temple's structure. The bend in between the pyramid's entrance passage and the horizontal passage is at the same place as the bend in the Temple axis.

This architectural design is so extraordinary that amount of mathematical complexity required for its creation and the incomprehensible imagination required to create it may well leave you wondering whether it is intentional on the part of the architects,

The temple of Luxor

The bent temple of Luxor placed alongside the Nile on the east bank in contrast to the majority of the other monuments in Egypt

plan of the
temple

The plan view of
the rotated subter-
ranean chambers
placed on top of
the ground plan
of the temple of
Luxor

or possibly the results of an over imaginative analysis of the work on my part. It would be a most rational position to take that it is indeed an over elaboration on my part, if it were not for the fact that the amount of supporting evidence that the architects have incorporated in the design is overwhelming, as we see in the following page. At this stage you, the reader, are in the same position that I found myself in when I first came across all of the elements which make up this section of the overall design plans. It simply does not appear credible. Effectively, what we are being shown is that by going down into the subterranean chambers of the Great Pyramid, and mathematically progressing through the chamber and into the dead-end passage, then we will come out in the avenue of the Sphinxes in the Temple of Luxor. With such an outrageous proposition we need to start to assemble the corroborating evidence.

The first place to start is by looking

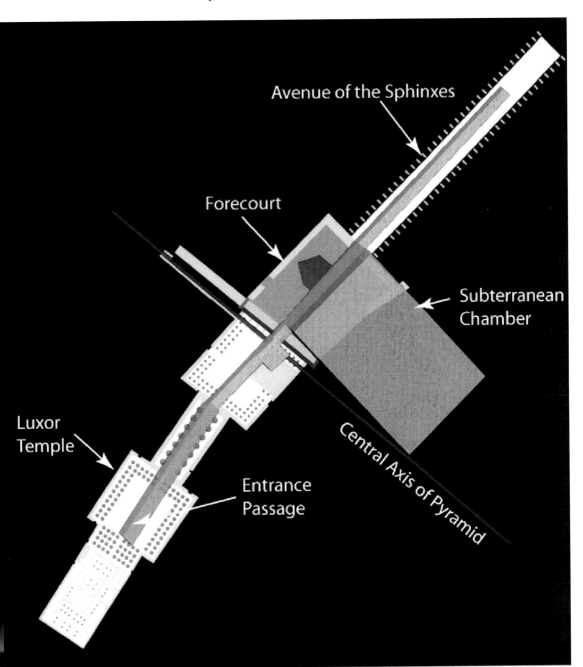

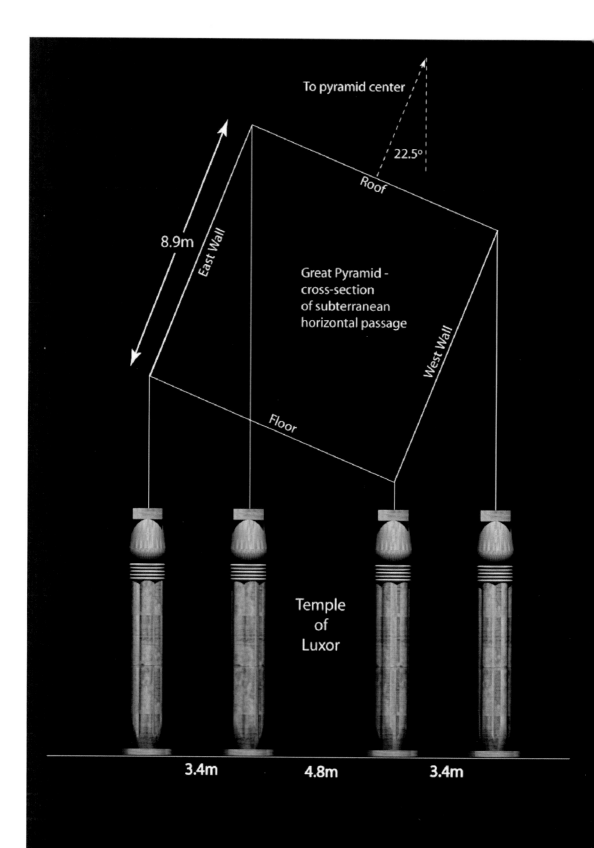

To pyramid center

22.5°

Roof

8.9m

East Wall

Great Pyramid -
cross-section
of subterranean
horizontal passage

West Wall

Floor

Temple
of
Luxor

3.4m   4.8m   3.4m

The pillar align-
ent in the temple

eft) The cross
ction of the
bterranean pas-
ge constitutes the
esign geometry
f the pillar layout
the temple

he deep shaft in
e chamber

ight) The dia-
ram of the shaft
ken from the
ork of Edgar

at the cross section of the horizontal passages in the subterranean area of the pyramid, since we have just performed a rotation upon them and their position after this rotation may well be significant.

The illustration opposite shows the cross section of the horizontal passage system after it has been rotated about the three angles. With the projection of the four corners of the square passageway marked on the plane of projection, or more simple language, marked on the floor. The rotation angle of the Earth's axial tilt dictates that the spacing between the four points will not be regular, as can be seen in the dimensions marked on the diagram. What can then be seen by comparing these distances to the temple layout in Luxor is that the pillar spacing in the Temple has been dictated by this geometric architectural principle. This pillar spacing by itself could be explained in many other ways if it were not for the fact that if we go back to the subterranean chamber you will recall that it contains a square hole, 10m deep and at an angle to the side walls of the chamber. This hole is shown in accompanying illustration which is taken from the work of the Edgar brother. As can be seen, the architects have angled the square cross section of the hole

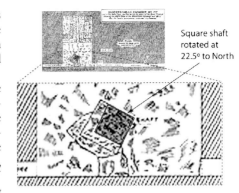

Square shaft
rotated at
22.5° to North

at about 22.5°, giving us our first piece of confirmation that what we have just done is probably both correct, and intentional on the part of the architects.

The vast amounts of other corroborating evidence can be found exclusively in the Temple of Luxor itself, and these will be explained in the next chapter, but before leaving the Great Pyramid we should tidy up a few of the details regarding this rotation that we have just performed.

When you perform a rotation around 3 axis, the order in which you carry out the rotations has an effect on the end result. It is therefore essential to explain before leaving this chapter the order in which

he rotation
ngles and order

he rotation of
he pyramid that
required in the
ecific order to
roduce the correct
round plan

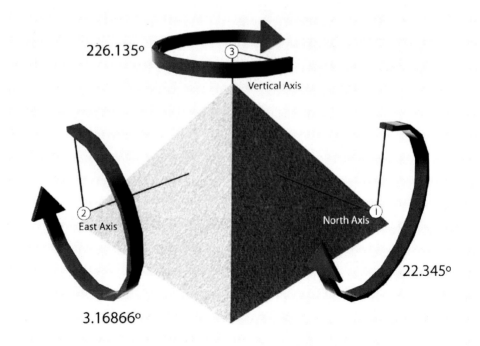

226.135°

Vertical Axis

East Axis

North Axis

22.345°

3.16866°

the rotation of the Great Pyramid has been carried out. The pyramid was first rotated around the north-south axis by 22.345° in an anti-clockwise direction when viewed towards the north from the perspective of the centre of the pyramid. This first rotation accounts for the resulting bend in the passageway system and aligns it perfectly with that of the Luxor temple.

The second rotation is around the east-west axis and is by 3.17° in an anti-clockwise direction when viewed towards the east from the centre of the pyramid. This small rotation, which is seemingly insignificant, accounts for the alignment of the pyramid's central axis with the axis markings at the Luxor temple. Thirdly is the rotation of 226° around the vertical axis in an anti-clockwise direction when viewed upwards from the centre of the structure. This rotation is the principle rotation which aligns the subterranean chambers with the temple passageways. *All of the angles that are quoted here are approximate angles that were used during the analysis* of this section of the architectural design, and no significance should be placed on there exact values. The exact numerical values of these angles are determined in a later chapter.

So we now have a most extraordinary situation on our hands where it appears that the hidden geometric exit from the Great Pyramid of Giza is in the underground chambers of the building, and that by taking this mathematical exit one emerges on the Avenue of the Sphinxes, just in front of the temple of Luxor. Quite clearly there is something that must link together the architecture of these two buildings, and to find out just what the link is we need to pay a visit to the temple of Luxor.

WELCOME TO LUXOR

*The temple of
Luxor*

*A view down the
avenue of sphinxes
taken from the exit
point of the Great
Pyramid's lower
passage*

The majestic avenue of Sphinxes which leads to the Temple of Luxor's main entrance is shown in the photograph below and its magnificence is entirely appropriate to the astonishing architectural construction which has lead us to this point. After years of analysis of the dark passageways of the Great Pyramid of Giza, this view of the Luxor Temple is provided to us by the architects of this quite incomprehensible architectural masterpiece The two colossal obelisks which mark out the temple's entrance, flanked on either side by immense statues of the Egyptian Gods, are the two largest obelisks in Egypt and the overall dimensions and architectural brilliance of the temple are breathtaking. The obelisks, which are clearly the primary archi-

tectural structure of the entrance area are covered from top to bottom in hieroglyphs and constitute the first written words that the architects have displayed to us since we started on our quest to understand the Giza plateau. As shown in the photograph, there is only one obelisk currently in place in Luxor, the second having been removed by French explorers and currently resides in the Place du Concorde in Paris.

The very first of the hieroglyphics, which appears on all sides of both of the obelisks and which is located 25 metres above ground level at the top of the obelisks, needs little formal academic education for us to understand its meaning. It is shown in the illustration overleaf, and is a picture of a man kneeling before a god - an entirely appropriate symbol bearing in mind the complexity of the design work that we have seen up to this point. It was the staggering three dimensional rotation of the Great Pyramid of Giza that has lead us to the temple in Luxor, the accuracy of that rotational geometry when superimposed upon the temple layout that leaves us with no doubt at all that this location, some 500km from Giza, is the next point in the architectural design that is being presented to us. However, despite the certainty of our determination of this location being linked to the Great Pyramid of Giza's

architectural design, we have as yet found no other logical proof within the architecture of why this should be so. There clearly must be something more than the rotational geometry which links the two structures to each other since we know that the architectural design of the Great Pyramid is based upon highly accurate astronomical measurements. To start to find out what this connection between the temple of Luxor and the Great Pyramid is, we need only go back to the principle design element of the pyramid.

Within the Great Pyramid the complex system of shafts and passageways led us eventually to the grand gallery, and the central architectural purpose of the monument was to give us precise astronomical data for the Earth. We concluded in a previous chapter that the building is designed to show us the aphelion of the Earth in its annual orbit around the sun. It would be in keeping with the architectural design to assume that the Luxor temple, to which our attention has been drawn, may well be a representation of another of the planets in the solar system. Since the monument is clearly the next in sequence from the Great Pyramid, which we know represents the Earth, then if we are correct in our assumption, the planet that is being represented in Luxor will be the nearest neighbour to the planet Earth. A quick check of basic astronomical data shows that the planet in question will be Venus, which lies considerably closer to the Earth than the planet Mars, our next nearest neighbour. In order to see if there is any validity in this assumption we need to look at two pieces of information.

The first of these is the location of the temple of Luxor for which we need to determine its exact geographic location within Egypt and from this determine its location relative to the Great Pyramid of Giza. Both of these pieces of data can be determined using information systems which we have already utilised in our analysis of the Giza plateau. We can determine the location of the temple by using a suitably accurate satellite mapping system, and then determine the distance between the two locations in question by making calculations using the highly accurate geodesic distance calculator that we first used when looking at the unfinished pyramid 5km to the south of Giza.

The illustration below shows a screen shot of the Luxor temple taken from the "Google Earth' satellite mapping programme. The latitude and longitude of the entrance to the temple (the centre point between the two obelisks) is shown in the lower left corner of the screen shot, and it is worth stating again that although this is not a specialist geodesic location programme, the errors contained within the latitude and longitude coordinates are negligible for the purposes for which we are using it.

The entrance to the temple, between the two obelisks, is located at 25° 42' 01.40" North, 32° 38' 22.42" East and by plugging these figures into our geodesic calculation programme we can determine that the temple entrance is located 496,788.9 m from the central axis of the Great Pyramid of Giza at an angle of 162° 16' 36.6396" when measured from Giza, or 342°58'49.3745" when measured back to Giza from the temple. When reduced down to the same quadrant, the difference between these two angles is due to the elliptical nature of the Earth's surface and the figures shown above are known as 'Forward Azimuth' and 'Reverse Azimuth' respectively.

We can scale up the distance between

The obelisk

Detail of one of the two obelisks located at the entrance to the temple

The obelisk location

Satellite imagery is sufficiently detailed to accurately locate the two obelisks

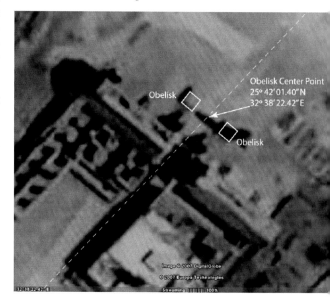

the Great Pyramid and the Temple of Luxor using the primary scale of the Great Pyramid's model of the Earth and determine that the distance between the Luxor temple obelisks and the central axis of the pyramid represent a real life distance of 43,070,307,577 m. To make sense of this value we need to look at the standard orbital elements of Earth and Venus and find the two values for the average aphelion of the two planets. The NASA planetary fact sheet for the Earth gives the average value of the aphelion of the Earth as being 152.1×10^6 km and the corresponding value for Venus as being 108.94×10^6 km , the difference between these values being 43,160,000,000 meters. Bearing in mind that the aphelion values for the planets vary on an annual basis by more than the difference between our calculated figure and the averaged figure, we can be quite certain that we have just found the connection between the two monuments. The Great Pyramid of Giza is a model of the Earth at aphelion, and the temple of Luxor is positioned perfectly at the aphelion of Venus.

Until we have more precise information to work from, there is nothing that we can do with the temple of Luxor's distance from the Giza monuments, because to have any idea of the accuracy of the measurement we would first need to know exactly where the planets were at an exact moment in time. And it is this thought that will lead us to the final conclusions of the work and lead us to the very place that the architects would like us to end up at.

The Giza plateau pyramids must not only be a model of the Earth and the Moon, they must also be a model for these celestial bodies *at a fixed moment in time*. Not only is that a quite astonishing concept, but it is also one which makes complete sense in astronomical terms. If you are trying to give precise astronomical data to someone over a long time span, it would be essential to first define an astronomical epoch with the exact positions and orbital data of the solar system's component bodies listed in immaculate detail.

And so with this in mind we can now head back to the Giza plateau and attempt to determine the exact date and time which **has** to be hidden inside the astronomical data that is built into the architecture of the monuments.

The Giza Pyramids astronomical epoch

THE GIZA PYRAMIDS
ASTRONOMICAL EPOCH

You may have noticed that as the chapters of this book have progressed, and we have followed the clues laid out in the architectural design of the monuments, that the scientific details have become more specific. We are now at the point in the work where there is sufficient information available to us to be able to search within our own modern astronomical records to see if we can finally make sense of the layout of the Giza Plateau.

We know that the Great Pyramid of Giza is a scaled model of the Earth, and from our correct interpretation of the temple of Luxor's distance when measured on that scale we now also know that the Earth must be at aphelion in its orbit. What we can now do is turn to the professionals, and examine the DE406 ephemeris tables which are provided to the scientific community via the Horizons web interface of NASA. These ephemeris tables are created by taking the currently known positions of the planets and moons of the planets in our solar system, and then integrating the equations of their motion with respect to time so that future and past locations of the bodies can be predicted. It is a science which has developed alongside our advancement in computer hardware, as the numerical crunching that is required to make the predictions requires colossal amounts of computer power. There are errors which are apparent in the ephemerides which are due to several factors, such as the unknown effect of large asteroids on the dynamics of the solar system. One way of eradicating some of the errors that are found in such tables is via the use of space travel, and the Apollo missions to the moon and some of the more recent voyages to Mars have left scientific equipment on these celestial bodies with the intention of allowing us to track their movements with precision. It is by carrying out such fantastic work that the space agencies around the world have managed, year on year, to eradicate more and more of the errors that appear in these ephemerides. We are now at the point where predictions of the solar system's major bodies are extremely accurate over a period of a couple of hundred years in either direction from the current date. However, when the time scales that we are concerned with in this book of 45 centuries are looked at, there are inaccuracies of several hours and several thousand kilometres inherent in the data. In terms of celestial distances and astronomical time frames these errors are negligible and the data can be relied upon when looking at information with the current error margins of the analysis of the Giza plateau, as the resulting scaled down distance errors would be in fractions of centimetres.

So the first step in trying to work out the final details of the Giza pyramids is to extract the aphelion data of the Earth from the DE406 ephemeris tables of NASA. This task is unfortunately slightly more difficult than one would imagine, as the ephemeris tables do not automatically list aphelion and perihelion data for any given time span, so I wrote a specialist piece of computer software which interrogates the Horizons system, and with this extracted the aphelion data of the Earth over a time period of 300 years from 2800 B.C.E. to 2500 B.C.E., a time period which covers the radiocarbon dating results for these buildings. If the work is correct up to this stage, then somewhere in that database there should be one particular date which corresponds perfectly with the information that we have at our disposal from the architects. The problem is that we have no way at this stage of knowing which of the lines of data is the correct one, and so we are going to have to look back at the Giza plateau for the final time and apply one last piece of logical analysis to the problem.

We know that the third pyramid of Giza probably represents the apogee of the moon, that is its furthest distance from the Earth during its monthly cycle. If we take Petrie's surveyed distance between the Great Pyramid and the third pyramid, and scale it up by the secondary scale, then we end up with a real size distance between the Earth and the moon of 405,812,657 as calculated in the earlier chapter. However, what we have not taken into consideration when calculating this distance is that the third pyramid of Giza stands in an elevated position in relation to the Great Pyramid. By referencing the work of the Italian Egyptologists Maragioglio and Rinaldi we can determine the elevation of the pyramid as shown on the illustration below, which is a cross sectional drawing taken along the line which connects the centres of the two pyramid in question. What is of note on this drawing is that when a line is taken from the base center of the Great Pyramid up to the top of the third pyramid that the angle is 4.7745 degrees. From our astronomical knowledge we know that the orbital plane of the moon is inclined at an angle of 5.145 degrees to the equatorial plane of the Earth, and therefore it is quite clear how the internal structure of the third pyramid has been designed. It is built in exactly the same manner as the second pyramid, with its geometric reference point situated at the apex of the pyramid. From this information we can calculate the distance from the base of the first pyramid to the top of the third as being 939.42m, which when scaled up gives us a distance between the Earth and the moon at apogee of 407,226,040 m.

What we can now do is interrogate the NASA ephemeris computers once more and append the lunar orbit data onto the corresponding date in the database that we previously constructed so that we then have both the Earth's and the Moon's orbital information at our fingertips. It should then be a relatively easy job to search through the database and determine if any of the entries for the Moon's range correspond to the value that we have just calculated from the architecture.

When this is done we find that there is not only no date where the lunar range matches our calculated one, but also come across the fact that the distance that we have calculated is actually larger than the furthest possible distance that the moon could ever be from the Earth. Something is clearly wrong, and it turns out to be a lack of understanding on our part that has lead to our inability to correctly determine the information from

the database. To understand quite where the problem lies we need to understand the ephemeris tables to a slightly better level.

If we search through the lunar ephemerides for the time of apogee we find that, as was just noted, the distance between the monuments is too large. However, the emphemeris data contained in the database is an instantaneous snapshot of the moon at a particular moment in time, and from its instantaneous velocity and other dynamic elements, *a theoretical maximum distance in orbit can be calculated*. This value, which NASA lists under the heading of 'apoapsis distance' varies by considerable larger quantities than the apogee distance, and it is therefore quite possible that the third pyramid is marking out this theoretical apoapsis distance - the computed theoretical apoapsis distance of the moon from the instantaneous dynamic data - quite an achievement 4500 years ago.

If we now go back to the database and search through the apoapsis distance information for the moon at each of the Earth's aphelion points over the 300 year range we find that there are a very small number of corresponding entries which match the value 407,226,040 that we are looking for. By plotting the astronomical data from each of these entries onto a CAD map of the Giza plateau we come across one particular day in one particular year where the whole of the Giza plateau's layout corresponds beautifully with the data from NASA. The illustration on the opposite page shows the data from the DE406 ephemeris for 10th May 2532 B.C.E. when the Earth was exactly at it point of aphelion, a time given in the ephemeris as 18:31:11 UTC. Definitions for all of the astronomical terms shown on this illustration can all be easily found by searching through the internet or by referring to astronomy books, and I will not attempt to explain each of them here.

Moon orbit on th plateau

The DE406 ephemeris data mapped onto an architectural plan of the Giza plateau.

Giza plateau pyramid elevations

The base level of the third pyramid gives an angle between the base center of the Great pyramid of just under 5°.

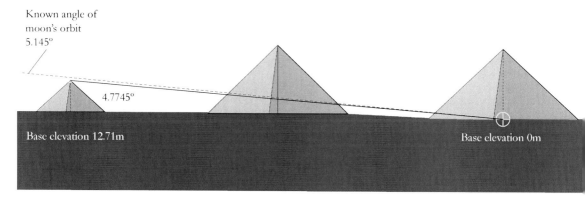

Known angle of moon's orbit 5.145°

4.7745°

Base elevation 12.71m

Base elevation 0m

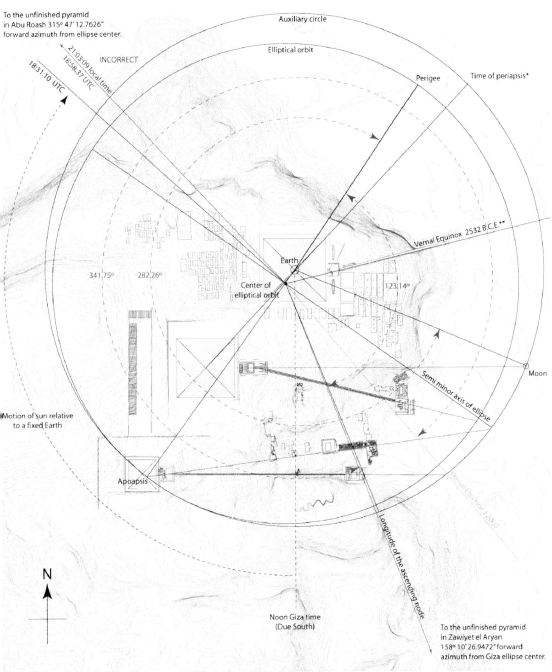

To the unfinished pyramid
in Abu Roash 315° 47' 12.7626"
forward azimuth from ellipse center.

Auxiliary circle

Elliptical orbit

INCORRECT

21:03:09 local time
18:58:37 UTC

18:31:10 UTC

Perigee

Time of periapsis*

Vernal Equinox 2532 B.C.E.**

Earth

341.75°   282.26°

Center of
elliptical orbit

123.14°

Semi minor axis of ellipse

Moon

Motion of sun relative
to a fixed Earth

Apoapsis

Vernal Equinox J2000

Longitude of the ascending node

N

Noon Giza time
(Due South)

To the unfinished pyramid
in Zawiyet el Aryan
158° 10' 26.9472" forward
azimuth from Giza ellipse center.

Moon Orbit at Earth Aphelion
2532 B.C.E. May 10th 18:31:11 UTC
JD 796740.271655062
(From NASA Horizons DE406 Ephemeris)

* The time of periapsis point is calculated by taking the time of periapsis in the ephemeris table, deducting the time of the ephemeris, and dividing the orbital
period by the resulting difference between the two times to obtain a representative angular rotation.
** The vernal equinox angle for 2532 B.C.E. is calculated using the standard formula of the IAU of 5,028.796195×T + 1.1054348×T² where T is the number of
Julian centuries relative to the J2000 epoch.

There are a number of interesting points to note about the illustration and the way in which the architecture fits the astronomical data.

First is that the longitude of the ascending node, because it is a reference point which is fixed against the stars, has been plotted from the center of the elliptical orbit rather than in the traditional way in which astronomers draw these quantities, centered on the Earth itself. Not only does this make complete sense from an astronomical perspective, but is also means that the rather unusual alignment of the causeway leading from the Great Pyramid at last makes sense to us, as it is also lined up with the ellipse's center point. It is highly appropriate that the majestic ramp leading up to the largest of all the Egyptian pyramids should be lined up with the vernal equinox of its date of construction. However, this alignment to the center of the ellipse also means that the bearing down to the unfinished pyramid in Zawiyet needs to be re-computed because the line does not emanate from the center of the Great Pyramid as we first assumed. This calculation can be done with relative ease since we know the scaling factor for the moon system and also know from the geometry of the elliptical orbit that the

Earth is at one of the foci of the ellipse. If we use the geodesic calculator in reverse, and determine the latitude and longitude shift for a nominal line length of 300m at Giza, then we can determine the geographic coordinates of the ellipses center point as shown in the illustration opposite. The ellipse's center has geographic coordinates of 29° 58' 43.40" North and 31° 08' 1.66" East, giving the bearing to the unfinished pyramid of Zawiyet as 158.1742° , and it is this bearing that has been plotted on the previous illustration.

The pyramid of Abu Roash, which is marked on the astronomical drawing and also shown in the illustration below, has not been covered in the work so far and it is situated some 8km north west of the Giza plateau. It is quite clear that this pyramid must be marking out the position of the sun in the system so that a time coordinate can be obtained for the aphelion position of the Earth. Since we have just be told quite clearly by the architects that the ellipse center is the point that they are using as the center point for the unfinished pyramid to the south, then it must also be that they are using the same point of reference for the unfinished pyramid to the north. If this is the case, and it would quite reasonable to assume that it is, then the NASA ephemeris is

Unfinished pyramid of Abu Roash

The geographic location of the center of the unfinished pyramid at Abu Roash

the ellipse center

the geographic
coordinates of the
orbital ellipse's
center point can be
calculated as shown
in the illustration.

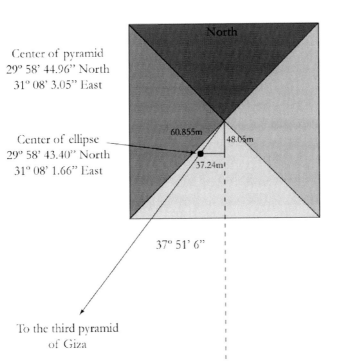

300m E/W = 0° 0' 11.19" of longitude at Giza

North

Center of pyramid
29° 58' 44.96" North
31° 08' 3.05" East

300m N/S = 0° 0' 9.75"
of latidue at Giza

Center of ellipse
29° 58' 43.40" North
31° 08' 1.66" East

60.855m

48.05m

37.24m

37° 51' 6"

To the third pyramid
of Giza

incorrect by about 29 minutes (an error which is quite plausible in their data) and we have an interesting situation to look at.

We know from our analysis of the Luxor temple that the rotation of the Earth around its North-South axis from which the temple avenue was formed was about 135 degrees, and for the Abu Roash pyramid to be showing the time of day for the astronomical system, the angle between the Great Pyramid and the Abu Roash pyramid **must be the same as the angle of the avenue of the Sphinxes in Luxor.** They both represent the same angle, which is the time of day angle of the Earth's aphelion. We can check this data on the satellite mapping programmes and geodesic bearing calculators and find that the two angles in question are

Abu Roash	44.21°
Luxor Temple	44.56°

where the first angle is shown as west of north, and the second as east of north. There is clearly a discrepancy between these two angles and if the work that we have done so far is correct then there shouldn't be. There is

clearly something wrong in the work that we have just done, and it is by analysing the astronomical illustration using pure logic that the error becomes apparent.

The time of day measurement is taken from noon time at Giza, and this quantity is shown in the top left corner of the earlier illustration along with a curved path showing the relative motion of the sun around the system. The drawing of the moon's orbital parameters is a snap shot taken at 9pm local time, which means that the ellipse center point from which we are taking our bearing up to Abu Roash is also located at 9pm local time. This is an utterly illogical situation - that we take the time of the aphelion relative to 12 noon, and then plot it from a point which is located at 9pm local time. The times simply do not match up. To correct this obvious fault, what we need to do is compute where the center of the ellipse would have been at noon local time, and plot the bearing up to Abu Roash from this point.

This calculation is an iterative calculation since by recalculating the position of the ellipse's center and then plotting a line up to Abu Roash, the resulting time of day measurement changes, and since this is the quantity that we are using to determine the center point's location, the operation has to be carried out iteratively until the angle becomes stable. The illustration below shows the location of the ellipse's center at noon Giza time with the geographic coordinates of latitude and longitude of the point calculated until they were stable in the 7th decimal place.

As can be seen from the illustration below, the bearing from the center of the ellipse to the unfinished pyramid in Abu Roash is 44.44° (west of north) and now matches the bearing down the avenue of the Sphinxes in Luxor considerably closer, the error between the two measurements being due to some other complexities regarding the center point of the Earth that have not yet been covered and the inherent errors in the locating of the Abu Roash pyramid center on the Google Earth programme.

So we can now redraw the astronomical chart of the moon's orbit correctly and in exactly the same manner that the ar-

chitects designed it, and this final layout of the Giza plateau is shown on the illustration opposite.

We have now arrived at the end of the puzzle that has been laid out before us, or more accurately we have just completed the initial assessment of the puzzle. We have established the exact date and time of what this wonderful construction represents, and therefore have the three rotational angles of the Earth available to us. The axial tilt of the Earth and its angle to the invariable plane of the ecliptic can be calculated from standard astronomical equations into which the date and time can be substituted, and the third rotational angle is simply the time of day measurement from noon that we have just calculated. The three rotational angles of the Earth at this moment it time are therefore

$$X= 24.001287461906°$$
$$Y= 1.804585974438°$$
$$Z=135.554775078781°$$

where X denotes a rotation around the North South axis, Y denotes a rotation around the

The map of the Giza plateau

The final, original astronomical chart of the Giza plateau

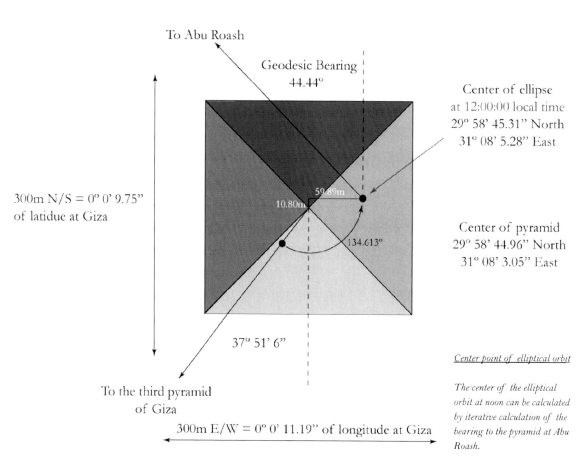

To Abu Roash

Geodesic Bearing
44.44°

Center of ellipse
at 12:00:00 local time
29° 58' 45.31" North
31° 08' 5.28" East

300m N/S = 0° 0' 9.75"
of latidue at Giza

59.89m

10.80m

134.613°

Center of pyramid
29° 58' 44.96" North
31° 08' 3.05" East

37° 51' 6"

To the third pyramid
of Giza

300m E/W = 0° 0' 11.19" of longitude at Giza

Center point of elliptical orbit

The center of the elliptical orbit at noon can be calculated by iterative calculation of the bearing to the pyramid at Abu Roash.

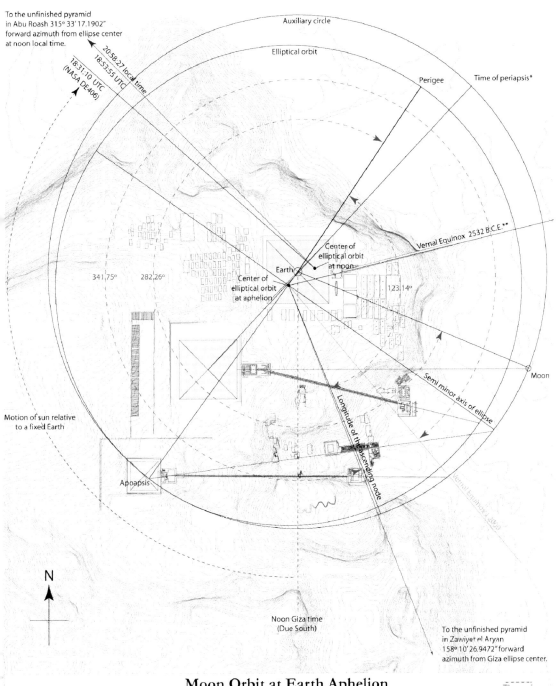

Moon Orbit at Earth Aphelion
2532 B.C.E. May 10th 18:31:11 UTC
JD 796740.271655062
(From NASA Horizons DE406 Ephemeris)

* The time of periapsis point is calculated by taking the time of periapsis in the ephemeris table, deducting the time of the ephemeris, and dividing the orbital period by the resulting difference between the two times to obtain a representative angular rotation.
** The vernal equinox angle for 2532 B.C.E. is calculated using the standard formula of the IAU of $5,028.796195{\times}T + 1.1054348{\times}T^2$ where T is the number of Julian centuries relative to the J2000 epoch.

East West axis, and Z a rotation around the vertical axis of the pyramid. What we can now do with these angles is go right back to the very start of the system, which is the primary model of the Earth that dictates the construction geometry of the Great Pyramid, and apply these rotations to the ellipsoid of the Earth. And when we do this we can then start to put together the final, highly complex internal structure of the pyramid's architecture, knowing for certain that the elliptical shape that we are now using is exactly the same as that which was designed by the architects all those years ago.

This final geometric construction is much more complex than the initial geometry that has been shown in this book as it involves orthographic projections of the ellipsoid, saddle points which are used as base points for the structure, and a number of complex rotated and translated ellipses. The resulting algebraic equations and geometric structures will take a considerable amount of time to construct and analyse, but when that work is finished we can be quite certain that the small granite ball which was found in the lower northern shaft by the Dixon brothers in the late 1800's will end up positioned perfectly within the pyramid at a distance from the central vertical axis equal to the Earth's aphelion on 10th May 2532 B.C.E.

Making Sense of It All

RADIOCARBON DATES OF OLD AND MIDDLE KINGDOM MONUMENTS IN EGYPT

Georges Bonani, Herbert Haas, Zahi Hawass, Mark Lehner, Shawki Nakhla, John Nolan, Robert Wenke, Willy Wölfli

During the nearly ten years that it took to write the content of this book I have had plenty of time to think through the philosophical nature of the work that I have been working on. I have attempted to maintain an entirely scientific and straight forward approach to all of the chapters in this book, so that the presentation of the findings is as clear and concise as could be. Yet the questions that arise from the discovery of this remarkable ancient construction's architectural design are perplexing, and I feel it is a responsibility of mine to at least share some of my thoughts regarding the likely origins of the architecture, what it means to us as a race of people, and where we may be heading in the future. This final chapter is therefore subjective in its nature, but written from a perspective of someone who has had sufficient time to get over the initial surprise of the discovery, and has a balanced outlook on the subject.

The first thing that we need to turn to when trying to make some sense of what we have on display is the radiocarbon dating of the ancient monuments that can be found in Egypt. The primary article on this subject is entitled

The radiocarbon dating of the Ancient Egyptian monuments

This document is authored, as can be seen, by some of the top names in Egyptology and its findings are fascinating. In the illustration below the radiocarbon dates of the fragments of organic material found lodged within the cement which holds the stonework of the pyramids together is shown as black horizontal bars. The right axis shows the name of the Pharaoh and the corresponding monument which has been attributed to that name, and the bottom axis shows the date B.C.E. The small blue rectangles show the dates of the Pharaoh's supposed reign and therefore the period in which the Egyptologists consider that each of the pyramids were built. It is as clear as daylight that the pyramids were built over a 300 year time span from 2900 B.C.E. to 2600 B.C.E., and all of the construction work was carried out simultaneously on all of the buildings. All of the radiocarbon dates of the pyramids fall into this 300 year band which is shown with the red dotted lines on the illustration.

So the world's top Egyptologists already know that the pyramid's dates of construction do not tally with the fictitous stories about these buildings having been constructed in 30 years by the Pharoahs of

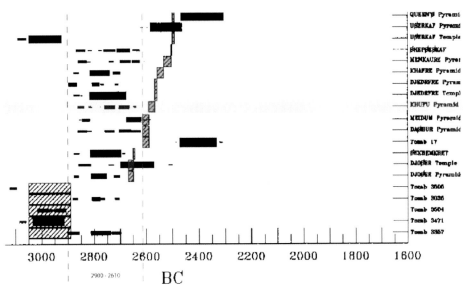

the old kingdom. The fact that the Egyptologists have chosen to disregard this evidence is of little consequence to us, as there is something within the radiocarbon data which is much more interesting. It is the fact that whoever built these building took 300 years to do so, and therefore we can be quite certain that they are not the creation of the 'Gods', who one would assume would have taken considerably less time and effort to make these buildings appear on the planet. Whoever built these buildings has laboured intensively to complete the construction, in much the same manner as we would do if we were to have undertaken the construction task. And it is in this statement that we can realise that whoever built these buildings appears to have the very same qualities that we possess as human beings. The pyramids have been realised through massive amounts of hard work, logistics and planning, and the characteristics of the architects and builders appears to us through that fact.

Another important piece of information that can be deduced from the radiocarbon dating is that the Great Pyramid of Giza's construction was started around 2875 B.C.E. and yet it contains the astronomical details of the Earth and Moon orbit for a date in 2532 B.C.E. From this we can be certain of two things. First is that whoever built the monuments knew for certain where the orbital positions of the planets would be some 250 years in the future, and since that is only possible through numerical integration of the instantaneous elements of the solar system planets and moons, we know the level of technology that was used in their construction. The calculations require sophisticated computer equipment. There can be no argument about this, regardless of how historically outrageous it may currently appear. The second fact that we can deduce is that the chronological details of the Old Kingdom must also have been created by whoever built the pyramids, because the date of the death of 'Khufu', the Pharaoh attributed to the Great Pyramid's construction, fits in so perfectly with the date of the astronomical details of the Giza plateau's monuments. Since it would not be possible to predict the date of the birth or death of someone 250 years in the future, then we can be quite certain that the Old Kingdom Pharoahs are also the creation of the building's architects, and are no more real than Mickey Mouse. This again tells us some more about those who built these monuments, because the art of elaborate story telling is another

trait that we can find within ourselves. Whoever built these monuments appears to have strong human characteristics.

It is worth addressing the problem that Egyptologists are going to have to confront over the coming years, since one of their arguments is bound to be that they have substantial archaeological evidence of the existence of Pharoahs from the Middle and New Kingdoms in ancient Egypt. There can be little dispute about these facts, but what needs to be realised is that the most likely series of events is that humans made settlements in Ancient Egypt amongst these fantastic monuments, and copied the culture and practices that were shown in the pictures on their walls. The Middle and New Kingdom Ancient Egyptians did indeed exist, are exactly as the Egyptologists describe them. What needs to be resolved, and it will only be achieved through the dedicated work of the Egyptologists, is where the cut off point lies between the real and the fictitous Ancient Egyptians. It will likely be a difficult task, as the real Ancient Egyptians will most like have copied the styles of the fictitous stories that they came across. It is not difficult to put yourself in the place of a nomadic tribesman, wandering through the desert some 4000 years ago and coming across the Temple of Luxor or the Great Pyramid. The location would become an obvious point of settlement, offering protection from nature's elements and protection afforded by the Gods - since there would have been no other way that the buildings could have been constructed in the eyes of the nomadic wanderer.

The next question that I would like to address is that of how far the system of construction stretches. We have seen in this work that the Temple of Luxor has been built at the position that one would expect to find the planet Venus within the astronomical system that is laid out on the Giza Plateau. The answer to the question of how extensive the system is is as remarkable as the content of this book has been, as it is possible to locate at least another six solar system planets using the methodology described in this work. Because the research work regarding these monuments is still ongoing I have decided not to publish their details at this stage, since I would like to have a more comprehensive analysis completed before doing so. A second reason for not publishing these additional details is that the historical anomalies presented within them are particularly more perplexing than those that we have come across on the

Giza Plateau. However, by way of illustration of the magnitude of the system, I would like to relate an episode which occurred during the work that I have carried out on the Giza Pyramids, and which illustrates the point quite simply.

I am British, and one of the questions that was posed to me by some of my friends and acquaintances during the work was 'what about Stonehenge', a question relating to the famous megalithic monument which can be found in the south of England. Despite my numerous replies to this question that "I am studying the pyramids of Egypt", the question arose on numerous occasions, and I eventually succumbed to the temptation to have a quick look at the layout of the monument. To my surprise, it took less than 2 hours to deduce that the monument was most likely part of the same geometric system that I was looking at, and to understand the simplicity of the solution to Stonehenge, one needs to understand the concept of geodesic bearings.

The geodesic bearings between Stonehenge and Giza

The illustration below shows the shortest line that can be drawn between Giza and Stonehenge, and is known as a geodesic bearing line. Because the Earth is an ellipsoid, the shortest path between two points is not a straight line, as we have already seen in the chapters of this book. It is a curved line which bends around the ellipsoid's surface, and as a result there are two bearings which have different numerical values between two points on the Earth's surface. The bearing from point A to point B is not the same as the bearing from point B to point A. The difference in these bearings when applied to the Stonehenge-Giza path is nearly 22° and is highly significant when trying do determine the design principles of the Stonehenge monument. As is shown on the illustration overleaf, the central axis of the Stonehenge monument has been set perfectly at right angles to the bearing of Stonehenge from Giza, as opposed to the bearing of Giza from Stonehenge. As a consequence of this it is impossible to un-

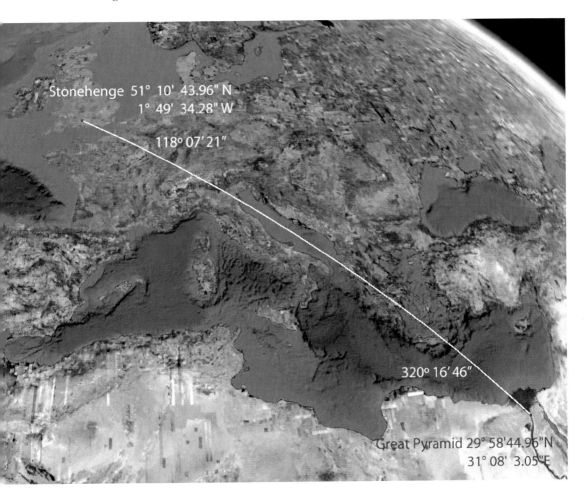

Stonehenge 51° 10' 43.96" N
1° 49' 34.28" W

118° 07' 21"

320° 16' 46"

Great Pyramid 29° 58' 44.95" N
31° 08' 3.05" E

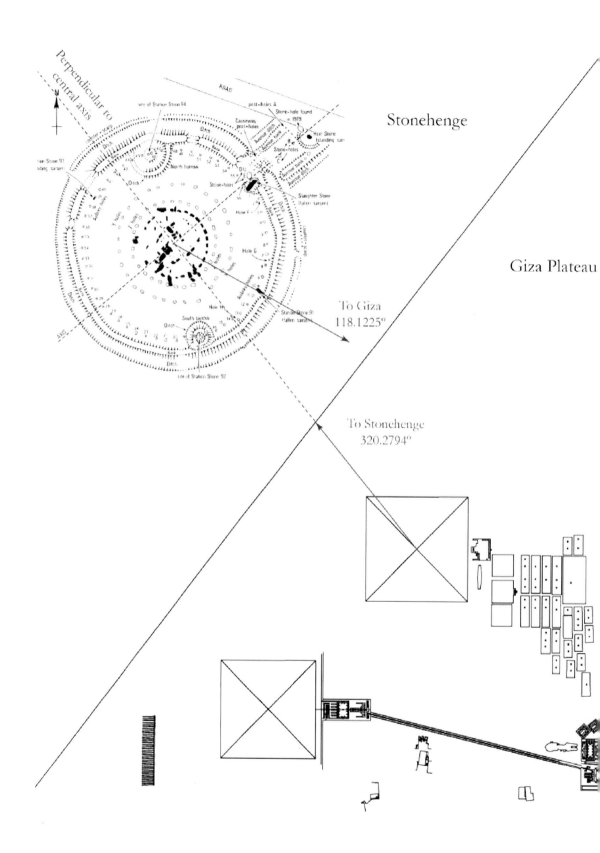

Stonehenge

Giza Plateau

To Giza
118.1225°

To Stonehenge
320.2794°

*Stonehenge's
central axis*

*The central axis
of Stonehenge is
perpendicular to its
geodesic bearing
from Giza*

derstand the Stonehenge circle if it is looked at in isolation. It would not matter how long one spent trying to deduce its inherent geometry, it would never yield its secrets. It is only after the Great Pyramid's inherent design has been understood that any sense can be made of the stone circle, and it is abundantly clear that it is connected to the Giza monuments. Within the space of a morning's work it was possible to determine that the central axis of the Stonehenge circle must have a bearing of 50.2794° without ever having laid a surveying tripod anywhere near the construction.

The logic of the connection between the two monuments is relatively easy to understand once it has been established that someone has built us a snapshot of the solar system taken on 10th May 2532 B.C.E. The Stonehenge stone circle is likely to be a representation of an asteroid which is significantly large enough to have an impact on the ephemeris calculations required to correctly map out the dynamics of the orbiting bodies within the solar system. It might seem a far fetched idea when viewed from the perspective of our current historical ideas about the world, but it is entirely logical and plausible when viewed in the context of what has been discovered during the work on this book.

All that remains to be considered is the immense question of the future, and what it holds in store for us. Once again it is possible to come to some highly rational conclusions on this subject matter by considering the work that has gone before us. One of the elements that continually surprised me during my work on this book was that the puzzles and mathematical systems never seemed to come to an end. You would have thought that once a cross sectional model of the Earth had been discovered within the Great Pyramid, that the project would have come to quite a rapid conclusion, but the opposite was the case. The more corroborating evidence that I discovered, the more work seemed to appear before me and even now, with this book completed, the final architectural plans of the Great Pyramid are still some distance away. But it was this experience that helped me understand what I consider the architects of these monuments have most probably done. They have built a model of the solar system in astonishing detail, which effectively is a map that they have designed for us to read. One would assume that somewhere on that map will be the iconic 'X marks the spot', which will be the exact position of something out

there in our solar system with which we will be able to communicate. To that end, the builders unit of the 'cubit' has been carefully selected to be a specific division of the light second, and therefore a precise transmission frequency.

The only snag with the whole system is that human beings tend to go into a state of shock when you tell them something as profound as the details contained within this book. So the one element that you need to design into the work is TIME - you have to make the puzzle so complicated and so full of small anomalies and quirks that it cannot be solved by just plugging the data into a computer. It needs to be solved by human beings, who will have to think profoundly about the systems and information which are on display, and this will take time. Most probably very large amounts of time, which I suspect may run into a couple of decades or so. And during this time, the population of the world will do what it has always done, and that is grow older and die whilst a new generation of children are born and grow up.

For that next generation of children, who will have been educated from their early years with the knowledge that we have quite a story on our hands within these ancient buildings, there will be considerably less of a problem accepting the situation. As they grow up and become scientists, teachers and politicians themselves they will have the task of deciding how to move forward, and quite possibly how and when to make contact with whoever built these monuments. That decision will be for that generation to take, but for the current generation our obligation is to understand and document that which is so clearly laid out infront of us.

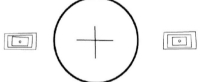

Appendix

The appendix to this work contains a small selection of the data that was collected during the writing and research for the book. During the nine years of work required to dissect the Egyptian monuments contained in the work I created over 18,000 computer files with a total of 38 Gb of storage space, and so the selection of data in this appendix is only a tiny fraction of that total. I have restricted the content to items which will be either of interest to the reader, such as the hieroglyph plots for the pyramid of Unas, or which will be important in the future for anyone pursuing the avenues explored in this work. In particular, the numbering system for the racks of hieroglyphs in the Unas pyramid should adopted as a standardised numbering system for that pyramid, as the inclusion of the missing racks from earlier works will allow a uniform reference system to be adopted, as well as being a template for other groups of hieroglyphs in other buildings, where the artwork and blank racks must be included in any analysis of the monuments if the architect's design is to be fully understood.

The stonework of the internal shafts of the Great Pyramid is included in this appendix so that anyone wanting to understand the intricate details of their construction can do so. The details of the positions of all of the stones within the Great Pyramid can therefore be fully compiled by anyone wanting to look through William Petrie's surveying data alongside this list.

The section of the appendix which covers the algebraic construction of the Great Pyramid of Giza is an essential starting point for understanding the monuments design principles, although it is far from an exhaustive analysis of the work. It covers the fundamental mathematical design elements which turn out to be little more than a sketch of the final, highly complex ellipsoidal geometry which is at the heart of the building's architecture. For anyone wanting to recreate the internal structure of the Great Pyramid, the algebraic solutions to the angles and points within the pyramid which are presented here are sufficient for such a drawing to be correct down to a few millimetres of accuracy, although insufficient to be able to extract the final astronomical data from the monument with the precision required to make factually correct deductions. The final mathematical plans of the pyramid, which will take considerably talent to produce and for which I will require the assistance of professional mathematicians, will be published in due course, once they have been diligently checked so as to ensure their authenticity.

The Conceptual design of the Great Pyramid of Giza

Lemma 1.1   The Great Pyramid of Giza is a geometric model of the Earth, the scale of which is equal to the numerical value of 1/365th of a sidereal year measured in sidereal seconds The length of the pyramid's base is half the circumference of the scaled elliptical cross-section of the Earth's meridian. The height of the pyramid is the scaled polar diametre of the Earth which, for the purposes of this document[1], bisects the base line and is perpendicular to it. The pyramid's geometric faces are designed by connecting the ends of the base to the upper end of the scaled ellipse's minor axis as shown in figure 1.

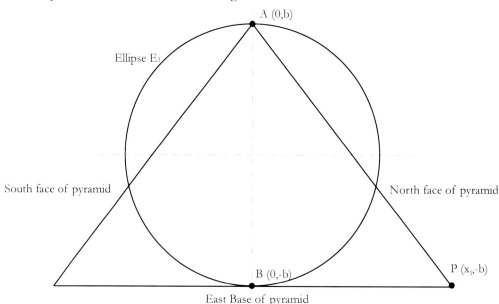

Proof : In order to prove this lemma by enumerating the algebraic geometry for the base length and face angles and then comparing the results to the surveying data of the pyramid, we need to calculate the radii of the ellipse in terms of the base length. For this, the circumference formula for an ellipse is required.

(a) The circumference formula for an ellipse

The exact value for the circumference of an ellipse is given by the formula

$$\sum_{n=\inf}^{n=0} \left(\frac{-1}{2n-1}\right)\left(\frac{(2n)!}{(2n.n!)^2}\right)^2 e^{2n}$$

---

1. *A more advanced analysis of the monument's underlying design indicates that the elliptical cross section refered to above should in fact be an ortho-graphic projection taken from an ellipsoid of the Earth, where the saddle point at the base of the ellipsoid is centrally placed on the pyramid's base. Rotations of the ellipsoid around its two axiis parallel to the ground cause the base saddle point to move off a line projected vertically down from the ellipsoid's center point. Since the building's design indicates that it is this saddle point which remains fixed to the base center during the rotation process, the apex of the pyramid is not located above the center of the base lines.*

here the letter e in the equation represents the eccentricity of the ellipse, and is defined as

$$e = \sqrt{1 - \frac{b^2}{a^2}}$$

he Indian mathematician Ramanujan produced a highly accurate approximation formula for
ι ellipse's circumference

$$c = \pi\left(3(a + b) - \sqrt{(3a + b)(a + 3b)}\right) \qquad (1.1)$$

·hich, when compared to the full formula for the circumference of an ellipse , is correct for
ιe first 6 terms of that series. In order to illustrate the size of errors which this formula cre-
·es when used in substitution for the full formula, it can be applied to the elliptical meridian of
ιe Earth as an appropriate reference. The following data for the dimmensions of the earth's
∥lipsoid is taken from the world geodesic reference datum GRS80 :

$$a = 6,378,137\text{m} \qquad \text{Equatorial (Major) Radius)}$$
$$b = 6,356,752.3141\text{m} \qquad \text{Polar (Minor) Radius)}$$

Jsing the full formula up to the fifth term in the series, the circumference of the Earth merid-
ιn is

$$c = 40,007,862.\ 9164813\text{m} \pm 0.0000001\text{m (Earth's meridian)}$$

ιnd using Ramanujan's approximation formula

$$c = 40,007,862.\ 9164813\text{m}$$

·he accuracy of Ramanujan's formula is apparent in the above result, producing an error less
ιan 1/10000th millimetre when applied to the Earth's meridian.

(b) Calculating the radii of an ellipse of known eccentricity from its circumference

·o calculate the radii of an ellipse of known eccentricity from its circumference using Ramanu-
ιn's formula we can introduce the term f to represent the fixed ratio of the two radii where a
= fb , giving

$$c = \pi\left(3(fb + b) - \sqrt{(3fb + b)(fb + 3b)}\right)$$
$$c = \pi b\left(3(f + 1) - \sqrt{(3f + 1)(f + 3)}\right)$$

·he term inside the brackets is a numerical constant for any given ellipse, and can be replaced
·y R_c, which I shall call Ramanujan's constant. To calculate the value of Rc for the Earth using
·he data from the GRS80 document

$$f = \frac{6378137}{6356752.3141}$$
$$f = 1.00336409$$
$$R_c = 2.003365502 \qquad (1.2)$$

Ramanujans equation can therefore be simplified to

$$c = \pi b R_c$$

Lemma 1 states that the length of the pyramid's base will be half the circumference of the ellipse and is therefore defining the circumference as

$$c = 4x_1$$

therefore

$$4x_1 = \pi b R_c$$

$$b = \frac{4x_1}{\pi R_c} \tag{1.3}$$

$$a = \frac{4x_1 f}{\pi R_c} \tag{1.4}$$

giving the radii if the ellipse (*a and b*) in terms of the length of the base line (x_1) .

(c) The face angle of the pyramid

The gradient of the face of the pyramid PA, has the algebraic quantity

$$gradient\ PA = \frac{-2b}{x_1} \tag{1.4a}$$

and substituting the value of b from equation 1.3 into this equation gives

$$gradient\ PA = \frac{-8}{\pi R_c}$$

This is, as you would expect it to be, a fixed quantity and its value and that of the corresponding internal angle of the pyramid are

$$gradient\ PA = -1.2711006$$

$$angle\ BPA = 51.807170^o$$

$$angle\ BPA = 51^o\ 48'\ 25.8'' \tag{1.5}$$

The surveying data for the pyramid is provided by William Petrie[2], and the weighted mean angle of the north face of the pyramid is given by him as

$$angle\ BPA = 51^o\ 50'40'' \pm 1'5''$$

(d) The scale of model

Lemma 1 states that the scale of the model of the Earth is based on a time constant, that being the number of sidereal seconds in 1/365th of a sidereal year. This value can be enumerated as follows :

if
$$1\ sidereal\ year = 365.256363004\ mean\ solar\ days^3$$
$$1\ sidereal\ day = 86,164.090530833\ \ mean\ solar\ seconds^4$$

2. Petrie, W. M. Flinders. *The Pyramids and Temples of Gizeh. 1st ed.* London: Field and Tuer; New York: Scribner & Welford, 1883
3 Simon et al., 1994, Astron. Astrophys., 282, 663
4. Aoki, S., B. Guinot, G. H. Kaplan, H. Kinoshita, D. D. McCarthy and P. K. Seidelmann: "The new definition of Universal Time". Astronomy and Astrophysics 105(2), 359-361, 1982, from equation 17

hen the scale of the model of the Earth is defined as

$$scale = \frac{365.256363004}{365} \times \frac{86400}{86164.090530833} \times 86400$$

$$scale = 86697.405800 \qquad (1.6)$$

value which is acurate up to the 6th decimal place.

(d) The length of the pyramid base

The base length of the pyramid can now be calculated from the scaling factor by determining he radii and circumference of the cross section of the Earth as described in Lemma 1. Using he data from the GRS80 geodesic reference document

$$scaled\ axis\ a = 73.5678\ m$$
$$scaled\ axis\ b = 73.3211\ m$$
$$scaled\ circumference = 461.4655\ m$$

and therefore the base length of the pyramid is

$$base\ length = 230.733\ m$$

This value can be compared to the surveying data by consideration of the following diagram of he foundation stones of the pyramid :

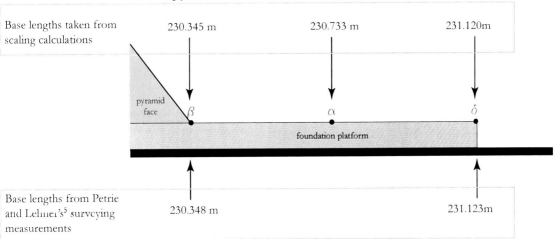

| Base lengths taken from scaling calculations | 230.345 m | 230.733 m | 231.120m |

| Base lengths from Petrie and Lehner's[5] surveying measurements | 230.348 m | | 231.123m |

Point α is half the elliptical circumferene as calculated above.
Point β is half a circular circumferece based on the polar radius of the Earth model
Point δ is half a circular circumference based on the equatorial radius of the Earth model
The line $\alpha\beta$ is 19.38cm in length and the line $\alpha\delta$ is 19.36cm in length
The foundation platform is an alignment tool allowing the model's scale to be determined.
The calculated points match the surveying points to 1.5mm of accuracy.

---

5. *Lehner, Mark. The Complete Pyramids. Thames and Hudson London. 1997 (page 213 diagram 4)*

By understanding the design of the plinth of the pyramid it is possible to determine how the stonework that makes up the pyramid's face was designed. If the stone construction starts from the point β on the previous diagram and extends up to the top of the elliptical cross section then the gradient of the line βA and the angle $B\beta A$ of the pyramid are given by

$$gradient\ \beta A = \frac{2b}{\left(\frac{\pi b}{2}\right)}$$

$$gradient\ \beta A = \frac{4}{\pi}$$

$$angle\ B\beta A = 51.85397^{\circ}$$

$$angle\ B\beta A = 51^{\circ}51'14''$$

thereby concealing the true side angle of the pyramid's geometric construction.

The principal mathematical theorem of the Great Pyramid of Giza

Lemma 1.2 The exit points of the upper shaftways of the pyramid are positioned in accordance with the following mathematics theorem:

Let E_1 be an ellipse with standard equation

$$\frac{x^2}{a^2} + \frac{y^2}{b^2} = 1$$

Let $A(0, b)$ and $B(0, -b)$ be the two ends of the ellipse's minor axis. Let the point $T(x, y)$ be the tangent point on the ellipse for a line emanating from the point $P(x_1, -b)$.

Let E_2 be an ellipse with standard equation

$$\frac{x^2}{a_1^2} + \frac{y^2}{b_1^2} = 1$$

which has the line PA as a tangent and whose minor axis has the end points $B(0, -b)$ and $E(0, y)$.

Then the intersect point of the lines PA and BT, $I(x_2, y_2)$, is also the tangent point of the ellipse E_2 with the line PA.

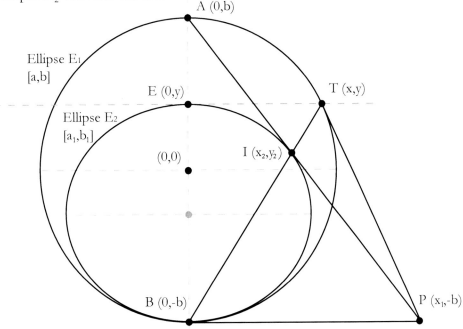

A (0,b)

Ellipse E₁
[a,b]

E (0,y)   T (x,y)

Ellipse E₂
[a₁,b₁]

(0,0)   I (x₂,y₂)

B (0,-b)   P (x₁,-b)

Proof : As the geometric system is dependent primarily upon the positioning of the point $P(x_1, -b)$ then all calculations will be in reference to this point. In order to prove the lemma, a) the steps required to calculate the intersect point of the lines PA and BT, $I(x_2, y_2)$ will be looked at first b) those to calculate the tangent point of PA and E_2 will be considered second and c) how the numeric values of the algebraic equations relate to the pyramid's shaftways will be considered third.

(a) The intersect point of the lines PA and BT

1) We first need to determine the algebraic coordinates of the tangent point T.

The tangent to an ellipse at the point (x, y) can be determined by differentiating the standard formula for an ellipse as an implicit function :

$$\frac{x^2}{a^2} + \frac{y^2}{b^2} = 1 \qquad (2.0)$$

$$\frac{2x}{a^2} + \frac{2y\frac{\partial y}{\partial x}}{b^2} = 0$$

$$\frac{\partial y}{\partial x} = \frac{-xb^2}{ya^2} \qquad (2.1)$$

On the diagram this algebraic expression represents the gradient of the line PT, which is also given by the formula for the gradient of a straight line between two points (x, y) and (x1, y1)

$$line\ gradient = \frac{y - y_1}{x - x_1} \qquad (2.2)$$

In this particular case $y_1 = -b$ by definition of the point P, and so equations 2.1 and 2.2 can be solved simultaneously giving

$$\frac{-xb^2}{ya^2} = \frac{y + b}{x - x_1}$$

$$-xb^2(x - x_1) = ya^2(y + b)$$

$$-x^2b^2 + xx_1b^2 = y^2a^2 + ya^2b \qquad (2.3)$$

Re-working the standard equation of an ellipse

$$\frac{x^2}{a^2} + \frac{y^2}{b^2} = 1$$

$$y^2 = \frac{b^2(a^2 - x^2)}{a^2}$$

$$y = \frac{b\sqrt{a^2 - x^2}}{a}$$

and substituting this value of y into equation 2.3 gives

$$-x^2b^2 + xx_1b^2 = \frac{b^2(a^2 - x^2)a^2}{a^2} + \frac{b\sqrt{a^2 - x^2}.a^2b}{a}$$

$$-x^2b^2 + xx_1b^2 = b^2(a^2 - x^2) + ab^2\sqrt{a^2 - x^2}$$

$$a\sqrt{a^2 - x^2} = xx_1 - a^2$$

$$a^2(a^2 - x^2) = x^2x_1^2 + a^4 - 2xx_1a^2$$

$$a^4 - a^2x^2 - x^2x_1^2 - a^4 + 2xx_1a^2 = 0$$

$$x^2(x_1^2 + a^2) + x(-2x_1a^2) = 0$$

This equation is now in the format where it can be solved using the standard formula for solving quadratic equations, giving

$$x = \frac{2x_1 a^2 \pm \sqrt{4x_1^2 a^4 - 4(x_1^2 + a^2).0}}{2(x_1^2 + a^2)}$$

$$x = \frac{2x_1 a^2 \pm 2x_1 a^2}{2(x_1^2 + a^2)}$$

$$x = \frac{2x_1 a^2}{x_1^2 + a^2} \quad or \quad x = 0 \tag{2.4}$$

This is the algebraic value of the x coordinate of the tangent point, and to determine the y coordinate we can substitute the non zero value of x back into the standard ellipse equation, giving

$$\frac{\frac{4x_1^2 a^4}{(x_1^2 + a^2)^2}}{a^2} + \frac{y^2}{b^2} = 1$$

$$\frac{4x_1^2 a^2}{(x_1^2 + a^2)^2} + \frac{y^2}{b^2} = 1$$

$$y^2 = b^2 - \frac{4x_1^2 a^2 b^2}{(x_1^2 + a^2)^2}$$

$$y^2 = \frac{b^2(x_1^2 + a^2)^2 - 4x_1^2 a^2 b^2}{(x_1^2 + a^2)^2}$$

$$y^2 = \frac{b^2 x1^2 + b^2 a^4 + 2x1^2 a^2 b^2 - 4x_1^2 a^2 b^2}{(x_1^2 + a^2)^2} \tag{2.5}$$

$$y = \frac{b(x_1^2 - a^2)}{x_1^2 + a^2}$$

Therefore the tangent point T(x,y) has the algebraic coordinates

$$T\left(\frac{2x_1 a^2}{x_1^2 + a^2}, \frac{b(x_1^2 - a^2)}{x_1^2 + a^2}\right) \tag{2.6}$$

2) Second we need to determine the equations of the lines BA and BT and thereby determine the their intersect point.

The gradient of the line BT can be calculated by substituting the known end points of the line into equation 2.2 where

$$y_1 = -b$$

$$x_1 = 0$$

$$y = \frac{b(x_1^2 - a^2)}{x_1^2 + a^2}$$

$$x = \frac{2x_1 a^2}{x_1^2 + a^2}$$

giving

$$\text{gradient } BT = \frac{\dfrac{b(x_1^2 - a^2)}{x_1^2 + a^2} + b}{\dfrac{2x_1 a^2}{x_1^2 + a^2} - 0}$$

$$\text{gradient } BT = \frac{b(x_1^2 - a^2) + b(x_1^2 + a^2)}{2x_1 a^2}$$

$$\text{gradient } BT = \frac{bx_1}{a^2}$$

The equation of the line BT is therefore

$$y = \frac{bx_1 x}{a^2} - b \tag{2.7}$$

The end points of the line PA are $(x_1, -b)$ and $(0, b)$, and substituting these into equation 2.? gives the line gradient as

$$\text{gradient } PA = \frac{-2b}{x_1}$$

so the equation of the line PA is

$$y = \frac{-2bx}{x_1} + b \tag{2.8}$$

The intersect point can now be found by simultaneously solving the two line equations 2.7 and 2.8 giving the point $(x2, y2)$

$$\frac{bx_1 x_2}{a^2} - b = \frac{-2bx_2}{x_1} + b$$

$$\frac{bx_1^2 x_2 + 2bx_2 a^2}{a^2 x_1} = 2b$$

$$x_2(x_1^2 + 2a^2) = 2a^2 x_1$$

$$x_2 = \frac{2a^2 x_1}{x_1^2 + 2a^2}$$

substituting this value of x_2 into the equation 2.7 gives

$$y_2 = \frac{bx_1 2a^2 x_1}{a^2(x_1^2 + 2a^2)} - b$$

$$y_2 = \frac{2bx_1^2 - b(x_1^2 + 2a^2)}{x_1^2 + 2a^2}$$

$$y_2 = \frac{b(x_1^2 - 2a^2)}{x_1^2 + 2a^2}$$

The intersect point of the lines PA and BT, $I(x_2, y_2)$ is therefore

$$I\left(\frac{2a^2 x_1}{x_1^2 + 2a^2}, \frac{b(x_1^2 - 2a^2)}{x_1^2 + 2a^2} \right) \tag{2.9}$$

(b) The tangent point of line PA and ellipse E_2

n order to find the tangent point of PA with E_2 we need to 1) find the general solution to a ine-ellipse tangent point, 2) transform the line PA into the coordinate system of ellipse E_2, 3) calculate the radii of ellipse E_2 in terms of the radii of ellipse E_1 and 4) solve the general line-ellipse tangent equation using the results of 2) and 3).

1) The general solution to a line-ellipse tangent point.

Re-working the general equation of an ellipse, 2.0, gives

$$y^2 = \frac{b^2(a^2 - x^2)}{a^2}$$

For the general formula for a straight line

$$y = mx + c$$

$$y^2 = m^2x^2 + 2mxc + c^2 \qquad (2.10)$$

so, at the intersect(s) between a straight line and ellipse

$$m^2x^2 + 2mxc + c^2 = \frac{b^2(a^2 - x^2)}{a^2}$$

$$m^2x^2a^2 + 2mxca^2 + a^2c^2 = b^2a^2 - b^2x^2$$

$$x2(b2 + m2a2) + x(2mca2) + a2(c2 - b2) = 0$$

and solving this using the standard solution for quadratic equations gives

$$x = \frac{-2mca^2 \pm \sqrt{4m^2c^2a^4 - 4(b^2 + m^2a^2)(a^2(c^2 - b^2))}}{2(b^2 + m^2a^2)}$$

$$x = \frac{-2mca^2 \pm \sqrt{4m^2c^2a^4 - 4a^2b^2c^2 - 4m^2a^4c^2 + 4a^2b^4 + 4m^2a^4b^2}}{2(b^2 + m^2a^2)}$$

$$x = \frac{-mca^2 \pm \sqrt{a^2b^2(b^2 + m^2a^2 - c^2)}}{b^2 + m^2a^2}$$

At the tangent point, where there must be only one solution for x and therefore the $\pm$ term must be zero

$$x = \frac{-mca^2}{m^2a^2 + b^2} \qquad (2.11)$$

and substituting this value of x into the general straight line equation 2.10 gives

$$y = \frac{-m^2ca^2}{m^2a^2 + b^2} + c^2$$

$$y = \frac{cb^2}{m^2a^2 + b^2} \qquad (2.12)$$

2) Transform the line PA into the coordinate system of ellipse E_2.

From the diagram, if the ellipse E_2 has radii of a_1 and b_1 then the distance d between the centres of the ellipses E_1 and E_2 is

$$d = b - b1$$

and by definition

$$2b_1 = b + y$$

The value of y in terms of x_1 was calculated earlier and shown in equation 2.5, so substituting this values into the equation above gives

$$2b_1 = b + \frac{b(x_1^2 - a^2)}{x_1^2 + a^2}$$

$$2b_1 = \frac{b(x_1^2 + a^2) + b(x_1^2 - a^2)}{x_1^2 + a2}$$

$$b_1 = \frac{bx_1^2}{x_1^2 + a^2} \tag{2.13}$$

therefore the distance d is given by

$$d = b - \frac{bx_1^2}{x_1^2 + a^2}$$

$$d = \frac{b(x_1^2 + a^2) - bx_1^2}{x_1^2 + a^2}$$

$$d = \frac{ba^2}{x_1^2 + a^2}$$

The equation of the line PA in the primary coordinate system is given in equation 2.8, and adding the value of d from above to re-base the line to a coordinate system centred on ellipse E_2 gives the line equation as

$$y = \frac{-2bx}{x_1} + b + \frac{ba^2}{x_1^2 + a^2}$$

$$y = \frac{-2bx}{x_1} + \frac{b(x_1^2 + a^2) + ba^2}{x_1^2 + a^2}$$

$$y = \frac{-2bx}{x_1} + \frac{b(x_1^2 + 2a^2)}{x_1^2 + a^2} \tag{2.14}$$

3) Calculate the radii of ellipse E_2 in terms of the radii of ellipse E_1

The algebraic value of the minor radius of ellipse E_2 in terms of the radii of E_1 has already been shown in equation 2.13. Equation 2.6 gave the tangent point $T(x, y)$ on the ellipse E_1, and by the same argument the tangent point $I(x_2, y_2)$ based to the coordinate system of ellipse E_2 must be

$$T\left(\frac{2x_1 a_1^2}{x_1^2 + a_1^2}, \frac{b_1(x_1^2 - a_1^2)}{x_1^2 + a_1^2}\right)$$

therefore the gradient of the line PA, by substituting the points P and I into equation 2.2 is

$$gradient\ PI = \frac{\dfrac{b(x_1^2 - a_1^2)}{x_1^2 + a_1^2} + b_1}{\dfrac{2x_1 a_1^2}{x_1^2 + a_1^2} - x_1}$$

$$gradient\ PI = \frac{b_1(x_1^2 - a_1^2) + b_1(x_1^2 + a_1^2)}{2x_1 a_1^2 - x_1(x_1^2 + a_1^2)}$$

$$gradient\ PI = \frac{2b_1 x_1}{a_1^2 - x_1^2}$$

and substituting the value of b_1 from equation 2.13 into the above equation gives

$$gradient\ PI = \frac{2bx_1^2 x_1}{(a_1^2 - x_1^2)(x_1^2 + a^2)}$$

This gradient must be equal to the gradient of the line PA in the transformed coordinate system, and shown in equation 2.14, so

$$\frac{-2b}{x_1} = \frac{2bx_1^2 x_1}{(a_1^2 - x_1^2)(x_1^2 + a_1^2)}$$

$$-(a_1^2 - x_1^2)(x_1^2 + a_1^2) = x_1^4$$

$$-a_1^2 a^2 - a_1^2 x_1^2 + x_1^2 a^2 + x_1^4 = x_1^4$$

$$x_1^2 a^2 = a_1^2 a^2 + a_1^2 x_1^2$$

$$a_1^2 = \frac{x_1^2 a^2}{x_1^2 + a^2}$$

$$a_1 = \frac{ax_1}{\sqrt{x_1^2 + a^2}}$$

(2.15)

4) Solve the general line-ellipse tangent equation using the results of 2) and 3) above.

The x co-ordinate of the tangent point of any line with any ellipse is given in equation 2.11 and we can customise this to ellipse E_2 to give

$$x_2 = \frac{-mca_1^2}{m^2 a_1^2 + b^2}$$

we can substitute into this equation the values just calculated of

$$a_1^2 = \frac{a^2 x_1^2}{x_1^2 + a^2}$$

$$b_1^2 = \frac{b^2 x_1^4}{(x_1^2 + a^2)^2}$$

$$m = \frac{-2b}{x_1}$$

$$c = \frac{b(x_1^2 + 2a^2)}{x_1^2 + a^2}$$

therefore

$$x_2 = \frac{\dfrac{2b}{x_1} \cdot \dfrac{b(x_1^2 + 2a^2)}{x_1^2 + a^2} \cdot \dfrac{a^2 x_1^2}{x_1^2 + a^2}}{\dfrac{4b^2}{x_1^2} \cdot \dfrac{a^2 x_1^2}{x_1^2 + a^2} + \dfrac{b^2 x_1^4}{(x_1^2 + a^2)^2}}$$

$$x_2 = \frac{\dfrac{2b^2 a^2 x_1 (x_1^2 + 2a^2)}{(x_1^2 + a^2)^2}}{\dfrac{4b^2 a^2 (x_1^2 + a^2) + b^2 x_1^4}{(x_1^2 + a^2)^2}}$$

$$x_2 = \frac{2a^2 x_1 (x_1^2 + 2a^2)}{4a^2 x_1^2 + 4a^4 + x_1^4}$$

$$x_2 = \frac{2a^2 x_1}{x_1^2 + 2a^2}$$

Substituting this value of x_2 into the original equation 2.8 of line PA gives

$$y_2 = \frac{-2b2a^2 x_1}{x_1(x_1^2 + 2a^2)} + b$$

$$y_2 = \frac{-4ba^2 + b(x_1^2 + 2a^2)}{x_1^2 + 2a^2}$$

$$y_2 = \frac{b(x_1^2 - 2a^2)}{x_1^2 + 2a^2}$$

The tangent point of the line PA with ellipse E_2 at the point $I(x_2, y_2)$ is

$$I\left(\frac{2a^2 x_1}{x_1^2 + 2a^2}, \frac{b(x_1^2 - 2a^2)}{x_1^2 + 2a^2} \right)$$

$$(2.16)$$

and it can be seen that 2.16 and 2.9 are identical.

(c) Comparing the principle theorem to the pyramid's upper shaft

To compare the geometric design to the architectural design we need to 1) evaluate the numerical values of the algebraic equations and then 2) compare these values to the surveyed points in the pyramid's architecture.

1) The numerical values of the algebraic equations

The tangent point of ellipse E_2 with the line PA was given in equation 2.16. To enumerate this equation for I_x, the algebraic value of a from equation 1.4 can be substituted into the equation giving

$$I_x = \frac{\dfrac{2.16 x_1^2 f^2 \cdot x_1}{\pi^2 R_c^2}}{x_1^2 + \dfrac{2.16 x_1^2 f^2}{\pi^2 Rc^2}}$$

$$I_x = \frac{32 x_1^3 f^2}{\pi^2 R_c^2 \left(x_1^2 + \dfrac{32 x_1^2 f^2}{\pi^2 Rc^2} \right)}$$

$$I_x = \frac{32 x_1 f^2}{\pi^2 R_c^2 + 32 f^2}$$

The numerical values that we have already calculated for the ellipse of the Earth and for the scaled model of the Earth are as follows

$$f = 1.00336409$$

$$R_c = 2.003365502$$

$$x_1 = 115.3664 \ m$$

and so the value of I_x is

$$I_x = 51.7438 \ m$$

The value of the y coordinate, I_y, can be found in a similar manner by substituting the values of and b from equations 1.3 and 1.4 into the algebraic value of I_y given in equation 2.16 giving

$$I_y = \frac{\frac{4x_1}{\pi R_c}\left(x_1^2 - 2.\frac{16x_1^2 f^2}{\pi^2 R_c^2}\right)}{x_1^2 + 2.\frac{16x_1^2 f^2}{\pi^2 R_c^2}}$$

$$I_y = \frac{4x_1}{\pi R_c}\left(\frac{x_1^2 \pi^2 R_c^2 - 32x_1^2 f^2}{\pi^2 R_c^2}\right)\left(\frac{\pi^2 R_c^2}{x_1^2 \pi^2 R_c^2 + 32x_1^2 f^2}\right)$$

$$I_y = \frac{4x_1\left(\pi^2 R_c^2 - 32f^2\right)}{\pi R_c\left(\pi^2 R_c^2 + 32f^2\right)}$$

$$Iy = 7.5496 \; m$$

o from the algebraic calculations

$$I(x2, y2) = (51.7438, 7.5496) \tag{2.17}$$

) The numerical values from the surveying data need to be extracted from the upper northern haft of the pyramid as shown on the diagram below.

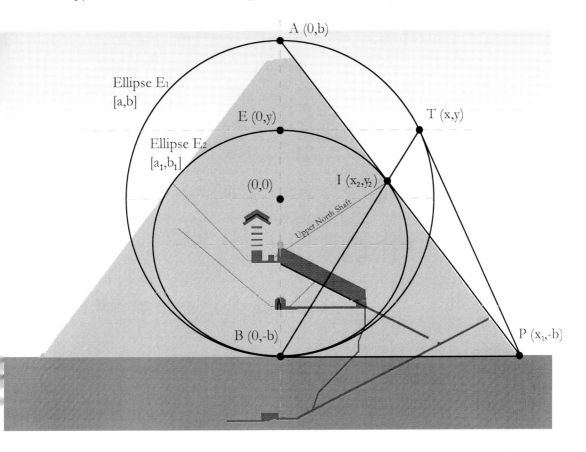

According to the lemma 2 this shaft emerges from the pyramid at the point $I(x_2, y_2)$ and since the external stonework around the shaft's exit is largely destroyed, it is necessary to use the straight shaft roof line as a reference, for which we will need its mathematical line equation.

The surveying data for this section of the pyramid comes from Rudolf Gantenbrink from which we can extract two arbitrarily chosen points on the shaft's roof. Since Gantenbrin used the base center as his coordinate center point, and we are using the ellipse center, the value from the survey needs rebasing to our coordinate system by subtracting the value of th ellipse's semi-minor axis of 73.3211m

	x coordinate	y coordinate	y coordinte transformed
Block 7 upper end	5.6016	51.4472	-21.8740
Block 25 upper end	39.5447	73.1544	-0.1667

The gradient and angle of the shaft's roof are therefore

$$gradient\ SHAFT = \frac{-0.1667 + 21.8740}{39.5447 - 5.6016}$$

$$gradient\ SHAFT = 0.6395$$

$$angle\ SHAFT = 32.599635°$$

and thereby the constant in the line equation of the shaft's roof is

$$-0.1667 = 0.6395 \times 39.5447 + c$$

$$c = -25.4563$$

and the equation of the shaft roof

$$y = 0.6395x - 25.4563$$

The equation of the pyramid's northern face, the line PA, can be evaluated from equation 2.8 giving

$$y = -1.2711x + 73.3211$$

and solving these two equations to find the shaft's intersect point with the face gives

$$0.6385x - 25.4563 = -1.2711x + 73.3211$$

$$1.9096x = 98.7774$$

$$x = 51.7267$$

and thereby the value of y as

$$y = -1.2711 \times 51.7267 + 73.3211$$

$$y = 7.5713$$

and so the surveying data gives the shaft exit point as being

$$I(x2, y2) = (51.7267, 7.5713) \tag{2.18}$$

Comparing the points from the algebraic calculations (2.17) and those from the surveying (2.18) shows discrepancies of 0.0171m on the x coordinte and 0.0217m on the y coordinate.

These discrepancies are sufficiently small to be able to state that lemma 2 is proven.

6. Gantenbrink, Rudolf *The Upuaut Project, www.cheops.org (cyber drawings - cheops shafts) Original DWF file*

The geometry of the upper shafts of the Great Pyramid

Lemma 1.3   The upper northern shaft, shown in the diagram below as the line IK, is a geometric construction showing continuity from the algebraic design of the pyramid proven in the previous section. Its angle is formed by taking a line from the point $I(x_2, y_2)$ to meet the line T_1B at a right angle. Its length is determined by the algebra from which it is created, with the vertical distance of the shaft being half the algebraic numerator of its gradient and the horizontal distance being half the algebraic denominator of its gradient. The upper southern shaft, shown in the diagram below as the line IL, is a geometric refernce line angled at 45°. Its length is determined from the algebraic geometry of the upper northern shaft.

The distance between the points I and K defines the length of the cubit measure which was used to construct the building.

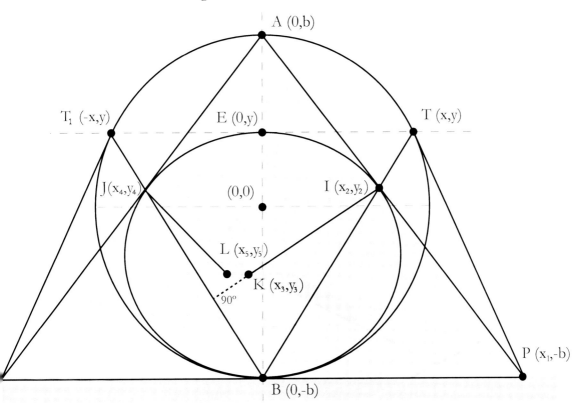

Proof : In order to prove this lemma we need to 1) determine the algebraic values of the points K and L and then 2) enumerate these points and compare the results to the surveying data.

1) The equation of the line BT was given in 2.14 and so the equation of the line BT_1, which for

---

7. *A more detailed analysis of the monument shows that the elliptical cross section shown above should in fact be an orthographic projection of an ellipsoid of the Earth which has been rotated around two axiis. This rotation causes the orthographic projection not to be symetrical around the vertical axis, and the simplified diagram above no longer holds true for reflection in the vertical axis. However, for the purposes of this work, the descrepancies in the numerical results are insufficient to make any fundemental difference to the proofs.*

the purposes of this document is simply a reflection of the line BT in the vertical axis[7], is

$$y = \frac{-bx_1}{a^2} . x - b$$

Since the extension of the line IK meets BT_1 at right angles, the equation of the line IK must be

$$y = \frac{-a^2}{bx_1} . x + c$$

where c is an unknown constant. Since this line passes through the point $I(x_2, y_2)$ then the constant in the equation can be determined

$$\frac{b(x_1^2 - 2a^2)}{x_1^2 + 2a^2} = \frac{-a^2}{bx_1} . \frac{2a^2 x_1}{x_1^2 + 2a^2} + c$$

$$c = \frac{b^2 x_1 (x_1^2 - 2a^2) - 2a^4 x_1}{bx_1 (x_1^2 + 2a^2)}$$

$$c = \frac{b^2 (x_1^2 - 2a^2) - 2a^4}{b(x_1^2 + 2a^2)}$$

and the equation of the line IK is therefore

$$y = \frac{-a^2}{bx_1} .x + \frac{b^2 (x_1^2 - 2a^2) - 2a^4}{b(x_1^2 + 2a^2)} \tag{3.1}$$

The gradient of this line can be rationalised by substituting the idendity $a=fb$ giving

$$gradient\ IK = \frac{-f^2 b}{x_1} \tag{3.2}$$

in which both the denominator and numerator are measureable quantities within the pyramid. Lemma 3 states that the vertical difference betwen the shaft's ends is half the numerator, and the horizontal difference is half the denominator, giving

$$vertical\ length = \frac{-f^2 b}{2}$$

$$horizontal\ length = \frac{x_1}{2}$$

and so the algebraic value of the point K can be determined from the point I as follows :

$$x_3 = \frac{2a^2 x_1}{x_1^2 + 2a^2} - \frac{x_1}{2}$$

$$x_3 = \frac{4a^2 x_1 - x_1 (x_1^2 + 2a^2)}{2(x_1^2 + 2a^2)}$$

$$x_3 = \frac{x_1 (2a^2 - x_1^2)}{2(x_1^2 + 2a^2)}$$

$$\tag{3.3}$$

and

$$y_3 = \frac{b(x_1^2 - 2a^2)}{x_1^2 + 2a^2} - \frac{f^2 b}{2}$$

$$\tag{3.4}$$

Lemma 3 states that the southern shaft line is set at 45° and so the coordinates of the point L can be determined by realising that the gradient of the line JL is given algebraicaly as

$$gradient\ JL = \frac{f^2 b}{f^2 b}$$

since the horizontal displacement of this shaft is the same as that of the northern shaft. Since the point J is known to be a reflection of the point I in the vertical axis, then the point L can be alculated algebraicaly as follows

$$X_5 = \frac{-2a^2 x_1}{x_1^2 + 2a^2} + \frac{f^2 b}{2}$$

(3.5)

nd

$$y_5 = \frac{b(x_1^2 - 2a^2)}{x_1^2 + 2a^2} - \frac{f^2 b}{2}$$

(3.6)

) Compare the algebraic shaft details to the surveying data

o compare these algebraic statements to the surveying data, first the gradient of the shaft can ￼e enumerated by substituting the numerical values of b, f and x_1 into the gradient algebra from quation 3.2

$$gradient\ IK = \frac{-1,00336409 \cdot 73.3211}{115.3664}$$

$$gradient\ IK = -0.6398$$

$$angle\ IK = -32.6125°$$

This compares to the angle reported in the surveying of -32.6023° giving an error between ￼he surveyed and algebraic figures of 0.01°, or 6mm horizontally and 10mm vertically over ￼he 68.5m length of the shaft. If we take into account that it was the floor of the shaft whose ngle was measured remotely in the survey and that the value reported was averaged out over ￼he length of the shaft due to minor degredations in the stonework, then the two values can be ￼tated as being identical within the margins of error of the surveying.

￼or the shaft end points of the line IK given in 3.3 and 3.4, the values of x_3 and y_3 can be calcu-￼ated by substituting the values of a, b, f and x_1 into the equations giving

$$X_3 = \frac{115.3664(2 \times 73.5678^2 - 115.3664^2)}{2(115.3664^2 + 2 \times 73.5678^2)} m$$

$$X_3 = -5.9394\ m$$

$$y_3 = \frac{73.3211(2 \times 73.5678^2 - 115.3664^2)}{2 \times 73.5678^2 + 115.3664^2} - \frac{1.0034^2 \times 73.3211}{2} m$$

$$y_3 = -44.4572\ m$$

￼or the shaft end points of the line JL, the y coordinate is the same as that of the line IK, so

$$y_5 = -44.4572\ m$$

￼nd the x coordinate is found by substitution of the numerical values into 3.5 giving

$$X_5 = \frac{-2 \times 73.5678^2 \times 115.3664}{115.3664^2 + 2 \times 73.5678^2} + \frac{1.0034^2 \times 73.3211}{2}$$

$$X_5 = -14.8362$$

The following diagramme of the bottom of the shafts shows where this point falls in the pyra-nid's architecture along with the corresponding point in the southern shaft.

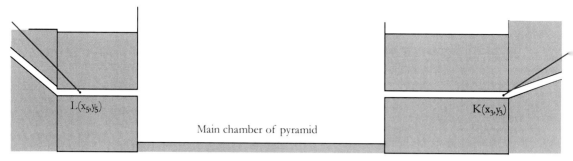

L(x₅,y₅)

K(x₃,y₃)

Main chamber of pyramid

Due to the bending of the shafts at the lower end where they deviate from the straight line that makes up the majority of their length, the geometric lines do not follow the stonework for the last few meters of the shaft. The lower end points are positioned just inside the horizontal sections of the shaft. The horizontal midpoint of the shafts was surveyed at -44.4621 m and therefore the points K and L are located 4mm below the surveyed shaft mid point.

The algebraic expressions for the horizontal x co-ordinates of the shaft end points were given in 3.3 and 3.5 and so the distance between these points, algebraically, is

$$\overline{LK} = \left| \frac{-2a^2 x_1}{x_1^2 + 2a^2} + \frac{f^2 b}{2} - \frac{x_1(2a^2 - x_1^2)}{2(x_1^2 + 2a^2)} \right|$$

$$\overline{LK} = \left| \frac{-4a^2 x_1}{2(x_1^2 + 2a^2)} - \frac{x_1(2a^2 - x_1^2)}{2(x_1^2 + 2a^2)} + \frac{f^2 b}{2} \right|$$

$$\overline{LK} = \left| \frac{x_1(x_1^2 - 6a^2)}{2(x_1^2 + 2a^2)} + \frac{f^2 b}{2} \right|$$

and substituting the numerical values of a,b,f and x_1 into the equation gives

$$\overline{LK} = \left| \frac{115.3664(115.3664^2 - 6 \times 73.5678^2)}{2(115.3664^2 + 273.5678^2)} + \frac{1.0034^2 73.3211}{2} \right|$$

$$\overline{LK} = 8.8967 \; m$$

It is an established fact that the main pyramid at Giza was constructed using the 'cubit' as its measuring unit and over the course of the centuries the value of the cubit has been established at 0.5235 m, as reference to any encyclopedia[8] will testify. The distance between the points L and K in cubits is therefore

$$\overline{LK} = 16.9947 \; cubits$$

The error margin in this value is effectively zero, since it is based entirely on scaled geodesic quantities which are known to great precission. Consequently, the cubit can be *defined* algebraically as follows :

$$17 \; cubits = \left| \frac{x_1(x_1^2 - 6a^2)}{2(x_1^2 + 2a^2)} + \frac{f^2 b}{2} \right| m$$

8. *Common knowledge reference on wikipedia, http://en.wikipedia.org/wiki/Ancient_Egyptian_units_of_measurement, 2010.*

$$cubit = \left| \frac{x_1 \left(x_1^2 - 6a^2 \right)}{34 \left(x_1^2 + 2a^2 \right)} + \frac{f^2 b}{34} \right| m$$

iving the exact[9] value of the cubit as

$$cubit = 0.5233379 \, m \pm 0.0000005$$

---

9. A more detailed study of the Giza plateau's mathematical construction shows that this value is not exact, but is in fact a very close approximation differeing from the actual value of the cubit by + 0.0000029 m.

The entrance passage geometry
of the Great Pyramid

Lemma 1.4 The entrance passageway is formed from simple algebraic adjustments to the major and minor diametres of the ellipse E_2 (a_1/f and b_1f) and by placing the adjusted minor diameter perpendicular to, and at the end of, the adjusted major diameter to form a T shape as shown in the diagram below. This construction is then positioned at the top of ellipse E_2 in the manner shown, and rotated until the extremity of the minor axis, the point G, touches the geometric face of the pyramid.

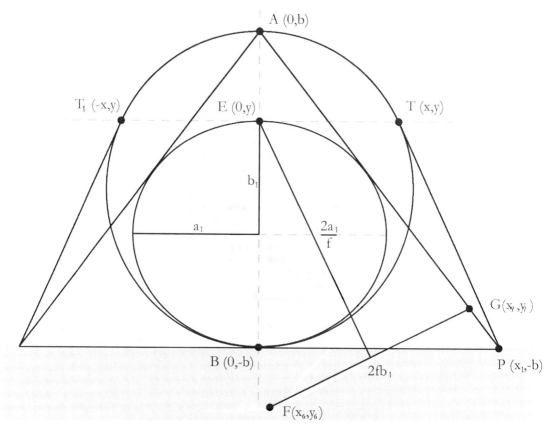

Proof : The method for calculating the points $G(x_7, y_7)$ and $F(x_6, y_6)$ and the gradient of the line GF is 1) calculate the general algebra of a circle and line intersect, 2) coordinate transform this geometry to be centered at the point E, 3) calculate the distance from the point E to the entrance point G, 4) calculate the algebraic value of the point G from the mathematics of the previous section, 5) calculate the algebraic value of the gradient of the entrance passage in terms of x_7 and y_7 and then determine the point F.

) The general algebra of a circle and line intersect.

At the intersect of a circle of equation $x^2 + y^2 = r^2$ and a line of $y = mx + c$

$$r^2 - x^2 = m^2 x^2 + c^2 + 2mxc$$

$$x^2(m^2 + 1) + x(2mc) + c^2 - r^2 = 0$$

and solving using the 'quadratic formula' gives

$$x = \frac{-2mc \pm \sqrt{4m^2 c^2 - 4(m^2 + 1)(c^2 - r^2)}}{2(m^2 + 1)}$$

$$x = \frac{-mc \pm \sqrt{r^2(m^2 + 1) - c^2}}{m^2 + 1} \tag{4.1}$$

?) Transform previous relevant algebra to be centered at the point E

The equation of line PA, equation 2.8, needs to be coordinate transformed to be centered on the point $E(0, y)$ which involves subtracting the value y of the point E from the constant in the line equation. The algebraic value of y was shown in 2.5 and so

$$y = \frac{-2bx}{x_1} + b - \frac{b(x_1^2 - a^2)}{x_1^2 + a^2}$$

$$y = \frac{-2bx}{x_1} + \frac{b(x_1^2 + a^2) - b(x_1^2 - a^2)}{x_1^2 + a^2}$$

$$y = \frac{-2bx}{x_1} + \frac{2ba^2}{x_1^2 + a^2}$$

or substituting the identity $a = fb$

$$y = \frac{-2bx}{x_1} + \frac{2f^2 b^3}{x_1^2 + f^2 b^2} \tag{4.2}$$

3) Calculate the distance from the point E to the entrance point G

Letting the distances of the adjusted diameters of ellipse E_2 be as shown on the diagram then the distance r from the top of the ellipse at point E to the entrance point $G(x_7, y_7)$ using Pythagoras' formula on the triangle, is

$$r^2 = \frac{(2a_1)^2}{f^2} + (fb_1)^2$$

$$r_2 = \frac{4a_1^2}{f^2} + f^2 b_1^2$$

Substituting the algebraic values of a_1 and b_1 from 2.13 and 2.15 then

$$r^2 = \frac{4a^2 x_1^2}{f^2(x_1^2 + a^2)} + \frac{f^2 b^2 x_1^4}{(x_1^2 + a^2)^2}$$

and substituting a = fb gives

$$r^2 = \frac{4b^2 x_1^2}{x_1^2 + f^2 b^2} + \frac{f^2 b^2 x_1^4}{(x_1^2 + f^2 b^2)^2} \qquad (4.3)$$

4) Calculate the algebraic value of the point G

To calculate the value of x_7 the values of the line gradient m and the line constant c from 4.2 and the distance r from 4.3 can substituted into equation 4.1 giving

$$x_7 = \frac{-\dfrac{-2b}{x_1} \cdot \dfrac{2f^2 b^3}{x_1^2 + f^2 b^2} \pm \sqrt{\left(\dfrac{4b^2 x_1^2 + f^2 b^2 x_1^2}{x_1^2 + f^2 b^2}\right)\left(\dfrac{4b^2}{x_1^2} + 1\right) - \left(\dfrac{2f^2 b^3}{x_1^2 + f^2 b^2}\right)2}}{\dfrac{4b^2}{x_1^2} + 1}$$

$$x_7 = \frac{\dfrac{4f^2 b^4}{x_1(x_1^2 + f^2 b^2)} \pm \sqrt{\dfrac{4b^2 x_1^2 + f^2 b^2 x_1^2}{x_1^2 + f^2 b^2} + \dfrac{16 b^4 x_1^2 + 4 f^2 b^4 x_1^2}{x_1^2(x_1^2 + f^2 b^2)} - \dfrac{4 f^4 b^6}{(x_1^2 + f^2 b^2)^2}}}{\dfrac{4b^2}{x_1^2} + 1}$$

$$x_7 = \frac{\dfrac{4f^2 b^4}{x_1(x_1^2 + f^2 b^2)} \pm \sqrt{\dfrac{16 b^4 x_1^2 + 16 b^6 f^2 + 8 f^2 b^4 x_1^2 + 4 b^2 x_1^4 + f^2 b^2 x_1^4 - 4 f^4 b^6}{(x_1^2 + f^2 b^2)^2}}}{\dfrac{4b^2 + x_1^2}{x_1^2}}$$

$$x_7 = \frac{4 f^2 b^4 x_1 \pm b x_1^2 \sqrt{16 b^2 x_1^2 + 16 b^4 f^2 + 8 f^2 b^2 x_1^2 + 4 x_1^4 + f^2 x_1^4 - 4 f^4 b^4}}{(x_1^2 + f^2 b^2)(4b^2 + x_1^2)} \qquad (4.4)$$

To find the value of y_7 this algebraic value of x_7 can be placed back into the original equation of the line PA giving

$$y_7 = \frac{-8 f^2 b^5 \pm - 2 b^2 x_1 \sqrt{16 b^2 x_1^2 + 16 b^4 f^2 + 8 f^2 b^2 x_1^2 + 4 x_1^4 + f^2 x_1^4 - 4 f^4 b^4}}{(x_1^2 + f^2 b^2)(4b^2 + x_1^2)} + b \quad (4.5)$$

5) Calculate the algebraic value of the gradient of the entrance passage in terms of x_7 and y_7 and then determine the point F

To determine the gradient of the entrance passage GF a detailed diagram of the geometry of the entrance passage is required

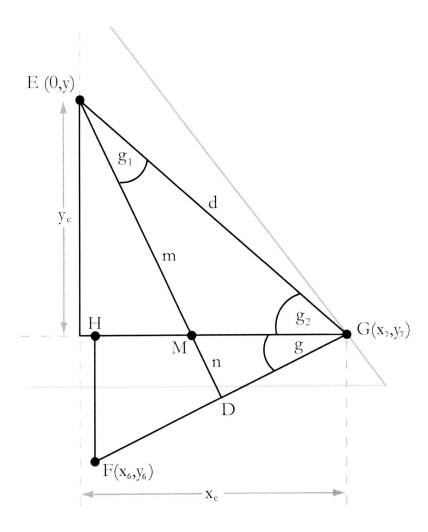

or the purpose of the analysis let the line ED have a length $2a_2$ and the line DG have a length $_2$. Then from the triangle GEM the law of sines gives

$$\frac{d}{\sin(g_1 + g_2)} = \frac{m}{\sin g_2}$$
$$d.\sin g_2 = m.\sin(g_1 + g_2)$$

ecause

$$\sin g_2 = \frac{y_e}{d}$$

hen

$$y_e = m.\sin(g_1 + g_2)$$

and from standard trigonomerty identities

$$y_e = m(\sin g_1 \cos g_2 + \cos g_1 . \sin g_2)$$

$$y_e = m\left(\frac{b_2}{d}.\frac{x_e}{d} + \frac{2a_2}{d}.\frac{-y_e}{d}\right)$$

$$-ye = \frac{m(b_2 x_e - 2a_2 y_e)}{d^2}$$

$$m = \frac{-y_e d^2}{b_2 x_e - 2a_2 y_e}$$

By definition

$$n = 2a_2 - m$$

so

$$n = 2a_2 - \frac{-y_e d^2}{b_2 x_e - 2a_2 y_e}$$

$$n = \frac{2a_2 b_2 x_e - 4a_2^2 y_e + y_e d^2}{b_2 x_e - 2a_2 y_e}$$

substituting

$$d^2 = 4a_2^2 + b_2^2$$

gives

$$n = \frac{2a_2 b_2 x_e - 4a_2^2 y_e + 4a_2^2 y_e + ye_2 b_2^2}{b_2 x_e - 2a_2 y_e}$$

$$n = \frac{b_2(2a_2 x_e + y_e b_2)}{b_2 x_e - 2a_2 y_e}$$

$$\tan g = \frac{n}{b_2} = \frac{2a_2 x_e + y_e b_2}{b_2 x_e - 2a_2 y_e} \tag{4.6}$$

Lemma 4 states that for the entrance passage of the pyramid

$$a_2 = \frac{a_1}{f}$$

$$b_2 = b_1 f$$

Substituting the values of a_1 and b_1 from 2.13 and 2.15 gives these values as

$$a_2 = \frac{bx_1}{\sqrt{x_1^2 + f^2 b^2}}$$

$$b_2 = \frac{fbx_1^2}{x_1^2 + f^2 b^2}$$

Placing these values into the equation of the entrance gradient 4.6 gives

$$\tan g = \frac{\dfrac{2bx_1 x_e}{\sqrt{x_1^2 + f^2 b^2}} + \dfrac{y_e f b x_1^2}{x_1^2 + f^2 b^2}}{\dfrac{f b x_1^2 x_e}{x_1^2 + f^2 b^2} - \dfrac{2bx_1 y_e}{\sqrt{x_1^2 + f^2 b^2}}}$$

$$\tan g = \frac{2bx_1 x_e \sqrt{x_1^2 + f^2 b^2} + y_e f b x_1^2}{f b x_1^2 x_e - 2bx_1 y_e \sqrt{x_1^2 + f^2 b^2}}$$

$$\tan g = \frac{2x_e \sqrt{x_1^2 + f^2 b^2} + y_e f x_1}{f x_1 x_e - 2y_e \sqrt{x_1^2 + f^2 b^2}} \qquad (4.7)$$

Letting the length of line HG be x_f and the length of line FH be y_f where

$$x_f^2 + y_f^2 = (2b_1 f)^2$$

$$y_f = \sqrt{4b_1^2 f^2 - x_f^2}$$

ince

$$\tan g = \frac{y_f}{x_f}$$

hen

$$\tan g = \frac{\sqrt{4b_1^2 f^2 - x_f^2}}{x_f}$$

$$\tan^2 g = \frac{4b_1^2 f^2}{x_f^2} - 1$$

$$x_f^2 = \frac{4b_1^2 f^2}{\tan^2 g + 1}$$

$$x_f = \frac{2b_1 f}{\sqrt{\tan^2 g + 1}} \qquad (4.8)$$

The value of *tan g* from 4.7 can be substituted into this equation to give the algebraic value of x_f in the following manner

$$\tan^2 g = \frac{4x_e^2 (x_1^2 + f^2 b^2) + f^2 x_1^2 y_e^2 + 4x_e y_e f x_1 \sqrt{x_1^2 + f^2 b^2}}{4y_e^2 (x_1^2 + f^2 b^2) + f^2 x_1^2 x_e^2 - 4x_e y_e f x_1 \sqrt{x_1^2 + f^2 b^2}}$$

$$\tan^2 g + 1 = \frac{(4x_e^2 + 4y_e^2)(x_1^2 + f^2 b^2) + f^2 x_1^2 (y_e^2 + x_e^2)}{4y_e^2 (x_1^2 + f^2 b^2) + f^2 x_1^2 x_e^2 - 4x_e y_e f x_1 \sqrt{x_1^2 + f^2 b^2}}$$

$$\tan^2 g + 1 = \frac{4(x_e^2 + y_e^2)(x_1^2 + f^2 b^2 + f^2 x_1^2)}{4y_e^2 (x_1^2 + f^2 b^2) + f^2 x_1^2 x_e^2 - 4x_e y_e f x_1 \sqrt{x_1^2 + f^2 b^2}}$$

$$\frac{1}{\sqrt{\tan^2 g + 1}} = \sqrt{\frac{4y_e^2 (x_1^2 + f^2 b^2) + f^2 x_1^2 x_e^2 - 4x_e y_e f x_1 \sqrt{x_1^2 + f^2 b^2}}{4(x_e^2 + y_e^2)(x_1^2 + f^2 b^2 + f^2 x_1^2)}}$$

and therefore

$$x_f = 2b_1 f \sqrt{\frac{4y_e^2(x_1^2 + f^2 b^2) + f^2 x_1^2 x_e^2 - 4x_e y_e f x_1 \sqrt{x_1^2 + f^2 b^2}}{4(x_e^2 + y_e^2)(x_1^2 + f^2 b^2 + f^2 x_1^2)}} \qquad (4.9)$$

giving the algebraic value of x_f in terms of known values. To determine the value of y_f we know that

$$y_f = x_f \tan g$$

and substituting the value of $\tan g$ from 4.7 gives

$$y_f = 4x_e b_1 f \sqrt{\frac{4y_e^2(x_1^2 + f^2 b^2) + f^2 x_1^2 x_e^2 - 4x_e y_e f x_1 \sqrt{x_1^2 + f^2 b^2}}{4(x_e^2 + y_e^2)(x_1^2 + f^2 b^2 + f^2 x_1^2)}} \cdot \frac{\sqrt{x_1^2 + f^2 b^2} + y_e f x_1}{f x_1 x_e - 2y_e \sqrt{x_1^2 + f^2 b^2}}$$

$$(4.10)$$

The geometry of the lower shafts of the Great Pyramid

Lower Southern Shaft

Lemma 1.5 The lower southern shaft, shown as the line UV on the diagram, is formed from the tangent to a third ellipse E_3 which is formed as a mathematical by-product during the formation of the primary ellipse E_1. Ellipse E_3 has its center at the point $(0,-b)$ and is rotated by an angle equal to that of the Earth's maximum axial tilt. The tangent line from which the shaft is formed eminates from one end of a base line of length equal to half the circumference of ellipse E_3.[10] This base line lies on the base line of the pyramid and has its center at the point $(0,-b)$.

The start of the shaft is formed from a second tangent line which starts from the southern end of the ellipse's rotated base line, the point S, and intersects the first tangent line at the point U.

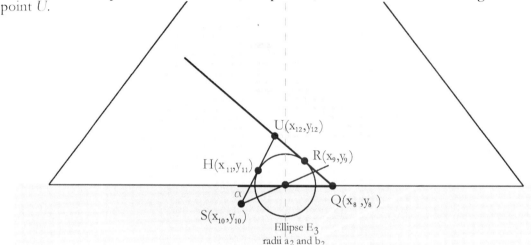

$U(x_{12},y_{12})$

$R(x_9,y_9)$

$H(x_{11},y_{11})$

α

$Q(x_8,y_8)$

$S(x_{10},y_{10})$

Ellipse E_3
radii a_2 and b_2

Proof

1) In the primary design of the pyramid's geometry, the ellipse E_1 was formed from the base length of the pyramid by using Ramanujan's circumference formula 'in reverse'. Equations 1.3 and 1.4 give the values of the ellipse's radii from the base length of the pyramid, and they involve the factor Rc which was defined as

$$Rc = 3(f+1) - \sqrt{(3f+1)(f+3)}$$

Whilst this formula produces the correct results for the ellipse's radii, the mathematics dictates that there must also be a second solution to this equation since there is a square root within it. Therefore

$$Rc' = 3(f+1) + \sqrt{(3f+1)(f+3)}$$

with this second solution giving the following numerical value for Ramanujan's constant for the ellipse of the Earth

---

10. *A more advanced analysis of the construction system of the pyramid shows that this base line length is proportional to the length of the pyramid's base, the length of which which varies when rotations are applied to the ellipsoid from which the whole system is designed.*

$$Rc' = 10.01682$$

The ratio between these two constants, which I shall call the Ramanujan ratio Rr, is another fixed quantity for the Earth's ellipse and has the value

$$Rr = \frac{Rc}{Rc'} = 0.2000001692$$

Therefore, when the ellipse $E1$ is formed from the base length, there must be a second ellipse formed at the same time, which I shall call E_3, which has the following radi

$$a_2 = a.Rr = 14.7136 \; m$$
$$b_2 = b.Rr = 14.6642 \; m$$

It is this ellipse that is used to form the lower shafts of the pyramid

2) Calculate the general solution for the tangent point on a rotated ellipse for a tangent line eminating from an arbitrary point x_1,y_1

The equation of a rotated ellipse is

$$\frac{(xCos\alpha + ySin\alpha)^2}{a^2} + \frac{(yCos\alpha - xSin\alpha)^2}{b^2} = 1$$

Substituting the identity $a=fb$ and solving for y and x gives

$$y = \frac{\pm\sqrt{2}f\sqrt{b^2(f^2+1)-2x^2+b^2Cos2\alpha(f^2-1)}+xSin2\alpha(f^2-1)}{1+f^2+Cos2\alpha(f^2-1)} \tag{5.1}$$

$$x = \frac{\pm\sqrt{2}f\sqrt{b^2(f^2+1)-2y^2-b^2Cos2\alpha(f^2-1)}+ySin2\alpha(f^2-1)}{-1-f^2+Cos2\alpha(f^2-1)} \tag{5.2}$$

Differentiating the rotated ellipse equation as an implicit function gives

$$\frac{\delta y}{\delta x} = \frac{-x(Cos^2\alpha + f^2Sin^2\alpha) + yCos\alpha Sin\alpha(f^2-1)}{y(f^2Cos^2\alpha + Sin^2\alpha) - xCos\alpha Sin\alpha(f^2-1)} \tag{5.3}$$

and equating this to the gradient equation of the tangent line gives

$$\frac{-x(Cos^2\alpha + f^2Sin^2\alpha) + yCos\alpha Sin\alpha(f^2-1)}{y(f^2Cos^2\alpha + Sin^2\alpha) - xCos\alpha Sin\alpha(f^2-1)} = \frac{y-y_1}{x-x_1}$$

It is at this point in the algebra that the calculations become too complex to perform by hand, and automated solutions are required.

Solving the above equation for x using a modern algebra solving computer program gives the following result

$$x = \frac{1}{2\left(Cos^2\alpha + f^2 Sin^2\alpha\right)} \cdot (x_1 Cos^2\alpha - 2yCos\alpha Sin\alpha + y_1 Cos\alpha Sin\alpha - f^2 y_1 Cos\alpha Sin\alpha +$$

$$f^2 x_1 Sin^2 a - \sqrt{(\,(x_1 Cos^2\alpha + (f^2-1)(2y-y_1)Cos\alpha Sin\alpha) +}$$

$$f^2 x_1 Sin^2\alpha)^2 - 4y(Cos^2\alpha + f^2 Sin^2\alpha)(f^2(y-y_1)Cos^2\alpha +$$

$$(f^2-1)x_1 Cos\alpha Sin\alpha + (y-y_1)Sin^2\alpha)) + f^2 ySin2\alpha)$$

into which the value of y from 5.1 needs to be substituted, and then the resulting equation solved for x.

Since it would be of no benefit to list the algebraic solution from this point onwards a it is highly complex, we need to turn to numerical solutions to the problem. The mathematica algorithms that solve these equations are programmed into CAD drawing systems, and so it is t these that we need to turn to to compare the mathematical design of the pyramid to the survey ing data.

Applying a rotation, equal to the Earth's maximum axial tilt[11] of 24.356932°, to the el lipse E_3 gives the following values to the points shown on the earlier diagram, using the bas center of the pyramid as the origin of the cartesian coordinate system.

$$Q = (23.07329, 0)$$
$$R = (9.8267, 11.33378)$$
$$S = (-21.29577, -8.88069)$$
$$H = (-13.02211, 6.84935)$$

giving the shaft start point and shaft angle as

$$U = (-4.582519, 22.89486)$$
$$shaft\ angle = 39.6197°$$

From the combined survey work of Petrie(for the shaft start) and Gantenbrink(for the shaf angle), the shaft start point and angle are

$$U_{survey} = (-4.56864, 22.92017)$$
$$shaft_{survey} = 39.6078°$$

The discrepancies between the mathematical and surveyed results are minimal, and are showr on the following scaled illustration

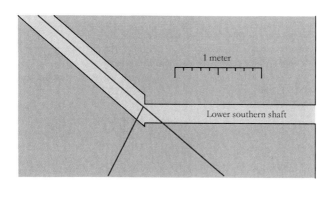

1 meter

Lower southern shaft

11. *The obliquity of the ecliptic, Wittmann, A., Astronomy and Astrophysics Journal, vol. 73, no. 1-2, Mar. 1979, p. 129-131. Equation 4a*

Lower Northern Shaft

Lemma 1.6 The lower northern shaft is formed from the geometry of the lower southern shaft shown in and proven from lemma 3.

The lower northern shaft start point, U', is a reflection of the lower southern shaft start point U in the y axis[12]. The upper section of the shaft and the shaft's angle are formed by taking line from the point S to meet the base line of the pyramid perpendicularly at the point V. A tangent line to the rotated ellipse E_3 forms the upper section of the shaft. The lower section of the shaft is formed by a line starting from the point U' and being parallel to the line VW.

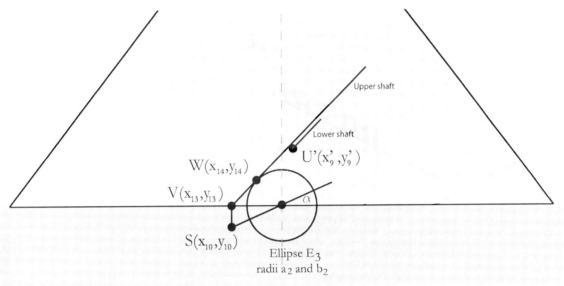

Prior to rotation, the point S has the coordinates

$$S(x_{10}, y_{10}) = \left(-\frac{\pi b_2 Rc}{4}, 0 \right)$$

and so after rotation has the coordinates

$$S(x_{10}, y_{10}) = \left(-\frac{\pi b_2 Rc}{4} Cos\alpha, -\frac{\pi b_2 Rc}{4} Sin\alpha \right)$$

The point V therefore has the coordinates

$$V(x_{13}, y_{13}) = \left(-\frac{\pi b_2 Rc}{4} Cos\alpha, 0 \right)$$

For reasons explained in the previous section, the algebra of the point W is too complex to present, and therefore numerical analysis has to be used.

From the CAD representation of the system, the points on the diagram evaluate to

$$S(x_{10}, y_{10}) = (-21.29578, -8.88069)$$
$$V(x_{13}, y_{13}) = (-21.29578, 0)$$
$$W(x_{14}, y_{14}) = (-10.16583, 10.63697)$$

giving the angle of the shaft line as

$$shaft\ angle = 43.7025°$$

The shaft start point, by reflection of the point U in the y axis[12], is

$$U' = (4.58252, 22.89486)$$

From the combined survey work of Petrie(for the shaft start) and Gantenbrink(for the shaft angle), the shaft start point and angle are

$$U_{survey} = (4.54216, 22.92017)$$
$$shaft_{survey} = 43.6678°$$

The descrepancies are again small, although it should be noted that in Gantenbrink's work he states that the angle of the shaft was still uncertain when he completed his work, presumably down to time constrainsts prohibiting its completion.

The geometric construction
of the ascending passage

Lemma 1.7 The ascending passageway is designed from similar geometry to the upper northern shaft, as shown in the diagram below.

Ellipse E_4 has its axiis parallel to the cartesian axiis, the lower end of its polar axis located at the point B and has the pyramid's geometric faces as tangent lines. At the tangent point, C, a line is taken to the point M, meeting the line line BD' at right angles. From the point M, a line perpendicular to the line BD is created to form the ascending passage angle of the pyramid. The line has no end point as it is used exclusively as an angular reference in the design of the pyramid's gallery section.)

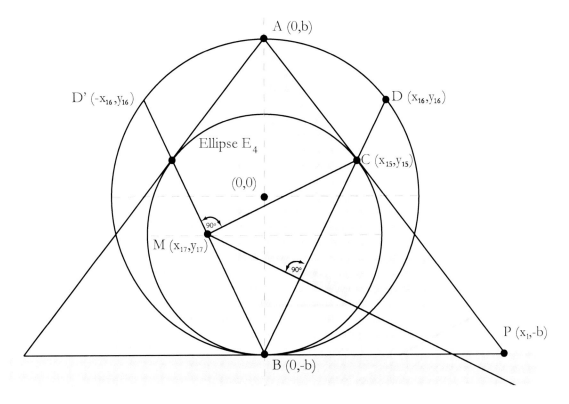

Proof

In 1.4a the gradient of the pyramid's face, the line PA, was given as

$$gradient\ PA = \frac{-2b}{x_1}$$

From the geometry of the system, at the point $D(x_{16}, y_{16})$ the tangent to ellipse E_1 will be the same as the gradient of the line PA and so from the equation 2.1

$$\frac{-x_{16}b^2}{y_{16}a^2} = \frac{-2b}{x_1}$$

$$y_{16} = \frac{-x_1 x_{16} b}{-2a^2}$$

and substituting the identity $a = fb$ gives

$$y_{16} = \frac{-x_1 x_{16}}{-2f^2 b}$$ (6.1)

From the general equation of an ellipse 2.0

$$x_{16}^2 = f^2 (b^2 - y_{16}^2)$$

and substituting the above value of y_{16} into this equation gives

$$x_{16}^2 = f^2 \left(b^2 - \frac{x_{16}^2 x_1^2}{4b^2 f^4} \right)$$

$$x_{16}^2 = f^2 \left(\frac{4b^4 f^4 - x_{16}^2 x_1^2}{4b^2 f^4} \right)$$

$$4b^2 f^2 x_{16}^2 + x_{16}^2 x_1^2 = 4b^4 f^4$$

$$x_{16}^2 = \frac{4b^4 f^4}{4b^2 f^2 + x_1^2}$$

$$x_{16} = \frac{2b^2 f^2}{\sqrt{4b^2 f^2 + x_1^2}}$$ (6.2)

Substituting this value back into 6.1 gives

$$y_{16} = \frac{-\dfrac{2b^2 f^2 x_1}{\sqrt{4b^2 f^2 + x_1^2}}}{-2f^2 b}$$

$$y_{16} = \frac{bx_1}{\sqrt{4b^2 f^2 + x_1^2}}$$ (6.3)

Substituting the values from 6.2 and 6.3 into the standard equation of a straight line gives the gradient, m, of the line DB as

$$\frac{bx_1}{\sqrt{4b^2 f^2 + x_1^2}} = m.\frac{2b^2 f^2}{\sqrt{4b^2 f^2 + x_1^2}} - b$$

$$bx_1 = m.2b^2 f^2 - b\sqrt{4b^2 f^2 + x_1^2}$$

$$m = \frac{x_1 + \sqrt{4b^2 f^2 + x_1^2}}{2bf^2}$$

and therefore the equation of the line DB is

$$y = \frac{x_1 + \sqrt{4b^2 f^2 + x_1^2}}{2bf^2}.x - b$$ (6.4)

The coordintes of the point C on the pyramid's face can be found by solving the equations of the lines PA from 2.8 and DB from 6.4 simultaneously giving

$$\frac{x_1 + \sqrt{4b^2f^2 + x_1^2}}{2bf^2}.x_{15} - b = \frac{-2bx_{15}}{x_1} + b$$

$$x_{15}\left(\frac{x_1 + \sqrt{4b^2f^2 + x_1^2}}{2bf^2} + \frac{2b}{x_1}\right) = 2b$$

$$x_{15}\left(\frac{x_1(x_1 + \sqrt{4b^2f^2 + x_1^2}) + 4b^2f^2}{2x_1bf^2}\right) = 2b$$

$$x_{15} = \frac{4x_1b^2f^2}{x_1(x_1 + \sqrt{4b^2f^2 + x_1^2}) + 4b^2f^2} \tag{6.5}$$

Substituting this value back into the line equation of PA gives

$$y_{15} = \frac{-2b}{x_1}.\frac{4x_1b^2f^2}{x_1(x_1 + \sqrt{4b^2f^2 + x_1^2}) + 4b^2f^2} + b$$

$$y_{15} = \frac{-8b^3f^2}{x_1(x_1 + \sqrt{4b^2f^2 + x_1^2}) + 4b^2f^2} + b$$

$$y_{15} = b.\frac{x_1(x_1 + \sqrt{4b^2f^2 + x_1^2}) - 4b^2f^2}{x_1(x_1 + \sqrt{4b^2f^2 + x_1^2}) + 4b^2f^2} \tag{6.6}$$

By the geometric principle of reflection in the y axis, the equation of the line BD' is

$$y = -\frac{x_1 + \sqrt{4b^2f^2 + x_1^2}}{2bf^2}.x - b \tag{6.7}$$

The equation of the line CM, which is perpendicular to $D'B$, is therefore

$$y = \frac{2bf^2}{x_1 + \sqrt{4b^2f^2 + x_1^2}}.x + c$$

where c is an unknown constant. The coordinates of the point $C(x_{15}, y_{15})$ from 6.5 and 6.6 can be plugged into this equation to determine the line constant giving

$$b.\frac{x_1(x_1 + \sqrt{4b^2f^2 + x_1^2}) - 4b^2f^2}{x_1(x_1 + \sqrt{4b^2f^2 + x_1^2}) + 4b^2f^2} = \frac{2bf^2}{x_1 + \sqrt{4b^2f^2 + x_1^2}}.\frac{4x_1b^2f^2}{x_1(x_1 + \sqrt{4b^2f^2 + x_1^2}) + 4b^2f^2} + c$$

$$c = \frac{x_1^2(-x_1 + \sqrt{4b^2f^2 + x_1^2}) - b^2(2x_1(f^2 - 1) + \sqrt{4b^2f^2 + x_1^2})}{b\sqrt{4b^2f^2 + x_1^2}}$$

and the complete line equation of CM is therefore

$$y = \frac{2bf^2}{x_1 + \sqrt{4b^2f^2 + x_1^2}}.x + \frac{x_1^2(-x_1 + \sqrt{4b^2f^2 + x_1^2}) - b^2(2x_1(f^2 - 1) + \sqrt{4b^2f^2 + x_1^2})}{b\sqrt{4b^2f^2 + x_1^2}}$$

$$\tag{6.8}$$

By solving the equations of the lines CM and BD' simultaneously, the coordinates of the point M can be determined

$$\frac{2bf^2}{x_1 + \sqrt{4b^2f^2 + x_1^2}}.x_{17} + \frac{x_1^2(-x_1 + \sqrt{4b^2f^2 + x_1^2}) - b^2(2x_1(f^2 - 1) + \sqrt{4b^2f^2 + x_1^2})}{b\sqrt{4b^2f^2 + x_1^2}} = -\frac{x_1 + \sqrt{4b^2f^2 + x_1^2}}{2bf^2}.x_{17} -$$

$$x_{17} = -\frac{2b^2f^2x_1(x_1(f^2 + 1) - (f^2 - 1)\sqrt{4b^2f^2 + x_1^2})}{\sqrt{4b^2f^2 + x_1^2}(2b^2(f^2 + f^4) + x_1(x_1 + \sqrt{4b^2f^2 + x_1^2}))} \tag{6.9}$$

Plugging this value back into the equation of the line BD' gives

$$y_{17} = -\frac{x_1 + \sqrt{4b^2f^2 + x_1^2}}{2bf^2} \cdot -\frac{2b^2f^2x_1(x_1(f^2 + 1) - (f^2 - 1)\sqrt{4b^2f^2 + x_1^2})}{\sqrt{4b^2f^2 + x_1^2}(2b^2(f^2 + f^4) + x_1(x_1 + \sqrt{4b^2f^2 + x_1^2}))} - b$$

$$y_{17} = b\left(\frac{2x_1(x_1(x_1 + \sqrt{4b^2f^2 + x_1^2}) - 2b^2f^2(f^2 - 1))}{\sqrt{4b^2f^2 + x_1^2}(2b^2(f^2 + f^4) + x_1(x_1 + \sqrt{4b^2f^2 + x_1^2}))} - 1\right) \tag{6.10}$$

The equation of the line MO, the ascending passage of the pyramid, can now be determined knowing that it is perpendicular to the line BD and passes through the point $M(x_{17}, y_{17})$ yielding the line equation

$$b\left(\frac{2x_1(x_1(x_1 + \sqrt{4b^2f^2 + x_1^2}) - 2b^2f^2(f^2 - 1))}{\sqrt{4b^2f^2 + x_1^2}(2b^2(f^2 + f^4) + x_1(x_1 + \sqrt{4b^2f^2 + x_1^2}))} - 1\right) = \frac{-2bf^2}{x_1 + \sqrt{4b^2f^2 + x_1^2}} \cdot -\frac{2b^2f^2x_1(x_1(f^2 + 1) - (f^2 - 1)\sqrt{4b^2f^2 + x_1^2})}{\sqrt{4b^2f^2 + x_1^2}(2b^2(f^2 + f^4) + x_1(x_1 + \sqrt{4b^2f^2 + x_1^2}))} +$$

from which the constant in the equation can be calculated, giving the line MO as

$$y = \frac{-2bf^2}{x_1 + \sqrt{4b^2f^2 + x_1^2}}x + \frac{2b(-4b^4(f^4 + f^6) + x_1^3(x_1 + \sqrt{4b^2f^2 + x_1^2}) - b^2f^2x_1(x_1(-1 + 5f^2 + 2f^4) + (1 + 5f^2 - 2f^4)\sqrt{4b^2f^2 + x_1^2})}{\sqrt{4b^2f^2 + x_1^2}(x_1 + \sqrt{4b^2f^2 + x_1^2})(2b^2(f^2 + f^4) + x_1(x_1 + \sqrt{4b^2f^2 + x_1^2}))} \tag{6.11}$$

The angle of the ascending passage from this geometry is

$$ascending\ passage\ angle = -26.02611$$
$$ascending\ passage\ angle = 26°\ 1'\ 34.006''$$

To compare this angle with the angle from the surveying work of Petrie we need to expand Petrie's work slightly.

He measured the angle of the gallery section of the pyramid and the ascending passage together, but in fact they have different angles, so we need to look at his methods of surveying and the tabulated results on page 65 of his work to resolve the problem.

He took measurements at three places in the passage, and noted the distance from a predetermined surveying line set at 26° 2' 30" to both the roof and floor in these three places. The illustration on the page opposite shows these three sets of measurements along the passage, and the floor and roof angles that can be deduced from them.

the algebraic construction of the shaft varies by 1 degree minute from the surveying data.

The vertical offsets of the algebraic line at the built ends of the shaft in comparson to the central passage line of Petrie's surveying are as follows :

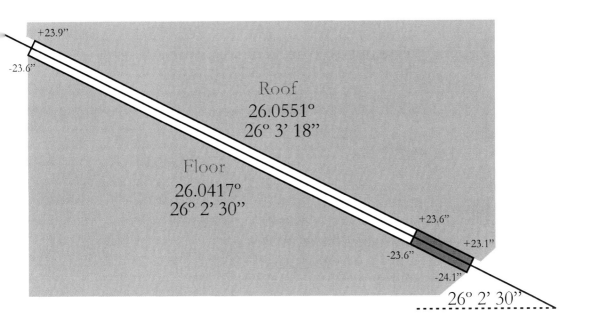

	Top of passage	Bottom of passage
Vertical Offset	+0.007 m	-0.003m

With an angular difference of 1 minute of a degree, and an average vertical difference of 5mm the algebraic calculations are sufficiently close to the surveying data to consider the lemma proven.

13. *In a more advanced analysis of the building's architectural design, the pyramid is formed from the orthographic projection of an Earth shaped ellipsoid, rather than the cross section used in this algebraic analysis. The small differences between the surveying data and the algebraic enumeration can be acounted for by this change in primary ellipse definition.*